M000267404

Theological
Reminiscences

Theological Reminiscences

John B. Cobb, Jr.

Toward Ecological Civilization Series

PROCESS CENTURY PRESS
CLAREMONT, CALIFORNIA 2014

THEOLOGICAL REMINISCENCES

© 2014 Process Century Press

All rights reserved. Except for brief quotations in critical publications and reviews, no part of this book may be reproduced in any manner without prior permission from the publisher.

Process Century Press
An Imprint of the Center for Process Studies
A Program of Claremont School of Theology
1325 N. College Avenue
Claremont, CA 91711

ISBN 978-1-940447-04-9
Printed in the United States of America

CONTENTS

PREFACE

Off and on for years I have considered writing something auto-biographical. Many of the people who live in my retirement community, Pilgrim Place, do so, as do some of my academic peers. But I have repeatedly postponed such an enterprise for a variety of reasons and might easily have kept postponing until my ability to carry it out was long gone. Current opportunities and needs always seemed more important. Indeed, I was not sure of what use any autobiography I might write would be.

What changed my mind was reading Thomas J.J. Altizer's *Living the Death of God*. He calls it, quite accurately, "A Theological Memoir." It is a reflection on his still ongoing theological journey. In three ways, reading it heightened my interest in writing some kind of theological memoir myself. First, it made me think about my very different theo-logical journey. Reading Altizer has always made me self-reflective, and reading this book pushed me to a brief renewal of what was once an intense and extensive interaction between us. I'll write about that later. Second, I decided that, for my own sake, I might make more sense of the variety of directions my thought has taken in a kind of *apolo-gia*. Overall, what have I been trying to do? Obviously, my hopes and dreams far exceeded any accomplishments. But here and there some of my initiatives have borne fruit. To what extent, then, have I "suc-ceeded"? Third, Altizer's book showed me that I might write something that would not *simply* be self-indulgent, although it remains that, but would also have its own theological weight and usefulness. It can be a proposal of a kind of theological program that few are pursuing. Perhaps it can even stimulate some readers to reflect about their own vocations, as I have been stimulated by Altizer to become more reflective about mine. I am not as original a thinker as Altizer; so my story is more typical of my generation of theologians than his. But no two stories are the same.

By calling my writing "reminiscences," I hope to free myself from heavy responsibility with respect to the detailed historical accuracy of what I say. I will write about how I see the development of my thinking from my present vantage point. No doubt I am now trying to fit things into an overall pattern that exists primarily in my current imagination. But I hope that there is also real connection to the past. I do not intend to write fiction.

(*Note.* The preceding preface was written about five years ago for an earlier version of this manuscript. The original plan for it fell through, and it gathered dust (or whatever comparably happens to documents on computers.) When I decided to resuscitate it, I found that more had changed in five years than I had realized. Part of the change was in my own perceptions and emphases. Two-thirds of the present manuscript comes from the earlier manuscript but, but there have been a few changes and considerable additions. It now expresses my present views. July 1, 2014.

This also gives me the occasion to thank some of the people who have helped me with various parts of the manuscript: Ignacio Castuera, Ronny Desmet, Tim Eastman, Hank Keaton, Catherine Keller, Gorgias Romero, John Quiring, and Vernon Visick. I have been particularly helped in the chapter on physics and metaphysics.)

CHAPTER ONE

Childhood and Youth

Theological reminiscences do not need to dwell on one's early life. On the other hand, at least in my case, basic beliefs and commitments root there. There is continuity between what I thought and cared about when I was a child and what I believe and care about now. That may mean that I have never been sufficiently critical of my childhood faith. I may cling too much to aspects of that faith that continue to seem valuable to me. It may still shape my vision and my hopes too much. However that may be, one of the norms I inculcated as a child is honesty. Accordingly, I need to acknowledge where I come from and how my early formation still informs me. And I continue to be grateful to my parents for the faith I imbibed through them.

So what was that faith? My parents were missionaries of the Methodist Episcopal Church South. They had expected to go to China, but in fact they were sent to Japan shortly after World War I, and they remained there (with a gap during World War II) until the mid-sixties. I was born there in 1925, the youngest of three children. My sister, brother, and I were all born in a Japanese-style house on the small campus of Palmore Institute, primarily a night school for Japanese who wanted to learn the English language. The next year the family moved to Hiroshima, and I lived there until my first time in the United States 1931-32.

My recollections of life in Hiroshima are very limited. I nearly died of scarlet fever when I was four. I remember the doctor telling my mother that unless I learned to gargle I would probably die. I apparently did learn. Of course, I was quarantined, especially from siblings, but my most vivid memory is of the adults preventing the family dog from

1

coming into the room. Another vivid memory was of participating with other kindergarten children in a race and being in the extreme rear. I have liked to blame my slowness on the scarlet fever, and this has been my dubious excuse for my poor physical prowess ever since.

Another memory is of Himura-san, a young man who was almost a part of our family. I remember climbing some outside stairs to his upstairs room. He is the person I would have most wanted to see when I was back in Japan in the army of occupation, but he was killed in Burma in continuing fighting just after the Emperor surrendered.

I was in Japan most of the time until December 1940, when war clouds led my parents to send me to Georgia to finish high school. They followed the next spring. The mission board judged that the presence of American missionaries in Japan, if war broke out, would be a heavy burden for the Japanese churches.

My parents were, in the broad sense, religiously conservative. But being a conservative Methodist in those days, even a Southern one, was very different from what we now identify as the religious right. Methodist conservatism then took the form of intense piety. As with Wesley, the concern was to order one's life so as to do as much good as possible and to be inwardly as pure as possible in one's devotion to God and humanity. To this day I consider those to be worthy goals.

These goals were closely connected in my childhood with a vivid sense of divine presence and companionship. I was never much for disciplined prayer, but when alone I often talked with God. I could talk with God about my feelings and my failures with an honesty that was inappropriate in other relationships. This conversation encouraged self-knowledge. Because Wesleyan piety centered on God's love, talking with God, even about what was wrong with me did not burden me with feelings of guilt. I assumed that God understood, forgave, and accepted.

Lest I seem to romanticize this piety, let me hasten to acknowledge some of its flaws. The most serious, I now think, was that it had no place for sexuality. I do not mean that a lot was said about sex of a restrictive or oppressive sort. Wesley himself was silent on this topic, and that silence was continued in the pietistic circles I knew. But such silence may be more oppressive than explicit legalism. Certainly I, like many other pious youth, was psychologically wounded by this form of Christianity.

In other respects such legalism as was part of this piety was not oppressive to me as a child. Because bridge was connected with gambling, we played "Rook," which was sometimes called "Methodist bridge." On Sunday, we avoided card games altogether and played board games such as Parcheesi. I delighted in family games, and just what they were on what days made little difference to me. I grew up assuming that Christians did not drink alcohol or smoke. I had no desire to do either. To this day I have never smoked, and I do not feel deprived. I am not an absolutist about drinking alcohol, but I have not developed any taste for it. I prefer a glass of coca cola to a glass of wine even now, though I recognize that the wine would be better for me.

My piety was based on home life rather than on any formal connections with the church. I understand that I was baptized as an infant by a Japanese Methodist bishop. I joined the church in Newnan, Georgia, where we spent furloughs every seven years. I was just seven, but the pastor thought I understood what I was doing and did not need to wait another seven years. I think he was right. In Japan I attended Kobe Union Church with my brother and sister, while my parents were busy in Japanese churches. But going there was more an accepted expectation than a source of inspiration or enlightenment.

Going to church, like going to school, involved riding a train and a good deal of walking. We made the roundtrip just once a week, Sunday morning. However, when the family was at home in Newnan during my adolescence, an evening youth group in which the young people took some real leadership was important to me as were summer camps and other activities. I found great satisfaction in working in these groups.

Frugality was a natural part of life during my youth in the Great Depression. We never wanted for what we needed, but we knew that money was scarce. My allowance, when I was in Georgia, was twenty-five cents a week. Of this ten cents was for Sunday school and five cents was for church. The remaining dime was disposable income.

I finished high school in Newnan in June of 1941. I went with my parents and siblings to Spokane, Washington, where my father became pastor of the Japanese Methodist congregation. In September I returned to Georgia to attend Emory at Oxford. This was located on what had been the campus of Emory College. When Vanderbilt, which had been the major university of the Methodist Episcopal Church, South, broke with the denomination, this little college was moved to Atlanta to become Emory University, the new university of the denomination (along with Southern Methodist University in Texas.) The old campus became a junior college of the new university.

My piety reached its zenith during those years. I had very little money, but I spent almost nothing so that I could send what I did have to a mission that worked with lepers in Africa. I knew very little about it, but it had caught my imagination as a way of helping people in desperate need. I organized a little group that met at night in the nearby woods to pray together.

Part of being a good Christian was complete honesty. I was not often tempted to lie or cheat, but on one occasion, confronting a quiz in English literature for which I was not prepared, I glanced across the aisle and copied an answer. At this point, I do not even know whether the answer I copied was correct. What I do remember is how deeply this dishonest act bothered me. That evening I went to the teacher's home to confess my crime. I received a zero on the test, but I felt better.

Whereas my piety strictly forbade dishonesty of the obvious kind, it actually encouraged dishonesty of another kind. I understood that as a Christian I should always be happy. In general I *was* reasonably happy, but nevertheless the idea led to presenting a public image that was not entirely accurate and to a certain amount of self-deception, too.

A related weakness showed up in another connection. At the end of my freshman year the college annual included cartoons, and one of the funniest depicted me with a halo and with spares over my arm. The limited and distorted nature of my piety displayed itself in my response, which was one of unreasonable anger. I still feel shame when I recall my total inability to appreciate the humor and to laugh at myself. I hope I have improved in this respect.

Theologically, this conservative pietism was quite open. I grew up assuming that the beliefs we held as Christians were the most sensible and advanced beliefs possible. It did not occur to me to view the natural sciences, or historical scholarship, or the beliefs of other religious communities as threats. I assumed that belief in a loving God was intellectually entirely secure, and that nothing else mattered much. When I was around twelve, a teacher gave me Van Loon's history of the world, which began with an account of evolution. I found it convincing and accepted it as a matter of course. This did not disturb my parents.

Conservative Methodist pietism supported social righteousness. That to be a Christian demanded commitment to peace and justice was taken for granted. There were vague tendencies toward socialism in the family.

Greatly as my parents admired Japanese culture and Japanese people, they were strongly against Japanese aggression in China.

In my childhood racism was self-evidently wrong. I don't know at what point my parents had rejected the racial segregation that was the dominant social institution of the South, but I certainly imbibed my opposition from them as part of my piety. When we were in Georgia, I got into occasional arguments. How often I was asked whether I would like to have Negroes (not always pronounced that way) living next door! By the time I was in college the answer was easy. The parsonage in which my parents lived in Spokane, Washington was under the same roof as the church, and the building was on a corner. The neighbors on one street were Japanese and those on the other street were Negroes. It was a thoroughly comfortable situation. The other popular question was whether I wanted my sister to marry a Negro! I truly had no objection to mixed marriages. I could only reply that at Canadian Academy, where I had studied in Kobe, many of my friends were of mixed race. They were often the best students.

At Emory-at-Oxford, the junior college to which I went at the age of sixteen, the more pious among my classmates and teachers agreed with me in opposition to racism, and acting through our youth group we invited some Negroes to come to the evening service at the church. Afterwards we were told we should not do that, but I'm glad to say that no one made a scene at the time. I already knew that it was often better to act and ask permission afterward.

On one occasion, after attending a national meeting of the Methodist Student Movement, I had the chance to speak at convocation. Issues of race had been a major topic at the meeting, and I focused on that. Many of my schoolmates stomped the floor and some later called me "nigger-lover," but I suffered no more serious consequences.

My second year at Oxford I was business manager of the annual and worked closely with the editor, George Brasington. We dedicated the annual to the only Negroes available, the custodian and his family. Such acts of protest obviously amount to very little, and I do not mean to claim complete freedom from racism, but I am glad that as a boy I did what I could. I am glad also that I did not have to struggle internally with this issue as I probably would have, had I grown up mostly in Georgia.

I mention these incidents also to indicate one feature of my youthful piety. If I thought something was true and right, I acted on it regardless of

its acceptability to others. I will come back to this topic in the chapter on
my army days, when I learned my limits. I have become more pragmatic
and diplomatic in my maturity, but I am not sure that is entirely a gain.

I mention these incidents also to clarify that the religiously conservative piety I knew in those days, not only for me, but for white Georgians
in general, correlated positively with the recognition of the injustice
of segregation and the willingness to oppose it. It was only later that I
discovered how piety could be used to support the acceptance of social
injustice. It was my personal experience that those who were devout in
their Christian faith opposed social evils and worked against them.

In high school and junior college my answer to the question as to
what I planned to do when I grew up was to go into government foreign
service. This expressed my social concern and its focus on international
relations. I thought that mistaken United States policies, above all the
exclusion act which blocked all immigration from Japan, were partly
responsible for Japanese aggression. I also blamed much of the destructive
nationalism of the time on the failure of the United States to enter the
League of Nations. More generally, in a world plunging into the Second
World War, I was concerned about world peace. Naïvely, no doubt, I
thought that spending my life in the U.S. Foreign Service would provide
a context for making a positive difference. It was not an unrealistic career
choice. A cousin with whom I roomed for a year, Arva Floyd, made that
choice and had a successful career, but I am glad that I was called in
another direction.

Growing up in Japan heightened my identity as an American. We
were certainly appreciative of the Japanese, and we were often critical of
U.S. policies, but basically we assumed that the United States was on the
side of the angels. We were proud to be Americans. The occasional sight
of an American flag on an American ship stirred my heart. There was not
the slightest question as to national loyalty.

My positive feelings toward Japan and the Japanese in no way raised
questions for me about serving in the U.S. Army against Japan. They
did affect particular actions and responses. Shortly after Pearl Harbor I
was invited to address a civic group in a town near the junior college.
I rehearsed the history of U.S.-Japan relations emphasizing how the
U.S. exclusion act had contributed to the rise of imperialism in Japan.
Looking back from the vantage point of the recent hostile response to
those who wanted to take the occasion of 9/11 to reflect critically about

American foreign policy, I give high marks to the group of business men in a small Georgia town who, shortly after the nation had been attacked, listened patiently and courteously to the talk of a seventeen-year-old boy who blamed U.S. policy in part for the Japanese attack.

My sympathies for Japan showed up in my disgust with the demonization of the "Japs" and the way they were caricatured. Also, later, I objected strongly to the demand for unconditional surrender, which blocked the efforts of the Japanese to surrender months before we dropped the atomic bombs. Probably the only condition on which they would have insisted would have been safeguarding the person of the emperor, and we did that any way. I felt deep horror at the subsequent dropping of the atomic bombs on Japan. The fact that as a small child I lived in Hiroshima for five years may have intensified my response to its obliteration. I ran a fever for several days.

My family connections were all in Georgia. In the Civil War generation, the Cobbs had been a politically important family. My father's grandfather had been a mere major in the Confederate army and was too young to play any political role. However his oldest brother, Howell, had been governor of Georgia and served on Buchanan's cabinet. He presided at the constitutional convention of the Confederacy. His other brother, T.R.R., was a lawyer who codified Georgia's laws. He commanded the center of the Confederate lines under Lee at Fredericksburg. Lee was victorious, but T.R.R. was killed. Some suspect that he was shot by one of his own troops. That this rumor gained currency does not speak well of his popularity with those he commanded.

I have wanted to take pride in my ancestry, but it is not easy. Some years ago I saw in *Books in Print* that a book by Howell Cobb had been reprinted. For a moment I was positively excited. Then I saw that it was a "Christian" defense of slavery republished for use in Black Studies programs. My feelings about the Cobb family were not improved by the assurance that they were pious Christians whose defense of slavery was based on the Bible. There was no doubt in my mind that I was a Southerner. For a serious Christian, a Southern identity is difficult. One can hardly affirm the "cause" around which so much of that identity is built. Yet one wants to be proud of one's people.

Southerners are the only Americans whose history includes defeat on our own soil. This leaves scars in the psyche that are familiar to Europeans but not to other Americans. The kind of innocence that characterizes so much of American consciousness is not possible for Southerners, at least in their identity as Southerners. It is our task to embrace a guilty legacy and a heritage of defeat. On the whole we have done this badly. I find it ironic that now, in both church and state, the South tends to dominate American politics. I like to tease my Northern friends by pointing out our superior political skills. But since I deplore its results, it is not really a source of pride.

I mention these matters to indicate that for me to be a loyal Southerner has never meant to accept or affirm the institutions and practices of the South. To be a loyal American has never meant to support American foreign policy. Later I could add, to be a loyal Christian did not mean to support what Christians had done and were doing. This was only later, because another weakness of the piety I imbibed was that it left me with a triumphalist view of Christianity, or at least of that branch of Christianity in which I grew up.

We had no trouble recognizing that the Crusades were wrong, but as far as I can recall, by being Protestants we thought we were free of that guilt. We knew there had been persecutions of dissenters, and that Christians had even used torture, but we thought all that, too, was a Catholic matter. My parents were mildly anti-Catholic; so I imbibed that feeling. I had virtually no contact with Jews, and my father had happy memories of Jews from his youth in Macon, Georgia. Further, Jews were not a threat to the religious freedom we prized, as we supposed Catholics might be. Hence I grew up with no negative feelings about Jews and had to learn later, sadly and painfully, of the terrible history of Christian relations to Jews.

Although my identity as an American was strong, my identity as a Christian was stronger. This did not involve negative feelings about Shinto or Buddhism. To Christian missionaries in Japan these did not appear as real religions but simply as part of a culture. We loved the aesthetics associated with both Shinto shrines and Buddhist temples, but all that we observed going on there seemed to be part of folk superstition. I'm not sure that my father ever knowingly met a serious practitioner of Buddhist meditation. We did know that there were groups who gathered to chant, but that seemed more magical than spiritual. Given the high visibility of sophisticated forms of Buddhist spirituality today, it is hard to imagine how invisible they were to most Japanese and to most foreigners in the previous generation. Perhaps if one imagined that in the United

States the only serious practice of Christianity was in monasteries, it might help to indicate how it seemed to most foreigners in Japan.

I attended a Japanese kindergarten, but otherwise received a Western education. Most of my schooling was at Canadian Academy. One lesson I learned early was that history may be read in many ways. In successive years we studied Canadian history, British history, and U.S. history. The textbooks were, of course, standard school texts in the three countries. Even as a child I was amused by the extreme differences in the treatment of the same event, such as the American Revolution. In the Canadian textbook the focus was on defending Canada against the invading forces from the south. There was some attention also to the acceptance by Canada of refugee loyalists fleeing persecution by the rebels. In the British text a couple of paragraphs indicated that while Britain was busy fighting France elsewhere, some of colonists in North America rebelled, and the British decided to let them go. I need not describe the quite different account in the American textbook. I now judge that this contributed to my distrust of the media and of the academy as well.

It has been my assumption that most of what I hear on the radio and TV and read in mainstream publications is partially propaganda. As a child I took this for granted with respect to the daily paper, the English version of the *Osaka Mainichi*. Reading it told us what our Japanese friends understood about what was happening, but we assumed that we knew better.

This feature of my upbringing is so important for my theological career that I will elaborate. With respect to textbooks, I have already given an illustration. I could have added the Confederate and Georgia histories at home. I should say that those who never encounter the Southern perspective typically do not realize the extent to which the war was fought over trade policies, with the South supporting free trade. Nor are they likely to appreciate that on strictly constitutional grounds, the South had the best of the argument. They are also likely to think that the North was committed to abolishing slavery, although histories today are less likely to give that impression. My point is not to defend the South or to express doubt that what I read in Southern histories was propaganda. I am glad we lost. But the reality is that it was not quite the good versus bad controversy that is sometimes presented. The fact that history is written by the winners is often forgotten. The horrors of the Confederate prison for captured Northern troops at Andersonville are far better known than the comparable horrors of the northern prisons for captured Confederates. The story told by winners is no less propagandistic than the suppressed story of the losers. I apply this today to World Wars I and II, and to the Cold War as well.

Recently I saw *Twelve Years a Slave*. It is painful for anyone to watch. For one like me, for whom family and tradition are emotionally important and whose ancestors may have been the largest slaveholders in the South, the pain is acute. That these ancestors like me were serious Christians adds to the problem. My reflection leads me to note that their racism was sincere. They probably never met whites who did not think that the white race was superior to the black. This view was shared by Abraham Lincoln and even by most abolitionists. Even in the North, abolitionists were a minority considered to be extremist. In the South, where the entire economy depended on slave labor, this form of extremism was beyond the pale.

The question of how serious Christians could support slavery and participate in the slave system is very much like the question: how could serious Christians support the Nazi government of Germany? However, I find another comparison more *à propos*. How can serious Christians support contemporary American imperialism and global capitalism? The answer in all cases is that we are brainwashed by the dominant propaganda. Southern whites in the period before what from the Northern point of view was the "Civil War," vigorously debated secession vs. unionism, and Howell Cobb was a leader of the unionist side. But there was no significant discussion of emancipating the slaves. Today many good American Christians seek to alleviate the suffering of the victims of imperialism and global capitalism, and they seek to moderate the destruction of democratic institutions. They side with political progressives. But they take the basic global capitalist system for granted. It is essential to our "way of life." There is no significant debate about it. My critique of my ancestors for acquiescing uncritically in a vicious system leads me to want to be less acquiescent in the equally vicious system now operative in my society. I do not want to be so easily socialized into the particular group-think that dominates our world.

In my childhood and youth I did not extend my skepticism to science. It was distressing to me to learn much later that what is called science also socializes people to think in certain channels and to be contemptuous of alternative theories. But as I encountered evidence of the propagandistic character of scientific texts and scholarly articles, it was easy to extend my critical habit of mind to these. I am grateful for childhood conditioning that freed me from the credulity that is almost inescapable for those who were not so fortunate.

I have always regarded my sister, Margaret, the oldest sibling, as the most psychologically normal and healthy of the three of us. She married while our father was serving as District Superintendent of Methodist work with Japanese as they returned to the West Coast from internment camps, and she had three sons. Our two families visited one another and camped together from time to time. Her husband died early of brain cancer, but she stayed in their home in Alameda. We tried to get together at least once a year, often spending a week in a timeshare, and these contacts were always reassuring. I happened to be with her when she died in the fall of 2009. Our children and hers and, to some extent, their children as well feel themselves to be part of one extended family.

My brother James was another matter. He was almost albino in appearance, and he never adjusted well to the realities of this world. Whether there was a connection I do not know. Some thought that his problems began with a mastoid operation at the age of two. Although we fought occasionally, our relations were generally good. But he was a source of embarrassment to me at school. During recess he would wander around the fringes of the playground, playing with a rock and humming to himself. Occasionally he would have episodes of jumping up and down. He was clearly in a world of his own imagination. I was not myself secure in my acceptance by my peers; so I avoided associating with him at school. One vivid memory is of watching a larger student beating him up and my doing nothing about it. I don't think any intervention on my part would have helped, but I still feel shame at not trying. Neither of us ever mentioned the incident to one another or at home.

At home I sometimes entered into imaginary worlds with him. We enjoyed making maps of imaginary countries on imaginary planets and recounting their histories. He devoured dictionaries and encyclopedias and could provide information on a vast number of topics. Instead of using the dictionary or encyclopedia ourselves, the rest of the family just asked him what we wanted to know. When we played family games, which sometimes went on sporadically for weeks, we rarely wrote down the scores, because James always remembered them. The possibility that he would distort them in his own favor simply did not exist.

My parents always thought that if they treated him as if he were normal, he would become more normal. I suppose it worked within limits. But the expectation was not realistic. In my generation, we would have sought psychiatric help as a matter of course. But this was not a part of my parents' world. Treating him as if he were normal meant sending him to school, and somewhat remarkably he graduated from college and even from law school at Emory University in Atlanta. I don't know what we expected to happen next. If no one intervened, he was supposed to shape up and take realistic responsibility for himself. Of course, that did not happen.

My parents were back in Japan, and I was going to school in Chicago. I received a call from an uncle who taught at Emory, expressing concern about James' whereabouts. He no longer had a dormitory room, of course. Since my sister was in California, it was my job to find him. No problem. I took the train to Atlanta and went straight to the city library where he was reading the newspapers. He had been sleeping in the park. I'm not sure where or what he was eating.

I made some arrangements for his living and make-work for which we would pay without his knowing it. My mother came back from Japan to make a home for him. Some years later, after our mother had returned to Japan, we arranged for him to see a psychiatrist. It may be that the psychiatrist forced him to face reality. In any case, shortly thereafter, he stepped in front of train. Perhaps it was the best solution. Certainly it made life easier for the rest of us. But it is hard for those who loved him to think so. Mother saw him in a dream, and he reassured her that all was well. I still choke up when I talk about him.

In some respects, as a child and youth, I was advanced for my age. I sometimes think I was one of those children who are more like small adults in a child's body. I generally preferred adult conversation. At fifteen my parents sent me back from Japan to Georgia by myself, a three-week trip by ship and train. I was an avid sightseer; so I planned a complicated trip across the continent from San Francisco, going as far north as Niagara Falls and as far east as Washington, D.C., before going to my grandmother's home in Georgia. In general I arranged to spend my nights on the train and to sightsee during the days. My parents raised no objections.

Because I lived alone with my grandmother for some time before my parents returned from Japan, I was quite close to her. About the time we left for my father's new assignment in Spokane, she was to have an operation from which there was no assurance that she would recover. I have never again prayed as hard as I did then—for her survival. She did survive, but from that time on she was extremely senile. Death would have been better. I wondered whether the prayer had been rightly formulated.

Later she moved to Macon to live with one of her sons who was a doctor. In her senility she would often cry out quite loudly—loudly enough to disturb the neighbors. My uncle took her to the hospital to have a minor operation that reduced the volume of her cries. The shock to her system brought back her authentic personality. It faded again in a few weeks.

I have included junior college in this account of childhood and youth, since I was only sixteen when I began my course there. Further, the ethos of the junior college was a continuation of the piety that has been my primary topic, and I have illustrated that piety from events that took place there. From a later perspective I marvel that I could have engaged in conscientious study of a variety of college courses without any recognition that the modern world is profoundly different from the world of piety in which I was raised. But in fact that was the way it happened.

CHAPTER TWO

The Army

I cut junior college short to volunteer for the army in the spring of 1943. Because I knew a little Japanese, I had arranged in advance to attend the army's Japanese language school at the University of Michigan. The whole program was just twenty months, the last eight at Camp Savage, Minnesota. The modest knowledge of the language that I brought with me allowed me to skip the first four months of the program. When we completed it, we supposedly could read and write two thousand characters and six thousand compounds, roughly equivalent to a Japanese high school graduate. In fact our knowledge of the language was quite limited, but it was enough to get us started in translating captured military documents. Our conversational skills were, of course, far less, but they had to suffice for some of my colleagues to begin interrogating prisoners near the front lines.

My own assignment was far from the front lines! I was sent to Camp Ritchie, Maryland, a bit further West than the now famous Camp David, on the highway from Washington, D.C., to Hagerstown. I can hardly imagine a pleasanter location. I had stints in the Pentagon itself and in Washington in a joint program with the navy. After the war, I spent four months in Japan in the army of occupation.

This gave me a chance to reconnect with a few personal friends but more important to reestablish relations that were important to my father. When Japanese Americans were released from internment camps and allowed to return to the West Coast, my father moved from the Japanese-language church he had been serving in Spokane to Alameda, where he was to serve as District Superintendent of the

Japanese-language churches. Of course, the task was to reestablish these churches that had been closed and to help the Japanese reestablish themselves. Very much on his mind, and a concern of the national church, was whether missionaries should be sent back to Japan. He wanted me to make some contacts with Japanese leaders and get their advice. So I served as a sort of advance reconnaissance.

My judgment based on conversations was that at just that moment the Japanese people would be very responsive. They found assimilating the defeat of the emperor psychologically, we may say religiously, very difficult. They were immensely surprised that the American occupation was relatively benign. They truly appreciated General MacArthur and almost transferred to him their reverence for the emperor. The gospel message would have been listened to with great seriousness. But I judged that the door would probably not be open long.

At least on the latter point I was correct. A few months after my term of service in Japan was over, my father was the first Methodist missionary to return and was warmly welcomed. The church recovered, but its growth was like that before the war, a matter of individual decisions, painstakingly considered. Whether a mass movement to Christianity, such as had occurred in Korea, was ever a possibility in Japan, I don't know. Nor whether that would have been a good thing.

During the war, our job was to translate such captured documents as General McArthur decided to send to the Pentagon. Since McArthur was unlikely to allow anything of value to escape his control, it is highly unlikely that our unit made any significant contribution to the war effort. There was one possible exception. I was given a transcription of an intercepted radio message. It was far more difficult to decipher because there was no indication of where words began or ended, and the same sounds can have many meanings. A written document makes the meaning clear by the use of Chinese characters. I have no memory of the content, but it may have been of some value to someone. I was given a ribbon for my work.

For these reminiscences my work with the Japanese language is important only because of the people with whom it brought me in contact. These were very different from the pious Georgia Protestants with whom I had previously associated. Indeed, in my new context, the world that had previously been mine was viewed with some amusement as an anachronism. In addition, at eighteen, I was much younger than most of the soldiers in this program. Still they treated me kindly.

A few of my fellow students and translators were persons who had lived in Japan like me. One of them, Wayne Oxford, had been a close childhood friend with whom I have remained in contact throughout our lives. He followed me to Camp Ritchie and brought with him a motorcycle that I learned to ride there.

However, most were men who had seen war coming and had decided they preferred to serve in academic ways rather than in the more usual military roles. Most were from New York City and had started Japanese language study there as civilians. So far as I recall, they were all either Catholics or Jews, whereas I had had no previous contact with either. I was told that our unit had the highest average IQ of any in the Army. Hence, in a quite atypical way, my first encounter with intellectuals took place in the Army. I found it exhilarating. The classmate who became best known was Robert Heilbronner, whose later work I greatly admire. I regret that I knew him only casually.

I was fortunate that my conversation partners were not thoroughgoing secularists. I was not ready for that. At Camp Ritchie I developed a friendship with Robert Langbaum. My literary education began with him, and to a small degree I was introduced through him to the rich and fascinating world of Jewish culture. Subsequently he had a career teaching and writing in the field of English literature, chiefly at the University of Virginia.

My closest companion at Camp Savage was a devout Catholic by the name of Jim Daly. I discovered that his thinking about matters of faith was far more sophisticated than mine. He introduced me to Thomistic thought. For a while I was largely persuaded that Thomas had been able to synthesize human knowledge and understanding at a uniquely favorable moment in history, and that the succeeding developments, beginning with nominalism, represented a steady decline. This depiction of Western intellectual history did not deny the contributions of the sciences, but it assimilated them into a worldview quite different from the reductionistic one that has dominated the modern world. I toyed with the idea of becoming a Catholic. Even today I see that way of reading the history of Western thought as having considerable plausibility—although I do not accept it and am glad I did not take the step of conversion. At least it ended any prejudices against Roman Catholicism that my earlier experience had inculcated.

Probably the reason that I did not convert was that I was encountering so many other ideas, wholly new and strange to me, that my thinking was in too much of a flux to make any definite commitment. One of the other types of literature that touched me deeply was mysticism. The book that had the greatest impact on me was Aldous Huxley's *Perennial Philosophy.* Although his interest is in showing that mystical thinking develops in all traditions, and that this testifies to its authenticity, in fact the form of mysticism he promotes is largely Hindu. Buddhism is notably missing from his quotations. But I noticed none of this at the time. I found Huxley's account profoundly persuasive. Although I stand somewhere else today, I will never disparage his vision.

None of this suggested to me that my own Protestant tradition had much to contribute. I read enough history to learn something about the Reformation and its leaders, but what I read at that time did not impress me with their intellectual stature. My loss of Protestant moorings was not especially disturbing to me, since my identity was as a Christian rather than as a Protestant. Whereas before I had assumed that the form of Protestantism in which I was nurtured was the purest and fullest form of Christianity, now I saw its limitations. Indeed, I saw them in exaggerated form because I made no contact with the brilliant history of continental Protestant theology. In any case, I could give up the idea that my own form of Christianity was the best without any personal crisis.

Nevertheless, it was fortunate for me that I did come across the writings of Reinhold Niebuhr. I worked my way slowly and with great difficulty through *The Nature and Destiny of Man.* This, too, I found overwhelmingly persuasive. It provided me with quite different glasses for looking at Christian thought and history, and ones that seemed very important to me at the time. I still consider them as such. This is not to say that Niebuhr was correct in all his historical judgments. Nor did he escape the Eurocentrism of the day. Also his realistic recognition of how effective policies and actions must take account of the universality of human sin has been used to justify opposition to much needed change and as support for Machiavellian rather than biblical thinking. But that our biblical heritage can offer an illuminating account of intellectual and political history and provide guidance even today is a lesson I learned from Niebuhr. He also brought me back to my youthful vocation to make a difference for peace and justice in international affairs.

This intellectual turmoil and growth had remarkably little effect on my personal piety. I still communed with God with very little of anything that could be called a spiritual discipline. Even my fascination with mysticism did not lead me in the direction of much formal meditation. I participated in church life when I could, but more as an expression of my piety than as a support or enrichment.

Four occurrences during Army days merit recall in these theological reminiscences. The first occurred while I was stationed at Camp Savage in Minnesota. On the weekends most of us went into the Twin Cities. I spent a good deal of my time around a Methodist church. I was particularly attracted by a group of conscientious objectors I met there. They were doing alternative service which consisted in being guinea pigs for the study of the effects of various diets on health. As far as I can recall, the Army wanted to learn more about what armies of occupation should do to prevent starvation or serious health problems among the people of the occupied country. Talking with them raised for me a question I thought I had settled: should I, as a Christian, serve in the Army?

That issue had been central at a national meeting of the Methodist Student Movement in Urbana, Illinois, during the Christmas holiday shortly after Pearl Harbor. We heard pacifist speakers and others who believed that fighting Japan and Germany constituted a just war. I leaned in the latter direction and found this tendency confirmed by our discussions there. At the time I was still sixteen; but the issue was not raised for me again before joining the army fifteen months later, soon after my eighteenth birthday. Now, talking with these deeply committed pacifists who were paying a high personal price for their faith, I faced the question with quite different intensity.

It seemed to me that they had chosen the better path. What should I do? It was all too characteristic of me as a youth that it hardly occurred to me to ask advice of others. The question was for me to decide. I decided that I *should* announce to my commanding officer that I could no longer serve. What would happen if I took that action? I had no idea. I still don't know what the results would have been.

The United States had reasonably generous provisions for those who refused to join the armed services on the grounds of conscientious objection. But so far as I knew there were no similar provisions for those who decided that they were objectors after having enlisted. I was nineteen at the time, and although I have claimed to have been rather mature in some respects, I was far from mature in others. And among other things,

I was easily intimidated by authority. The prospects of dealing with such authorities on this matter were appalling to me.

My solution was to postpone action. I could have rationalized the postponement as giving myself time to think it over, but as far as I recall I did not do so. I continued to believe that I should refuse to serve any longer whatever the consequences. But in fact I did nothing about it, and the moral urgency faded. I learned something about myself. It was the first time that I had clearly decided that something was the right thing for me to do and then deliberately failed to do it.

I trust no reader will suppose that I considered that I had previously been sinless. The kind of piety that shaped me called attention to a pervasive sinfulness that expressed itself in many thoughts, words, and actions. The goal of having one's life governed by love of God and other people is a lofty one, and the aspiration for such a life throws a light that calls attention to constant and repeated failures. But this was different. This was a fully voluntary act of wrongdoing, repeatedly willed, day after day. I had not previously known that I was capable of such behavior.

Within a few months, when contact with this group of admirable conscientious objectors had ended and its memory had faded, I was glad that I had failed to act. My sense of World War II as a just war and of the appropriateness of participation in such a war recovered dominance. My respect for conscientious objectors remained and remains high, but except for that brief period I have never been a pacifist. What I learned through this experience was that my piety was not sufficient to overcome my fear. In a strange way, I am grateful for my weakness, a weakness that I know has continued with me throughout my life. There are limits to the risks I will take regardless of my convictions.

Years later when I studied John Wesley's theology, I understood that in his terms I had forfeited my status as a Christian. To be a Christian is not to be perfect—far from it. But for Wesley, to decide consciously and intentionally to do what one thought one should not do, or to fail to do what one thought one should do, was an unchristian act. Later Methodists called it backsliding. Wesley thought one would then need to reenter the Christian life. I am glad I did not know Wesley's theology at the time. It never occurred to me that my failure to act separated me in any way from the love of God. I assumed God understood my weakness and nevertheless accepted and forgave me. I think that reflects the deeper currents of Wesley's own teaching.

Knowing the limits of my virtue, I hope, has reduced my tendency to judge others. It has also heightened my admiration for the many who do take real risks to oppose historical evil. I wonder whether I am capable at all of doing so. I would like to think that if I had lived in the days of slavery I would have resisted it in some way. I would like to think that if I had been in Germany in the Hitler days, I would have taken some risks to oppose him. But I am doubtful. It would have been too easy to postpone any dangerous action.

And living today in the heart of the American empire and of a global capitalism I abhor, I wonder what risks I am even now willing to take in my opposition. I marvel that it costs so little to voice objections, but I know also that this cost-free action is unlikely to be effective. What would it take to make a difference? And if I could answer that question, would I act? Sadly, I doubt it. Today, the question is what actions am I prepared to take to oppose global warming? I have excused inaction on the grounds that my wife needs my presence with her. Now she is cared for by others. How far am I prepared to go to oppose suicidal policies?

A second experience was very different. It taught me a very different lesson. When I was stationed at Camp Ritchie, Maryland, rather than attend services in the chapel there, I walked a couple of miles each Sunday to a Presbyterian church across the border in Pennsylvania. I offered to teach a Sunday school class and was assigned junior high boys. The class met on the front seat of the sanctuary. I thought of myself as a complete failure in this role, since the boys showed no sign of interest in anything I had to say. But I have learned that I am no judge of when what I do has an effect. On the whole, what influence I have had has probably had little to do with my conscious intentions and hopes. In this case, many years later I learned that two of those boys went into the Presbyterian ministry and gave that class some credit for the decision.

A third experience was of considerably greater importance for my own career. One Sunday morning as I was walking to church, thinking about nothing in particular, I suddenly stopped in my tracks. Whereas I had been telling anyone who was interested that I planned to serve in the United States Foreign Service, in that moment I knew that I would work in some church-related job. What it would be was completely open.

There is nothing surprising that my piety would lead me to choose a church vocation. That I would change from one plan to another at the age of twenty is certainly understandable. But I still marvel at the way it happened. Because of my sense of failure with my Sunday school class, I was not enjoying my experiences in church at the time. I was under no pressure to make a vocational decision and had felt perfectly comfortable with the one I had long announced. Indeed, I do not recall giving any thought to the possibility of a church vocation prior to that moment. After it, I had no doubt about the decision, and I never again considered the Foreign Service. I felt no need to announce the decision, though I was quite ready to tell anyone who inquired. No other decision in my life has had that character.

A fourth experience also came "out of the blue." I was living in Arlington while working in Washington, D.C. I have mentioned that I have rarely been disciplined in forms of piety, but at that time I was engaged in a simple spiritual practice of holding before God, for a moment, people I met or saw, asking God's blessing on them. I mention that as the only possibly relevant context I can think of for what I am about to recount.

One night I knelt beside my bed for a perfunctory moment of prayer before going to sleep. Suddenly the room seemed filled with the divine presence. I felt a warmth, a love, a total acceptance I have never experienced before or since. It may have lasted a minute before fading. The memory of that pure joy remains precious to me.

In the area of sexuality I was terribly naïve and immature throughout adolescence and even as a young adult. Joining the Army had little effect in this department. I remember an occasion when I was twenty, and another soldier and his wife invited me to their home for an evening. I had been reading *Perennial Philosophy*, and I was expatiating on the rejection of all legalisms. One of them asked me if that meant there were no restrictions on sex. I remember how I flushed and stammered—"except that." Even at the time I felt like a fool, but my response expressed the terrible lack of integration of the sexual dimension of life into my piety, and I might begin to say, into my theology.

As I was being separated from the Army in September 1946, I was promoted to captain for my final two-week leave, and I was also asked whether I would like to join the reserves. Being a captain in the reserves would have given me prospects of a little income, of which there was otherwise only the GI bill. For a moment I was tempted, but emotionally I wanted to have nothing more to do with the Army. I am very grateful for that split-second decision to follow my emotions rather than my practical reason. Those who chose otherwise were called back into service during the Korean War.

I returned to my grandmother's home in Newnan. There I picked up a relationship that began in childhood. At the age of six, now eighty-three years ago, I had met Jean Loftin. She lived around the corner from my grandparents' home. I liked her then, but she had already been "going steady" with another fellow, Manly Bowen. When I came back to Newnan after a seven-year absence, they were still going together. I jokingly assert that I wanted a steady relationship myself, and that I married Jean because she had proved herself capable of that.

Dating at Newnan high school, at least in my case, was largely an arranged affair. Newnan was a quite social town, and there were many parties for high school students. During that furlough year I became fifteen, and when invited to a party, I would be asked whether I would bring a particular girl as my date. Manly's sister, Sally, was one of the girls with whom I was paired. The Bowens were Presbyterians, and Sally and I enjoyed arguing about predestination. But I was particularly pleased when, occasionally, I was paired with Jean.

I returned to Japan in the fall of 1940 for what turned out to be only a few months. Back in Newnan to complete high school, a year before Jean, I saw more of her, gradually displacing Manly. We kept up some connection through college and while I was in the army.

Manly went to Annapolis and became a career naval officer. Sally taught Latin in high schools in Newnan and was a leading citizen in the town. We remained friends with both of them until Sally died and have continued our relation with Manly to the present.

Like many World War II soldiers, I was eager to marry and settle down when I completed my service. So a couple of months after separation I proposed, and Jean agreed to marry me. We set the wedding date for June when I could return to Newnan from Chicago.

I entered marriage still in a state of confusion and naïveté with respect to sex. But somehow, thanks to a sensible and emotionally healthy wife, we have made marriage work for sixty-seven years. We had four sons during the first eight years, and we now have five grandchildren and two great-grandchildren. The family story would be a different book.

CHAPTER THREE

The University of Chicago

Altogether I spent three and a half years in the Army. They did not change me greatly at the level of fundamental self-understanding. My piety remained intact even if it fed on additional sources. But I did know that I did not want to go back to the sort of academic context I had left. I learned that at the University of Chicago I could go directly into graduate school, and that prospect greatly appealed to me.

The reason was that under Robert Maynard Hutchins a student could start college at Chicago two years earlier than elsewhere. Hutchins thought that bright students wasted a lot of time in high school, and he arranged an intensive four-year program that produced prodigies. I have heard that on examinations the graduates of the college at Chicago did as well as graduates of Harvard College even though they had had two years less schooling.

College was followed at Chicago by a three-year masters program. If one had two years of college credit one could take an exam and be admitted to this program. Although my work at Emory at Oxford and my Japanese studies at the University of Michigan certainly had not prepared me for graduate studies at Chicago, they did jointly give me the two years credit I needed. I hoped that my reading during Army days gave the knowledge I needed.

I was attracted to Chicago also by what Army friends had told me of Mortimer Adler and his work with the great books. Much of the college program was in fact based on the reading of classic writings. I confusedly and mistakenly thought that this applied to the graduate programs as well. In any case, this added to my interest in Chicago.

23

Although my decision for a church-related profession meant I would eventually attend a theological seminary, the Divinity School at Chicago was not part of the university's attraction for me. Indeed, what little I was told about it by Army friends repelled me. What I learned of its teaching was alien to my own piety even after the intellectual developments of my Army years. My scattered encounters with significant forms of thought led me to hunger for deeper rootage in the great intellectual and religious traditions. What I heard of the Divinity School suggested that it was committed to the most contemporary forms of thought. What little I knew of these did not appeal to me.

I suppose that in reminiscences, even theological ones, the author may be allowed an amusing digression. A very minor factor in my preferring Chicago among the universities I might attend was that my father had gone there once for summer school. For that reason I heard it mentioned as a child. Because he was planning on missionary work, my father was not drafted in World War I. When he graduated from Mercer College in Macon, he was offered a teaching job at Kentucky Wesleyan College. Because most of the younger teachers had been drafted, his responsibilities would include coaching the football team.

Unlike me, he was a fairly good athlete, a city champion in tennis, but he knew little about football. Hence, to prepare himself for his new responsibilities, he included among his studies at Chicago that summer a course in football with Alfonso Stagg. Since in my day Hutchins had abolished intercollegiate athletics at Chicago, this was wholly irrelevant to my reasons for going.

Years later my oldest son, Ted, a sports buff, learned of his grandfather's role in intercollegiate sports. He inquired how the team had done, but my father had been far more interested in courting my mother that year and did not remember. So my son did research and, to his delight, found that his grandfather's team had won two out of their three intercollegiate games. Perhaps Stagg's teaching had helped.

Although my reading and discussions in the Army had not shaken my childhood faith, they had made me realize that faith of that sort had little support in the intellectual world. I did not want to organize my life around indefensible beliefs. Hence, I went to Chicago thinking that I would spend three years immersing myself in the intellectual world and testing my faith in that context.

I fully expected my faith to survive this encounter. So I planned that, after completing the MA in the Humanities Division, I would go to seminary. As a Georgia Methodist, I planned to attend seminary at Candler School of Theology at Emory University. In due course I would be ordained in the North Georgia Conference.

Schooling was made possible by the GI Bill. I received $500 a year for tuition and books and $70 a month for food and lodging. It is amazing, from today's perspective, that in those days that sufficed. The University had acquired additional space to accommodate the flood of veterans, and I was able to share a big room with seven other men. I had $1.25 per day for food, and I was able to eat on that, although I did lose weight. When I married at the end of the first two quarters, the stipend increased to $90 a month, and when we had a baby boy, it became $120. I supplemented that with occasional part-time work, and I believe that the Mission Board that employed my parents helped a little. As children of the depression Jean and I were accustomed to frugal living; so this was no hardship. We did not have to touch the money I had saved in the Army until it became necessary, at the end of our time at Chicago, to buy a car.

In the graduate divisions there were a number of interdisciplinary committees. The Committee on Social Thought was well known. In the Humanities Division there was a Committee on the Analysis of Ideas and the Study of Method. My choices were to select one department within the division or to work in such a committee. If I had chosen a department, it would have been philosophy. But I was aware that there were other intellectual currents countering the Christian faith to which I should be exposed, for example, in literature and psychology. I applied to the latter Committee.

To be admitted to this program I needed to submit a topic for study during the three-year program. My proposal was to study all the reasons for not believing in God in the modern world. I was admitted. The only public exposure this committee ever had, so far as I know, was through Robert Pirsig's book, *Zen and the Art of Motorcycle Maintenance*. Pirsig began his studies in the committee in 1962.

I do not know whether the faculty members connected with this committee ever met. During my time within it, student enrollees did not. As far as I can recall, I only met one who identified himself as such. Hence admission to this program did not as such contribute to social or intellectual life. It affected me only in two ways. My academic advisor was a member of the committee and approved my courses. And some courses in the Humanities Division were starred in the catalog as particularly appropriate for students in this program.

I found my human, intellectual, and religious companionship separately. I probably was something of a pest to my fellow students because of my need to talk about what was going on in the classes. Chicago provided many interesting discussion partners.

The man with whom I ended up spending the most time during the first six months, as far as I recall, was a committed Communist. To me, student politics at Chicago seemed quite radical in those days. There were two large Democratic groups, one oriented to Americans for Democratic Action, and the other to the Progressive wing of the party. These were flanked by two small clubs of approximately equal size and influence: the Republican and the Communist. One can note that the "center" has moved a long way since those days. My guess is that among University of Chicago students today the center is considerably to the right of Americans for Democratic Action. However that may be, my friend found the whole school oppressively conservative. He left to study in Prague. I have no idea what became of him.

I joined two Christian groups. One was for Methodist students, the Wesley Foundation. It was largely social, although some very interesting faculty members were invited to come to talk with us. My first contacts with the Divinity School faculty came about in this way.

The other group was Intervarsity Christian Fellowship. Theologically it was much more conservative than I, but it was also much more scholarly and intellectually serious than my fellow Methodists. Despite my theological disagreements, the others accepted me graciously. Even though the theological gap may have widened since then, I have retained great respect for Intervarsity.

It was only gradually that I realized that the committee I had joined was the brainchild of Richard McKeon, who was also the dominant figure in the philosophy department and quite influential in the college. I became acquainted with him in my first quarter. One of his courses was starred; so I thought I should check it out. It was entitled: "Problems of Logic: Grounds of Inference." It was properly labeled as an advanced course, and I should have had the good sense to avoid it. However, on the first day of class I walked in and asked whether I could take the course.

In retrospect I blush to recall my claim to competence. When McKeon asked what I had done in philosophy, I told him that I had read Will Durant's history of philosophy and that of Bertrand Russell. He admitted me on this ridiculous basis, despite the fact that I had no academic work in philosophy at all and had done no reading whatever in logic. We were assigned four books to read on the problem of inference. I remember that three of them were by Bradley, Bosanquet, and Johnson. I do not recall the fourth. I had no understanding of what problem they were undertaking to resolve and accordingly could make very little sense of any of the texts. I'm not sure that I would do much better today. The task of the class was to compare the several solutions.

I wrote in the previous chapter about learning my moral limitations. In this first quarter at Chicago, I learned my intellectual limitations. In my readings in the Army I found that though ideas were new to me, patient care enabled me to grasp them, at least to some extent. In this course I realized that however patiently I studied the texts and however carefully I listened to the lectures, I understood very little indeed. I have encountered my limits frequently since then, but this first experience was the most painful.

I was saved from complete failure by McKeon's being called to a UNESCO conference in Paris before the quarter ended. Several of my classmates were professors in the college, and one of them led the class for the last month before Christmas. I then discovered that I was not alone in my bewilderment. Even our substitute teacher was having difficulties. The more elementary discussions we had in McKeon's absence combined with the extra time allowed to complete the course on McKeon's return saved me from a disastrous start in my work at Chicago. I managed to write a paper that McKeon graded as a B-. I have never been prouder of a grade.

I was fascinated by McKeon. I gradually realized that what he was teaching was the philosophy of the history of philosophy. One needed to know that history quite well before one could engage it at the level of his interests. Not having the background, I never did well in his courses. I just survived. But I kept taking them. Indeed, I studied more with McKeon than with any other professor. From him I learned that certain patterns of thinking come and go in the history of Western thought. They remain possibilities for thinkers through the centuries. He had very little sense of progress in this history, only of fresh expressions of much the same patterns.

He developed some very elaborate schemes for classifying philosophers. I do not remember any of those. I do remember a very simple one.
He pointed out that there are philosophies that take thought as their primary object, others, that take things, and still others, that take terms. The
first two I had no trouble understanding, but at the time I could hardly
imagine that anyone would regard language as the primary horizon of
inquiry. At that time linguistic analysis had made no inroads in Chicago. Accordingly, I was ill-prepared for the overwhelming success of the
linguistic turn. To this day I cannot quite believe that anyone supposes
that the English language is the primary reality for philosophical investigation, but I have regretfully learned how many can be absorbed into this
mode of philosophy. My incredulity is not McKeon's fault. Although he
was not committed to this himself, he presented it as a co-equal alternative with idealism and realism.

The permanent effect of McKeon on my thought is the recognition of
a basic pluralism in philosophy. There is, for example, no neutral perspective from which to judge that thoughts, things, or terms are the primary
object of philosophical investigation. There are many other issues of this
sort. Any claim that philosophical argument has actually shown something to be true, in some final or definitive sense, fails to convince me.

Nevertheless, I have become far more interested in the irreversible
historical changes that have occurred than was McKeon. Modern science
is an example, as is the rise of historical consciousness. The pluralistic
stance toward philosophy is itself something of importance that is new.
Further, whereas McKeon's stance was that of a detached observer, I have
become strongly committed to promoting and pursuing one particular
type of philosophy as critically needed in our time.

I mentioned that Pirsig was enrolled in the Committee on the
Analysis of Ideas and the Study of Method. He also found McKeon fascinating and kept going back for more. I can understand how McKeon
drove him over the edge. McKeon's teaching style consisted of throwing
out questions. But he rarely (perhaps never) fully accepted any answer.
My reaction was to be as inconspicuous as possible and never offer an
answer. Pirsig, on the other hand, kept trying. No doubt he found it
extremely frustrating never to have his carefully considered answers
treated as adequate.

In my first two quarters at Chicago, in addition to courses in the
history of philosophy, enrollment in the committee allowed me to study

the history of academic psychology, Freud, and literary criticism. I was studying very intensively, and I learned a lot. But the really important consequence of my study was quite different.

Perhaps the most straightforward description of my experience at that time is that God ceased to be existentially and religiously real to me. This was not because of any specific thinker whose anti-theistic writings were convincing. Of course, there are good reasons to reject many ideas of God, but to this day I have not found particularly convincing arguments against the existence of something that can reasonably be called God. The change occurred more from my way of studying. I have always tried to enter into the point of view of the one I study, to look at the world provisionally in his or her way. I did this with thinker after thinker, most of whom lived in intellectual worlds in which God played no role. At some point I could no longer return to what had been my own God-filled world.

Something like this, I assume, happens in the education of many youth brought up in the church. The university socializes us into a world without God. It so takes for granted the self-enclosed system of the world that it senses no need to argue for its adequacy. There are many disputed issues, but the disputes take place within this context. There are many loose ends in most of the systems that are proposed, but the possibility that these loose ends point to God is not considered. To speak of God at all as a possible explanation of anything that happens in the world simply shows that you are not part of the legitimate discussion. You are allowed privately to harbor some kind of belief as long as you recognize and accept its disconnect from serious scholarship and thought.

For those for whom belief in God has never been of great importance, socialization into this way of thinking will hardly be noticed. Others may build successful defenses against it. For still others, like me, this loss of God was existentially of great importance. With it went the sense of life's deepest purpose.

Further, the practical matter of my planned line of work was also at issue. But that did not weigh heavily on me. I thought I could become a college teacher, probably in philosophy. But it would be just a job, not a vocation.

During the sixties and seventies I sometimes spoke of my own "death-of-God" experience early in my time at Chicago. However, this labeling may be misleading. I came to understand that the cultural historical experience to which that term refers contains a large element of liberation of humanity from an external authority. It frees people from guilt, and releases their creativity. I felt none of this. It was simply a loss. The loss included a reduced interest in critical reflection and intellectual exploration. Such reflection and exploration no longer seemed particularly important. I was "liberated" from freely chosen purpose and meaning. The "emptiness" into which I felt that I was falling had nothing in common with the Buddhist "emptiness" about which I learned later. I felt closure rather than openness. This all came to a head toward the end of my second quarter, just before my wedding. I tried to set it aside for this occasion, but a real crisis of faith does not allow itself to be set aside.

After returning to Chicago for the summer quarter, I had to deal with realistic matters. Of course, I talked with Jean, but this was all too strange to her experience for her to do more than give personal support. As in the case of previous personal crises, it did not occur to me to discuss this with others. Of course, that is just what I would recommend to other people in need, and I am not sure why this did not seem appropriate to me. On the other hand, I'm not sure who could have helped me.

One thing was clear. There was no point in continuing after that summer for six more quarters to pursue the study of reasons not to believe in God. Nor did it make any sense to drop out of Chicago and head to Emory to study for the ministry.

There seemed to be one somewhat promising alternative. I had taken one course with a theist. His name was Charles Hartshorne. I sensed that he knew the thinking of the modern world far better than I and still found reasons to affirm God. When God had been real to me, it had been all too easy to accept what he said. He sharply challenged the orthodox theological tradition, but what he objected to there was of no importance to me. What he defended seemed far more congenial.

Before giving up on what had been the center of my life, I thought, I should expose myself further to those who had immersed themselves in the world of modern thought and still affirmed some kind of God. I had also taken a course with James Luther Adams specifically on modern atheism. He taught in Meadville Theological Seminary, which was part of the Federated Theological Faculty. I had had slight contacts with other members of that faculty such as Joachim Wach. There seemed to be a group of people who were obviously fully aware of the modern intellectual climate and yet in one way or another remained believers. Perhaps it was time to shift from a focus on reasons not to believe and find out more about how others who did believe managed to do so.

At this point just what had repelled me from the Divinity School at Chicago when I had learned about it earlier, that is, its immersion in modern thought, made it a beacon of hope. I inquired about the possibility of being admitted without a college degree. I learned that the Divinity School admitted students with three quarters in one of the graduate divisions, and at that time I was in my third quarter of study. I joyfully applied and was admitted.

CHAPTER FOUR

The Divinity School

Leaving the MA program in the Humanities Division to start a new program in the Divinity School continued a pattern. I left Emory-at-Oxford without completing junior college in order to enter the Army. I never completed any college program. Often I am the only adult in the sort of gatherings I attend who is not a college graduate. This seemed then and has always seemed a matter of trivial importance.

One practical advantage of being in the Divinity School was that Jean and I were provided an apartment. During the preceding summer we had quite unsatisfactory arrangements, and by September Jean was pregnant. We were delighted to be able to share a large apartment with another Divinity School student, Gabe Fackre and his wife, Dot. We have cherished their friendship ever since. A special bonus was that this was almost across the street from Lying-In Hospital where Jean could get excellent medical attention and our first son, Theodore, was born. Jean could walk home, and we carried Ted in our arms.

My needs and the Divinity School under the deanship of Bernard Loomer were a remarkable match. I needed a community of support for a completely open-ended investigation of the possibility of belief in God at that time in history. Loomer made of the Divinity School a community of inquiry and discussion in which this and related questions were of central importance. He invited the new students to his apartment, and what he said assured me that I had never made a better decision. After some months of depression, my spirits lifted.

I found in the Divinity School an intensity of intellectual life I had not discovered elsewhere in the university. That it focused on questions of radical importance for me was more than I had dared to hope for. I had truly found my home.

That did not mean that I limited myself to courses in the Divinity School. In those days the Divinity School had no course requirements. The only requirement was the passing of a set of seven comprehensive exams. How one prepared for them was up to each student. Of course, I took or audited a good many courses in the Divinity School, but I also continued to take work in the philosophy department, especially with McKeon. Whether I learned much from him I am not sure, but I remained fascinated. I also took courses with Charles Morris and especially with Charles Hartshorne.

My continuing engagement with philosophy expressed my sense that I could not settle for myself the question of belief in God without knowing the history of Western thought better, and to an exaggerated degree, I identified that with philosophy. The reality of God is, of course, a metaphysical question, and metaphysics was more directly the topic of traditional philosophers than of theologians. This was true even when the topic of God was a minor one in their writings or absent altogether. So I prepared in rather haphazard ways for my Divinity School exams while preoccupied with philosophical issues.

Of course, there are many important theological questions that are not directly and obviously focused on God. I profited greatly from exposure to many of these discussions. But without settling for myself the metaphysical question of the reality and nature of God, I could not consider these questions as central or absorbing. I later regretted having failed to appreciate fully what my teachers had to offer.

The Divinity School faculty was itself quite philosophically oriented, but the metaphysical dimension was, for the most part, touched on lightly. The context for theology was provided more by radical empiricism and pragmatism. The most influential thinker for the faculty was Henry Nelson Wieman, who had recently retired.

Wieman frustrated me. His most important book, at least for my purposes, was published about that time—*The Source of Human Good*. It was a brilliant and highly original book about what he understood to be God. Since for him, as for the Divinity School faculty generally, "God" belonged to theological discourse, the basic definition of God grew more out of Christian experience and teaching than out of the metaphysical tradition where I had been seeking it.

For Wieman it was very important to avoid speculative thought in defining God. Christians needed to have confidence in the reality of that which they trusted and to which they committed themselves. Philosophy of a metaphysical sort could not provide a basis for this confidence. God must be found in indubitable experience.

It was equally important to understand experience in the "radical" sense. Wieman was not at all trying to discern reality through sense experience as so many empiricists did. Experience is much richer and more extensive than that. Actual human experience is profoundly relational and qualitative, and it is in these relations and qualities that human good is found. In a normal and healthy life, this human good grows. The question is how? What is the source of human good and its increase?

If Wieman's examination of this question had led him to believe that the growth of human good came about when people took control of their own lives and willed such an increase, I doubt that he would have spoken of God at all. Human good, he concluded, arises in the process of interaction that yields results that none of the parties to the interaction can either predict or control. The emergence of new patterns of relationship and new qualities of feeling cannot be predetermined or even aimed at, because they are not known until they occur. What people can do is to open themselves to the sorts of interactions through which growth occurs and trust the process even when it may be threatening to those goods they have brought into it. This analysis resonates well with Reformation teaching about grace and faith. Accordingly, Wieman felt fully justified in identifying as God the process of creative transformation through which good grows.

Wieman was not interested only, or even chiefly, in the theoretical question. He wanted to make a difference in the lives of students and others he touched. He saw all too many students, many like me, no doubt, unsure of whether there was anything to which we could or should wholeheartedly give ourselves. He saw a secular world in which people were trying to make themselves into whatever they wanted to be, and failing. He saw Christian churches in which faith had been turned into believing particular ideas of little help in practical life and destructive of intellectual integrity. He believed that he had found the alternative to all this and he promoted it practically within the Divinity School. He was one of the initiators of the sort of small group interaction that became especially important in the fifties and sixties both within and outside the churches. There is in my mind little doubt that many benefited from the open and honest interactions encouraged in these small groups. I include myself.

On the other hand, what Wieman called God was so different from what I had known as God and what I was seeking metaphysically that his work did not answer my questions. For me, much depended on the onto-logical status of what he called "God." This was not his explicit topic, but that did not reduce its importance for me. The ontological question was crucial to my ability to appropriate his thinking and find in it an answer to my own quest.

Accordingly I chose this topic for my master's thesis. I concluded that Wieman's God could only be understood ontologically in two ways. If God was concretely real, then each instance of creative transforma-tion was God and there were in fact innumerable Gods. Alternately God could be understood as the pattern actualized in all these instances and so well analyzed by Wieman. In that case God's ontological status was that of an abstraction.

I did not then think, nor do I now, that Wieman intended either of these results. His earlier writing had a metaphysical dimension that could give unity to God. My point was that the avoidance of this metaphysical dimension, required by the refusal to go beyond what is given in experi-ence, left him systematically without any way to avoid this result. I still think that is the case.

This does not undermine the value to be gained by entering trust-fully into honest exchange with others. But it does weaken the justifica-tion for using the word "God" to identify this process. Actually in later years Wieman cared less and less about using this word; so this criticism does not apply to his later position. But for me the inherent limitations of what could be learned from his radical-empirical method meant that I needed to continue my search.

I was encouraged in my search for a metaphysically real God by my contacts with Charles Hartshorne. His approach was at the opposite extreme from Wieman in some respects. This can be illustrated by his affirmation of the ontological argument for the existence of God. This argument goes from the idea of God to God's reality. In Hartshorne's version the argument begins with the idea of perfection and moves to the actuality of perfection. He developed the argument at great length and with great sophistication. I was interested, but its apparent formal logical success failed to have much effect on my actual beliefs.

What did affect me deeply were Hartshorne's many revisions of
classical theism. The God of my childhood certainly did not conform to
classical theism; so these revisions were readily acceptable to me. Equally
important, he led me to see that many of the reasons that God had been
rejected by sophisticated modern thinkers followed from an idea of
God which there was no reason to defend. One could agree that in one
aspect God is immutable, for example, while also holding that God is
supremely mutable in another, concrete aspect. If one takes seriously the
idea that God loves the world, then one can hold that God is always, and
unchangeably, loving in just the sense that means that whatever happens
to God's creatures, God fully empathizes with them. For God to empa-
thize with all the creatures as they come and go is for God to be having
new experience continually. In this way God is ideally mutable.

Although encountering a more coherent and credible idea of God
formulated in a thoughtful and persuasive way was a matter of great
importance to me, it did not sweep away my doubts. Hartshorne's elaborate arguments, other than the ontological one, also helped, but not decisively. More important was my gradual entry into a worldview that was
basically different from the modern one that had increasingly excluded
any possible role for God.

The modern worldview that had seeped into me and destroyed my
youthful faith was the materialist, empiricist one that had become so
closely identified with science. It is a worldview that has little place for
human subjectivity. Even though in some ways it inconsistently takes
the reality and importance of the human subject for granted, it does not
allow it a causal or explanatory role. I was, of course, aware of the idealist
alternative, but it seemed incredible to me. And I was never attracted to
Cartesian dualism.

I do not know just how I would have put matters at the time, but, as
far as I can recall, my problem was something like this. I could not doubt
the reality of the world studied by scientists. They viewed this world as
self-enclosed and self-explanatory. In general modern thinkers accepted
this view. In such a world I was to be explained in the same way as everything else as part of this self-enclosed world. My sense of freedom and
responsibility, indeed my very existence as a subjective being, were viewed
as illusions or, at best, epiphenomena.

I could not quite believe this. But I did not know how to articulate
my disagreement. I did not have the self-confidence to assert my refusal

even to myself. It seemed that to be honest and open-minded, accepting the best thinking of the modern world drew me into this closed system. I remember auditing a course with Rudolph Carnap. His closed system was even narrower and tighter than most. When he was asked how he could live in terms of his system, he made no claim to do so. It was the system required for thought—impossible for life. This seemed very wrong, but I did not know how to respond.

Through my faculty in general I became aware that there were other ways to think, even for modern persons who fully accepted the authority of science and historical scholarship. But it was only from Hartshorne that I learned a coherent alternative. Instead of interpreting the world in terms of matter in motion, one may interpret it as a field of interrelated events. Instead of thinking of these events as they appear to others, one can think of them as they are for themselves. Hartshorne called this panpsychism. I have never been attracted to that label, since the term psyche suggests something quite elaborate, something that is clearly lacking in most events. But in Hartshorne's use it meant only that an event must be something in and for itself before it is something for others. In this sense every event is a subject taking account of other events before it is an object being taken account of by others.

Whereas human subjectivity is excluded from the world of matter in motion, it exemplifies the world of interrelated events that are momentarily subjects. In such a world, I could find myself and appreciate the roles of other human beings without what felt like "escaping" into idealism or dualism. Moving from the dominant worldview to this one felt like an advance beyond modernism rather than a defensive reaction to it. At that time this seemed to me an important option to explore. Today I am thoroughly convinced of its superiority.

Although the shift is easy to describe, it was not easy to actualize. I know that others also find it difficult. Our Western sense of reality is so bound up with the objects of vision and touch that we try to make any new ontological assertion fit what we get out of those experiences. Even when I completed my work at Chicago, I still struggled with this.

Nevertheless, the first glimpses of this very different possibility were profoundly liberating. I felt that exploring this way of understanding and experiencing the world was an entirely honest and responsible activity. That was very important to me, because whenever I felt that I was resisting evidence and argument and the wisdom of better thinkers, I was stopped by my inner need to avoid wish-fulfillment and illusion. The very fact that I preferred this different way of thinking and perceiving made me deeply hesitant to give it full credence. But I became convinced that its attraction to me was not a reason to reject it. Perhaps truth need not lead to nihilism after all. I can hardly exaggerate the debt I owe to Hartshorne for introducing me systematically and rigorously, but also in a deeply human way, into this understanding of reality. It has shaped my life existentially, as well as my career.

Although I learned this from Hartshorne, it was reinforced by much that I heard from my theological professors. It fit well with radical empiricism. It offered a context for understanding Wieman. Without this reinforcement I might not have had the courage to internalize this way of thinking, which was so alien to what I learned elsewhere in the university and to the modernity I encountered in other departments. It was hard for me to trust ideas that did not find resonance with others, and I continued to be shaken by the fact that these ideas have been widely ignored if not ridiculed. Hartshorne's personal confidence was wonderfully helpful.

Hartshorne tended to present this picture of the world as *the* truth about it. I was too much influenced by Richard McKeon to think that any one philosophy was *the* truth. Also I was persuaded by Richard Niebuhr that we all think from our particular points of view, individual or collective, in such a way that theology is always "confessional." We confess what we see, what seems true to us. My own teacher, Daniel Day Williams, called this "perspectivalism." To me it was enough that this different metaphysics could offer me a valid perspective from which to think about many things, including my theology.

At that time I was prepared only to affirm that there was nothing in this different vision incompatible with scientific knowledge and investigation. Today I would argue that the metaphysics science has inherited is an impediment to its advance and that the alternative vision I learned from Hartshorne can be of great help in the advance of science. I incline today to make strong statements about the gross inferiority of the scientistic metaphysics inherited from the seventeenth century. Nevertheless, I retain reticence about claiming to be in possession of *the* true metaphysics.

One tension that I felt deeply was that between the dominant currents of theology and what seemed so important in my own quest. The broader theological climate in the post-World War II days was neo-orthodox. To be part of the theological discussion one must deal with

Karl Barth, Emil Brunner, and Rudolf Bultmann, as well as Paul Tillich and Reinhold Niebuhr, who were more popular among my teachers. For the most part, these thinkers eschewed metaphysics. Insofar as Tillich adopted a metaphysic, he seemed to take it as an inescapable ground. My view was that there was no inescapable metaphysical ground but that one's beliefs were inevitably bound up with diverse metaphysical positions. Accordingly, I thought everyone was involved with speculative beliefs, whereas hardly anyone acknowledged that.

This gave me a topic for my dissertation. I entitled it "The Independence of Christian Faith from Speculative Belief." My intention was to examine whether anyone succeeded in formulating a theology that actually had that independence. I showed to my own satisfaction that theologians make assumptions that should be acknowledged to be speculative. I was not critical of their doing so—only of their failure to acknowledge what they were doing. If the near inevitability, and, I thought, desirability, of employing speculative ideas were accepted, theological discussion would take a different form. An explicit debate about basic assumptions would be possible. Years later, my second book, *Living Options in Protestant Theology*, dealt with much the same topic in an expanded form. A small part of my dissertation is reproduced in it.

Although my excitement at discovering another way of viewing reality besides the materialistic, mechanistic, deterministic, reductionistic one was partly separable from my obsession with the question of God, it was certainly not disconnected. Hartshorne immediately connected the two. Some aspects of what he said about God could be accepted by people who were not participants in the wider worldview. But in my judgment, the persuasiveness of his theism is necessarily bound up with the persuasiveness of his broader metaphysics. As I appropriated the latter, I could appreciate his arguments much more. I began to think of God again unapologetically, if still without Hartshorne's full conviction. My dissertation included some Hartshorne-influenced speculations about God.

The gradual recovery of the intellectual belief in God and of the ability to speak about God was of great importance to me. It did not restore my youthful intimacy with God. Indeed, that has never returned, even as my assurance of the reality of God has grown. No doubt much of that intimacy depended on naïve projection, but I think that its loss is also of something real and valuable. God is in fact very present to all of us. Intimately so!

My ability to speak again with some conviction about God played into my hopes for a career in college teaching. I imagined that I would have many students whose encounter with the thought world of higher education would threaten the belief in God with which they came to college. I looked forward to sharing the way I had found to deal with that crisis. I remember that in the process of studying for my theological examination I read a book by Edgar S. Brightman, long the leading Personalist philosopher of religion. I thought the book would make a fine text in a course on philosophy of religion. I looked forward to teaching it and also showing how the arguments could be strengthened by making use of Hartshorne. I was excited by the prospects of such teaching.

CHAPTER FIVE

Whitehead

The influence of Alfred North Whitehead has been too pervasive on my thought, my piety, and my career to include as simply a part of my experience at the Divinity School of the University of Chicago. It began there, but whereas other influences of Chicago have generally faded, that of Whitehead has grown ever deeper. If I treated Whitehead as part of my Chicago experience I would have to try to think just how I experienced him then. I will make some effort in that direction, but what I say in this chapter will reflect my later perspectives as well.

Whitehead was an important influence in Chicago both in the Divinity School and through Hartshorne in the Philosophy Department. The influence of Whitehead in the Divinity School dated back to the twenties. The faculty, under the leadership of Shailer Matthews, was keenly interested in developing theology in a way that was credible to scientists and those whose worldview was largely shaped by science. They saw that, in the early decades of the twentieth century, some scientists were envisioning new ways of thinking that broke with the narrow scientism of the past. When Darwin showed that human beings are part of the natural world, many thought that the natural world could no longer be limited to objectivity and mechanism. Some scientists were involved in the effort to rethink nature in light of our inclusion within it. The faculty of the Divinity School hoped that religious thought could make contact with this newly emerging worldview. Most of the professors identified themselves as neo-naturalists.

I now think the term was apt and am happy to claim it for myself. At the time I did not fully appreciate the importance of the new naturalism.

Because of its connection with a non-metaphysical approach, I was dissatisfied. After a period of exploration of this option, mainstream science re-entrenched itself in seventeenth century ruts, but in the early decades of the twentieth century, theological observers had reason to hope for something else. In my view now the failure of the university to revise its understanding of nature was a tragic mistake of enormous historical importance. The question of metaphysics was in this practical context less important.

One of the neo-naturalist philosopher-scientists who impressed the Chicago faculty was Alfred North Whitehead. This was the Whitehead of *The Aims of Education*, *The Concept of Nature* and, especially, *Science and the Modern World*. Obviously, the theologians were particularly pleased when Whitehead wrote a book specifically on religion: *Religion in the Making*. But they were also startled by the content of that book. They had assumed that the religious thinking that could be continuous with new scientific thinking would not be theistic in any traditional sense. Matthews, for example, had identified God with "the personality-making forces of the universe." But the God who appeared in *Religion in the Making* seemed quite personal. They wondered whether Whitehead had lost his rigor or whether they misunderstood him.

They invited Henry Nelson Wieman to talk with them about the book. His success in satisfying them led to his appointment to the faculty, and for some time he taught Whitehead appreciatively. However, as he became more convinced of the importance of avoiding speculation and more fully aware of the centrality of speculation in Whitehead, he turned against him. Some of his later writings about Whitehead are almost vitriolic. However, Divinity School professors continued to cite various parts of Whitehead with appreciation, and his influence continued. At least when I was there, they left the teaching of his philosophy to Hartshorne. Later, I am told, Bernard Loomer regularly gave a year-long lecture course on *Process and Reality*.

Hartshorne developed his basic philosophy before he encountered Whitehead. However, he served as Whitehead's teaching assistant at Harvard, and he heard some of Whitehead's lectures. He found that some of his own ideas could be enriched and better formulated with the aid of Whitehead's conceptuality. Indeed, he associated his thought so much with Whitehead that his students often had difficulty distinguishing them. Today it is clear that there are extensive differences as well as extremely important agreements.

One major difference was that Whitehead came to philosophy with questions honed by his efforts to understand physics, especially relativity theory. His *magnum opus, Process and Reality,* is subtitled "an essay in cosmology." He did not eschew metaphysics, but he regarded it as an extreme limit which he visited only occasionally. What he sought primarily was a way of thinking that could accommodate what was known scientifically but also the immediate witness of our experience. He was motivated to develop new categories of thought partly by his conviction that many scientific theories, including those of Einstein, were incoherent. He feared that scientists were giving up the effort to make sense of the world.

Hartshorne, in contrast, was basically a metaphysician. Instead of metaphysical doctrines growing out of reflection on scientific theories, he developed them through thought and immediate experience. Once established they had consequences for science, and Hartshorne did pursue some of these. He certainly was concerned that metaphysics not be disconnected with science or incompatible with it. But he did not seek to develop a cosmology.

What narrowed the gap between them was that Whitehead decided a complete cosmology must accommodate all dimensions of experience. Most of all that meant that subjective experience must be included along with the physical world as objectively known. He thought that the deepest knowledge of the values and meanings to be found in human subjectivity were enshrined in religious teaching. Hence the intuitions and experiences that come to expression there were important data for his cosmology. His cosmology included, therefore, both philosophy of science and philosophy of religion. God played a role for him in both, but the full development of the doctrine has a religious basis. And there are remarkable parallels between his idea of God and that of Hartshorne.

Nevertheless, here, too, there are differences. The most important, I now think, is related to the difference between cosmology and metaphysics that I have noted. Hartshorne from childhood saw the world in a theistic way. He began his mature thinking with reflection about the religious and metaphysical tradition, primarily, but not exclusively, the Western one. He argued for improvements in that tradition, calling his position at times "neo-classical." He thought that the weaknesses of traditional arguments for the existence of God could be overcome by

making the doctrine more internally coherent and more consistent with
the remainder of our knowledge.

Whitehead understood himself to be making a new beginning in his
reflection about God. He had been a serious atheist for some time. But
his cosmological work had pushed him to metaphysics, and there he felt
the need for what he called a "principle of limitation" or of "concretion."
He did not come to this out of religious interests, and he did not think
that his initial formulations had anything to do with the theological and
metaphysical traditions of the West. Medieval and modern philosophers,
he complained, have paid God metaphysical compliments in order to
establish God's religious importance. He clearly intended to avoid this.
In this he understood himself to be renewing a mode of thought that had
ended with Aristotle. He did not use this language, but he thought that,
like Aristotle, his reasons for speaking of God, and much of what he had
to say about God, belonged to the sphere of the profane.

For Hartshorne, God is ultimate and absolute. God is also relative,
because perfect relativity belongs to the divine perfection. Although the
arguments are profane, what they argue for is the sacred reality that has
been identified with God for thousands of years.

For Whitehead, the rhetoric and sensibility were different. In *Process
and Reality*, God does not appear in the category of the ultimate or
indeed in any part of the categoreal scheme. The philosophical ultimate is
creativity. God is a "creature of creativity" or even an "accident of creativity." In the structure of *Process and Reality*, God appears as a "derivative
notion." Whitehead emphasized the importance of the "secular" function of God, which he claimed had been neglected. All of this points to a
fundamentally different way of thinking about God, even if some of the
resultant ideas are not so different.

One way of putting this is to say that, for Whitehead, God as the
Sacred One is dead. Accordingly he can develop a cosmology and a
metaphysics neither favoring nor fearing the inclusion of God. One
simply follows where the evidence leads. After one has identified what
is involved in the constitution of the world, one is free to consider how
to label what one has identified. Whitehead chose to use "God" to
name the "principle of limitation." However, it is also important to note
that this choice was dictated by the conviction that the word "God"
has religious connotations and should not be used where those are not
appropriate.

In the decision to name the principle of limitation "God," therefore, Whitehead was guided by his understanding of religious experience and thought. He rejected the alternative of identifying the metaphysical ultimate ("substantial activity" in *Science and the Modern World*, "creativity" in *Religion in the Making* and *Process and Reality*) as God, because that would make God equally responsible for good and evil. It was his judgment that religious traditions are oriented to a basis for distinguishing good and evil, and this indicated the principle of limitation instead. Once he had decided that religious intuitions are related to this principle, then he could look to these as a source for further knowledge of God. Thus treating God in a profane manner did not exclude actual religious experience from evidence.

In principle this profane approach to God should provide a third way between conventional theism and conventional atheism. Theists cling to remnants of the sacred they believe they can still discern. They like to talk about mystery and transcendence. God is sometimes affirmed as a limit phenomenon. Sometimes God is associated with the universal Ground. Often the idea of something absolute plays a role. God's actual role in human life or in the world frequently becomes vanishingly small. Yet God typically remains sacred in the sense of forbidding full analysis or examination. Trying to know or to say too much about God is inappropriate to the sacred object. In one way or another, the sense of awe and wonder must be preserved.

Atheists fear the interference of this remnant of the sacred. They remember all too well when it exerted enormous power psychologically and sociologically, and they see that there are large communities in which this still occurs, sometimes in dangerous ways. They want the world to be securely free from that, and that means it should be unequivocally atheist. Some see no loss entailed. Of these some believe that science can provide reliable answers to all our questions. Some believe that reason can deal somewhat separately with the realm of values without introducing anything theistic. Still others recognize that with the negation of God there is a threat of nihilism. But if human beings are to mature, they argue, they must face and endure that threat.

Whitehead proposed that when we are truly free from the power of the sacred, we need no longer fear that God or religious beliefs will threaten us with boundaries or with irrational demands. They are part of the profane world and constitute no limit on our freedom of inquiry.

Instead they contribute to the intelligibility of this profane world and to finding necessary meaning and purpose within it.

It is striking that those who cling to the sacred in an increasingly profane world are typically more and more minimalist in what they have to say about God, or religious reality generally. Often they avoid the word "God" altogether, sometimes replacing it with "the sacred" or simply "mystery." Whitehead, on the contrary, in his most technical writing speaks frequently and without embarrassment about God as a necessary factor in the world, performing crucial roles. Further he develops a rich and complex theory of God with manifold religious implications.

The price that Whitehead has paid for this extensive profane talk of God has been high. It turns out that the sacred lives on in still powerful and effective ways. Those who cling to it are offended by Whitehead's doctrine. They are uncomfortable with his comfort with the word "God." That comfort reflects the fact that God is not, for him, sacred. They prefer to believe less and less as long as they can connect what they say to the sacred or else disconnect their talk of God from their understanding of what actually happens in the world.

The enemies of the sacred cannot believe that Whitehead's God is on their side. That Whitehead speaks of God leads them to assume that he is softheaded or out of touch with the intellectual currents that have driven the sacred out of the world of the university and of intellectuals generally. They cannot entertain the possibility of giving religious community, intuitions, and values a major place in life and society while excluding the sacred.

Nevertheless, the time may come in the not too distant future when the situation will change. Some religious practices and modes of thought are finding a place in the high culture of our time. This is especially true of some forms of Buddhist meditation and thought. They can be experienced as wholly profane and as remarkably beneficial. Perhaps we are still too close to our Christian past to be ready to appropriate its wisdom and ideas in this profane way. But some segments of our culture have been largely free from this form of the sacred for generations. Recovery of Christian wisdom in a profane context should be possible.

Indeed, much of this work has already been done. The quest for the historical Jesus fully desacralized Jesus and presented him, precisely in this profane form, as one from whom one may well learn and one may decide to follow. Recently Marcus Borg, in *Meeting Jesus again for the*

First Time, again introduced the desacralized Jesus to the church in a respectful and persuasive manner. The response has been widely positive. Reinhold Niebuhr's *Nature and Destiny of Man* brought Christian wisdom to bear on the affairs of profane history without coloring them in a sacral light. Whitehead's profane God fits with these and many other moves. A profane Christianity need not be a minimalist or impoverished tradition. It can be very rich, and it can address the deepest needs of a profane world. Clinging to the remnants of the sacred or fanning the sparks of the sacred into new life will not accomplish this. Indeed, there is great danger for humanity in the currently widespread re-strengthening of the sacred and its absolutization of particular traditions, especially the Abrahamic ones.

One may argue that if the traditional religions are desacralized, the sacred will reappear in a new form. Nation states have clothed themselves in the aura of the sacred. This religious nationalism has done great harm culminating in World War II and the genocide of the Shoah. Sadly, one sees that the Jews who suffered most from national and Christian sacralizations are engaged in sacralization of themselves as the chosen people and the land as their divine right. If something must be sacred, perhaps it is better that it be the God of the Abrahamic traditions. But we have seen, and now see, the terrible dangers that result from this.

Equally disturbing is the sacralization that is involved with secularism. There are wide swathes of the university community, for example, in which the view that the natural world is self-contained is no longer discussable. It provides the context for the only acceptable conversation. Those who violate it or even challenge it are excommunicated. The task of desacralization shold not be limited to religious ideas or nationalism. No, our task is to desacralize altogether.

Paradoxically, one might say that if everything is desacralized, the profane will be sacralized. How we respond to this depends on our understanding of the "sacred." One approach is to focus on a particular dimension of experience, such as the numinous and the *mysterium tremendum*. In this sense, it is simply a fact of experience like others and should be contained in a fully profane account. Why should we question the reality of such experiences? The task is to understand them and consider how they are related to other experiences.

My critique of the sacred is based on understanding it to be that which is understood as absolute, that which brooks no comparison with other things, that which forbids rational analysis and eludes rational explanation. In this sense, what is profane ceases to be profane when it is sacralized. That is what I complain of with regard to the modern scientistic worldview.

On the other hand, we could understand "the sacred" as that which is most important for human life, that which gives it meaning, calls forth trust and compassion, and leads to generosity and commitment. In this case the profane God, the profane Jesus, and the profane Christian ethic can well become for some the new sacred. Similar statements can be made about other religious traditions. However, rather than redefining the "sacred" in this way, I think it is better to oppose it altogether. I wish we could also avoid the word "religion" except in a negative sense, but that would be more difficult. In any case, I favor speaking of wisdom traditions, systems of thought, worldviews, communities of faith, ways of life, convictions and commitments. We can talk about devotion to God and faithfulness to Jesus in this context without suggesting absolutes that are beyond critical evaluation.

Although I would not have written in this vein in my student days, I do not think I misrepresent even my early encounter with Whitehead. I was not offended by his apparent reducing of God by calling God a "creature of creativity" or by denying God the status of the ultimate. I appreciated the fact that he was affirming God because he found good reasons to do so rather than because he personally and religiously needed God as I did. I could trust his reasoning as I could not trust my own.

But my primary response to Whitehead, and especially to *Process and Reality*, was one of awe. It was clear to me that Whitehead was a thinker who wrestled with questions at a level far deeper than any to which my thinking had brought me. Despite my great fascination with McKeon and my great appreciation for Hartshorne, I did not see in either a comparable depth. Whitehead inspired in me a confidence that the deeper I went the more I would learn. I found a unique comprehensiveness of vision that dealt with extraordinary originality and insight with questions of physics, of personal faith, and of education as well as much else. I encountered a combination of technical rigor and human wisdom that I have not found elsewhere.

The vision of the world that I learned from Hartshorne and other process thinkers—as a field of interrelated events, rather than as lumps of matter in relative motion—was strengthened profoundly. I anticipated that many of the questions I could not yet answer had answers, and that many questions that had not yet even occurred to me also had answers in this text. Decades later new discoveries and insights seem more to confirm his vision than to supersede it.

After working through his *magnum opus, Process and Reality,* repeatedly, over a half century, I now know its limitations. Whitehead changed his mind as he wrote and did not bother to remove what he had written from an earlier point of view. He introduced new ideas that are not reconciled with elsewhere established principles. There are many loose ends. Nevertheless, I have never been disappointed. The richness of the analysis and the profundity and rigor of the thinking still challenge me to study yet again. Each time I study the book I see the superficiality of some aspect of my previous interpretation.

I dare to believe that at a fundamental philosophical level, with all its faults and weaknesses, it is the most important book of the twentieth century. Obviously this does not mean that its influence has thus far been comparable to that of numerous other works. Far from it! For a while I feared that the book would fall into obscurity and that the course of thought would proceed as if it did not exist. I am now less fearful of this fate—more hopeful. In the twenty-first century Whitehead's conceptuality is finding a resonance that seemed largely absent in the twentieth. If my personal vocation proves to have had any real historical significance, it will be in having helped to keep interest in Whitehead alive through a highly uncongenial period.

If Whitehead's writings gain the influence they deserve, there will be many "Whiteheads." Already there are many versions of Whitehead around and there are neo-Whiteheadians and post-Whiteheadians. Since Whitehead's system has important loose ends, modifications are inevitable. Also, no philosopher has been more emphatic than Whitehead that every system has its time and will be superseded by one that can absorb its insights and take account of new information as well.

Thus far, however, beginning with Hartshorne's modifications, I do not see the many changes that have been proposed as advances. I tried my own hand at making his position more coherent in *A Christian Natural Theology.* I now judge that, at least on most points, a fuller reading of Whitehead leads to a wiser and richer vision than I proposed. I am grateful that Westminster John Knox has allowed me to publish a significantly revised version that defends a position much closer to Whitehead's.

Some want to appropriate Whitehead's general cosmology without including any talk of God. Some want to make Whitehead's doctrine of God more like traditional understandings. Some want to replace his idea of God with an enriched view of creativity. Some want to absorb creativity into God. Some want to locate God in the future. Some want to abolish Whitehead's "eternal objects" so that there will be only process. Some want to interpret these eternal objects in a far more Platonic way than Whitehead intended. Some want to replace Whitehead's unitary actual entities with larger events that have no definite boundaries. Some want to treat Whitehead's conceptuality as more suggestive and less descriptive than Whitehead thought of it. Others want to insist more rigidly on its literal precision than did Whitehead. Some want to follow the early Whitehead, rejecting his later developments. Fortunately, on some of the most important contributions of Whitehead, such as his remarkable doctrine of physical feelings or prehensions, there is little disagreement.

That there are such discussions and proposals is healthy. Each modification brings Whitehead into closer alignment with some other currents of recent thought. Out of the resulting discussion there may indeed come enrichments and advances in Whiteheadian thinking. However, it is my current judgment that all of these changes, and most of the others I have heard proposed, reduce the adequacy of Whitehead's conceptuality to the entire range of data. Until the richness of Whitehead's thought has been more fully mined, I doubt that anyone will be able to make major improvements on what he has done. I see my own role therefore more as clarifying and recommending his thought as I understand it, as supporting efforts to relate it to other philosophies, and especially as encouraging its application in new fields. However, I think that identifying its loose ends and inherent problems is also an important task.

My greatest interest is in the applications. Of course, the application to theology has been my primary work and has been of special importance to me in my own religious struggle. But today I see the future of life on this planet as threatened in many ways. I believe that the dominant worldviews are partly responsible for the continued destructiveness of national and international policies. I believe that features of the Whiteheadian worldview, most of which are shared in the family of Whiteheadian philosophies I mentioned above, could redirect human energy in much more positive ways. This seems urgent. I am far less concerned about getting the details of the system right than about using its basic insights to reshape the way modern Western thought has led us to view the world. Many of the following chapters will pick up on these wider concerns.

In concluding this chapter I should probably make explicit the position to which I have come. I have not rejected what I learned from McKeon about the diversity of systems of thought and how they repeat themselves in history, but I do not believe that Whitehead can be classified as belonging to any one of these types. I now think that in a fundamental sense Whitehead has provided a comprehensive system in which they can all find a kind of fulfillment.

I have said that he is the most important thinker of the twentieth century. I actually have come to the conclusion that one should acknowledge more. He has overcome modernity as a whole; so he cannot be put on the plane with various modern philosophers. Even Kant and Hegel are not his equal. We have to compare him instead with Descartes, and they are a match in proposing a fundamentally changed way of understanding reality. However, Descartes' way requires the rejection of much of the inherited wisdom of his time. Whitehead can assimilate the gains of modernity while retrieving the wisdom it discarded. My real belief is that Whitehead's achievement is in a class by itself.

I know that such assertions are unacceptable in our pluralistic day. I was schooled in this pluralism and remain in many ways a pluralist. But I find my actual convictions moving me to stronger evaluations and judgments. I have now unburdened myself of my true conviction. I consider myself very fortunate to have been introduced to the work of this towering figure at a formative period in my own development and to have been able to live with it throughout my career.

CHAPTER SIX

Young Harris

I entered the Divinity School at Chicago, not to respond to my calling to work for the church but to deal with my personal spiritual crisis. I could not do this best in the BD program, which quite properly included professionally oriented requirements. In any case, at that time it was a marginal factor in the school. Accordingly, I took the purely academic route leading to the MA and PhD degrees. I received the MA in 1950 and was already far on my way to the PhD when my GI bill gave out at the end of that summer. I needed to get a job in order to support my wife and first son. To make that possible I completed course work and exams that spring.

Although my personal crisis was sufficiently eased that the idea of a career in the church made sense again, I had not properly prepared for ordination and ministry. In any case, at this point I wanted very much to teach; so I looked hopefully in that direction. I thought I could finish my dissertation while teaching. I could then consider at leisure whether to seek ordination.

However, wanting to teach and finding a job were two quite different matters. There were few jobs to apply for. Colleges had expanded their faculty to respond to the flood of veterans after the war. By 1950 their numbers were greatly diminished; so faculties were more likely to shrink than to expand. Teaching religion was limited largely to church-related liberal arts colleges. I had no inside track anywhere.

Furthermore, there were family considerations. My mother had come back to Georgia to make a home for my brother James. She wanted to rejoin my father in his missionary work in postwar Japan. We thought that if I returned to Georgia, I could give sufficient help and supervision. Accordingly, I contacted the North Georgia Conference of the United Methodist Church, asking for an appointment. I would seek ordination through what was called the "Conference Course of Study" to supplement what I had studied at Chicago, especially in terms of courses about pastoral work for which I was not prepared.

To begin the process of joining the Conference required filling out forms and writing a theological statement. It also involved going to Georgia to meet a committee. The procedure was not simple and the outcome was uncertain. A few years earlier the conference had admitted a Chicago graduate whose beliefs and teaching had caused a good deal of controversy. There were those who did not want to admit another, and my theological statement was not altogether reassuring. Actually, I think someone had lost it before I met with the committee. Probably what tilted the scales in my favor was that an influential member of the committee, Bill Cannon, vouched for me chiefly on the basis of having known me when he was pastor and teacher and Emory-at-Oxford and I was a student there. The bishop, Arthur J. Moore, knew and respected my father, who as a missionary in Japan had eventually joined the South Georgia Conference. The situation was stressful, but I was allowed to start the process toward ordination. This meant I would receive an appointment. I avoided the dreaded situation of joblessness.

There was a small Methodist school in the mountains of North Georgia called Young Harris College. It combined the last two years of high school with junior college. Dr. Dow Kirkpatrick had been appointed to be the preacher at the church there and to teach the Bible courses in the college.

A couple of years later he was asked to head up a conference-wide fundraising program for the college. To give him time for that additional work, he was to be released from teaching. I was assigned to pick up his teaching while serving what had previously been a nearby student charge, the Town County Circuit.

I still had one quarter left on the GI bill. I had not begun writing my dissertation and feared that writing it entirely away from the context of the university would be difficult. I arranged to return to Chicago for the summer quarter, coming to my new appointment before classes began at Young Harris College. This provided an occasion for learning again about my limitations.

Of course, I had known students who told me they had "writer's block." I suspected that either they did not know what they wanted to write or else that they lacked discipline. I hope I did not express my opinions condescendingly.

Having gone to great lengths to secure a couple of months to start on my dissertation, I went to the library to start writing the first morning after returning to Chicago from Atlanta. I had paper and pen and lots of ideas about what I wanted to write. But for the first time, I was unable to make myself write a single word. I gave up and went home. A couple of days later I was able to get back to work, but that first day my body and my psyche simply refused to obey my will. At least this made me a bit more sympathetic toward the problems of others.

Of course, before this time I had done a lot of work that led into my dissertation. Building on this, I got the bulk of the writing done during the summer. I was able to complete the dissertation in the fall and send it to my dissertation advisor, Bernard Loomer, at the end of the Christmas holidays of 1950. In a week or so I began eagerly hurrying to my mail box in hope of some acknowledgment of receipt or even some initial comment about the content, but I heard nothing. I finally got a friend in Chicago to make sure the dissertation had been received. But I heard nothing from Loomer until the spring of 1952. He was going through a difficult time as dean of the Divinity School, but this long silence also expressed something about his own temperament. He was more concerned to deliberate thoroughly than to meet schedules. I have been committed to avoid imposing any such anxiety-ridden period of waiting on my students.

When I did hear, it was clear that his response to the dissertation was positive. He had one suggestion for a change that involved just a couple of words. He wanted me to come for my oral exams on the dissertation, and it was clear that these would not be a real problem. Actually, he wanted to bring me back to Chicago to teach. This would have followed a pattern that had been common at Chicago for generations, that is, holding on to a few of their graduates. This was the way the Chicago school, as a distinctive type of theology and scholarship, had continued and renewed itself. After Loomer, the practice largely ended, and the Chicago "school," in the older sense, is no more.

The invitation Loomer wanted to give me never came. In my understanding, it was opposed by the president of Chicago Theological

Seminary, A.C. McGiffert. The faculty of the Divinity School was part of the Federated Faculty at that time; so new faculty must be approved by the four institutions involved, of which CTS was one. CTS was oriented chiefly to preparing students for pastoral ministry, whereas the Divinity School was oriented to doctoral studies. CTS blocked an appointment that it saw as simply furthering the one-sidedly academic nature of the faculty. Not too much later CTS withdrew from the Federated Faculty altogether. Ironically, years later it invited me join its faculty.

Actually, I am grateful that I did not have to make a decision about Chicago while in Towns County, Georgia. Professionally there could hardly be a comparison between the Federated Faculty of the University of Chicago and Young Harris. I doubt that I would have willingly turned Chicago down! But Jean would have been extremely resistant. For her, Chicago was not an attractive place to live and raise a family. She was deeply pleased to be back on more familiar turf in Georgia. Probably she would have agreed to return to Chicago, but only with great reluctance. Still, I sometimes wonder what my life would have been like had I returned so soon to Chicago. I might have been able to help keep the Chicago tradition of process theology more prominent in the American scene, but in other respects I suspect my opportunities would have been more limited.

Meanwhile my appointment was to what Methodists call a six-point charge. Although I preached at all of the churches, it turned out that only two of them were viable Methodist congregations. One preaching appointment was in a supposedly union church, composed of Methodists and Baptists. However, it was really a Baptist church attended by one Methodist family. I preached there once a month but recommended dropping it from the Methodist list thereafter. Several churches were attended by tiny congregations of from two to eight people. They all had organs powered by foot pedals, but usually there was no one to play them. Jean transferred her piano skills to these. I went to each just once a month. I preached at the other two each week.

To put it mildly, these churches were all very rural in their ethos and practice. There was no Methodist church in the county seat, Hiawassee. This town had a population of only a couple of hundred at that time, but a few people had moved into the town who wanted a Methodist church there. I began services for them every Sunday as well. We began the process of planning a building. Long after I moved on, this grew into a healthy congregation supporting its own pastor. This could happen because the area around Hiawassee now has a prosperous tourist business.

By far the largest congregation was located on Hog Creek. The church was called Union Hill. The name serves as a reminder that Appalachia was divided in its loyalties during the Civil War. In general the mountaineers had seen little reason to fight for the plantation-owning aristocracy. The sympathies of many were with the Union. The neighboring county is called Union County. In the days of the Democratic "solid south" these counties tended to be Republican.

More relevant to my churches was the fact that three of them, including Union Hill, had been related to the (northern) Methodist Episcopal Church and three to the Methodist Episcopal Church South. Since these denominations had united, they now constituted one charge or circuit. It would be good to suppose that this Union and northern sympathy meant improved attitudes toward blacks. Sadly, this was not the case. The mountaineers solved the racial problem by forbidding a black to spend a night in the county.

Union Hill provided much of my education in Appalachian church life. My predecessor on this student charge had led in the building of a parsonage. His insistence on an inside toilet had split the church. This seems ridiculous, but after all, few if any of the members had a luxury of this kind. Still, we were very grateful for his insistence. Unfortunately, he had not quite finished the construction. There was no door on the toilet. This would not have been an urgent matter except that the pastor who had taken care of the charge during the summer was still staying there after we arrived. A door was my first purchase. Also there were no asbestos shingles on the back of the house; so insulation was very poor. When the temperature went below freezing, the water in the bathroom froze, lifting the lavatory off its supports and depositing it on the floor. Water came from a well, and Jean refused to drink it. As its odor became worse, she refused to use it to wash clothes. So finally we had it cleaned. This consisted in part of removing the bodies of rats in various stages of decomposition.

Jean and I lived that year well below the poverty line. By adding the value of the milk, butter, fruit, and chickens we were given, our total income may have come to $1800. On this we had to support a car to navigate the dirt roads to the churches and the parishioners homes. But we had also a nice new, almost finished home. We had no telephone, but we had access to one at the school. And we still had some of the money I had saved when in the Army. Clearly we were not really poor.

Most of my people were. The Tennessee Valley Authority did much good, but it flooded the bottom lands of these poor farmers. They continued to scratch a living from the hillsides. Some lived in one-room wooden homes so poorly constructed that one could see through cracks in the walls and the roofs. So far as I was aware, none of them lacked food, but their diets were typically poor, as was their health. Few had motor vehicles of any sort, and I discovered that one role for the pastor was to take the sick to a hospital in Atlanta, a hundred miles away. Some families survived by sending one wage earner to work in a town. But they did not complain of lack.

One story I cannot forbear to tell also concerns the preacher with whom we first shared the parsonage. He was a Baptist preacher. During the summer he had led Union Hill in a revival. Soon after my arrival I was asked whether I planned to hold another revival that fall. The "revivals" I had experienced elsewhere in Georgia were weeks with daily preaching services. That I could handle, but I knew that would not cut it in Hog Creek. I acknowledged my limitations. The church members who were requesting the revival were, I think, relieved. Immediately they told me that the Baptist preacher who had led the summer revival was ready to lead another one. I agreed, wanting to observe so as to see whether I could be capable of leading revivals in the future.

I decided for both theological and personality reasons that I would not lead that kind of revival, and actually the issue never came up again. Nevertheless, the revival was very successful with numerous conversions. Of course, the great majority of the converts were already members of the church, having been converted before, perhaps several times. In traditional Methodist teaching, some people "backslide" after conversion and must start the process of sanctification anew; so church membership was no obstacle to conversion.

There were, however, also some boys around twelve to fourteen years of age who had been converted and were ready to join the church. I think there were twelve of them. They were disappointed that I insisted on their having some instruction first. Their attendance at my educational sessions was, at best, desultory, but I decided not to be rigid in requirements. We set the date for joining as the Sunday after Thanksgiving.

There would have been no problem, except that these Methodists held to Baptist views of baptism. They rejected infant baptism and
insisted on immersion. Actually they did the local Baptists one better.
Whereas the Baptist church in Hiawassee had an indoor baptismal pool,
they wanted immersion in the lake across the road from the church. I
have never felt that, at this point in history, these differences are important, and the Methodist church is very tolerant. So I accepted all of this
and borrowed a wetsuit from the Baptist pastor.

We went to Jean's parents home in Newnan for Thanksgiving. When
we returned we found the lake frozen. No one wanted to break the ice for
immersion. Baptism was postponed to spring.

None of this would matter much had it not been for the events that
winter. The Baptist preacher stayed in the area, setting up a competing
service. One weekend he got drunk, stole a car, and ended up in jail.
That ended the competition. But it had another, more serious effect. All
but one of the boys decided that they had not been genuinely converted
after all, and they would not go ahead with baptism and church membership. If this simply postponed membership until the next revival, this
may have made only a minor difference in their lives. But I do not know
what it would take to give them the needed assurance of authenticity.
Since the church was the only community organization in Hog Creek,
inability to join would be a real loss. In retrospect I think it might have
been better to skip the class and simply fit into the local pattern. Since I
have maintained very little contact with that community, I can only hope
that the boys found a way to join.

In the neighboring county was a Methodist minister, Jack Waldrep,
who had committed his life to helping the mountain folk mature in
their faith. He was an all-but-dissertation alum of the sociology department of the University of Wisconsin, and he had been serving the
ten-point Union County circuit for perhaps ten years when I arrived in
Towns county. I saw his ministry as the responsible alternative to what
I was doing. I admired him greatly and gladly accepted his advice, help,
and cooperation.

There was very little educational program in any of my churches, and
no programs for youth. I knew no way to create anything of that sort in
individual congregations, but I arranged with Waldrep for our youth to
become part of a sub-district of the Methodist Youth Fellowship with
the youth of Union County. In the spring a good many of them went

to a meeting there. The meeting included folk dancing. This split the churches in Towns County again.

I had worked hard to overcome the hard feelings from the previous split over the indoor toilet in the parsonage, and thought I had made progress. The new split distressed me greatly. These churches needed what Jack Waldrep was offering in Union County. But even if I had felt qualified for such a task, and I certainly did not, I did not want it. If this was what it would mean to serve the church as a pastor, I was ready to give up. After just one year I wanted out and even considered a radical redirection of my life. I am embarrassed to say that a childhood fascination with farming reasserted itself, and I half-seriously considered going in that direction. Such a decision would have quickly led to total disaster.

The idea of a farm was somewhat connected to providing for my brother, James. One reason for returning to Georgia was to free my mother to rejoin my father in Japan. By being in Hiawassee I was able to keep in touch and make some arrangements for him. But that was hardly ideal.

My commitment to helping my brother was real, but not absolute. I did not seek a teaching job elsewhere, but when expressions of interest came to me, I did not turn them down. One somewhat amusing incident indicates that I had not given up professional ambitions. Dr. Lyons, the president of Pomona College, was travelling in the East to recruit faculty, including a teacher of religion. He wanted to interview me, but the only time available on his schedule was on the train between Atlanta and Birmingham. I agreed.

It became quite clear that the interview was pointless. Between the time Lyons invited me for the interview and the interview itself he had found at Yale the man he wanted for the job. Later I learned it was Fred Sontag whose colleague I became years later when I moved to Claremont.

If I had been offered the job, I would almost certainly have accepted it and tried to work out something for James, however unsatisfactory. Actually James' suicide occurred just a few months later. If it had followed soon on my departure to California, I could not but have blamed myself more. There is enough self-blame as it is.

Fortunately, Young Harris College solved my problem by offering me a full-time teaching position. I jumped at the chance. Although my relation to the college had not been my major preoccupation during the first year, it had been a welcome relief from my general failure to be a good pastor to people who needed a kind of help I did not in fact provide. I had enjoyed my teaching there. Since teaching religion at a little Methodist college was an appropriate ministerial appointment, I could set aside all the concerns about my relation to professional ministry.

Since the college could not provide housing, and there was virtually nothing available in the tiny town, we decided to build a home. We had a great time studying plans and devising our own. We planned a few features that were quite original, and I still think they were good ideas. In the transition from the Hiawassee parsonage to our home in Young Harris, we rented for a few months. That was our only experience living with an outhouse. We were very glad to move into our new home before winter.

Jean was pregnant with our second son, Cliff, and we went to Atlanta for a checkup on October 1951, a few weeks before he was due. Because we lived so far from the hospital, the doctor decided to induce his birth then. We just barely got our new home ready for him to come to.

My teaching at Young Harris in fact expanded my education. Whereas the part-time job the first year limited my teaching largely to Bible courses, the full-time job of the next two years was based on my willingness to teach whatever the school needed. I taught courses in world history, American government, and psychology. The fact that I myself had had less than two years of regular college work meant that most of the courses were quite new to me. I taught chiefly by keeping a little ahead of the students in the textbooks. I'm sure I learned more than they.

I did turn down one course. I was asked to teach chemistry. I had never had a course in that, and I inquired whether I would be in charge of chemistry lab. The answer was affirmative, and I persuaded the dean that for the safety of the students I should be excused. In one sense I regret this, since my modest education in physics and biology badly needs supplementation with a smattering of knowledge of chemistry. I might have acquired that by teaching an introductory course. However, I still believe that concerns for safety properly trumped any possible gain for me.

Young Harris College was not the sort of institution that particularly encouraged publication. Still, while teaching full time there, I had a little time to do my own work. I wrote one article that was published in *The Journal of Religion*. I take no special pleasure in that article today, but at the time it seemed wonderful to see a copy of the journal with my name included on the cover.

From what I have said the reader will judge correctly that my years at Hiawassee and Young Harris were not theologically stimulating. This does not mean that there were no people around of high intellectual abilities. Kirkpatrick, or "Dow" as he wanted everyone to call him, had been a Rhodes Scholar. He went from Young Harris to some of Methodism's leading pulpits. Years later he spent time in Latin America and became a passionate, committed, and effective advocate of liberation theology and all its political implications. I wish I had known him better then. But when he was at Young Harris, he seemed confidently ensconced in neo-orthodox patterns of theology that I could not share and to have little interest in the social issues that seemed important to me. I did not think much was to be gained from theological conversation, and he showed no interest in discussion.

My responsibilities and personal interactions were too far removed from my private religious and intellectual concerns for the latter to be much affected by the former. I realize that my failure to make connections was a weakness. Perhaps at a later date I could have done so. I recall that during my first year, when I was serving a seven-point charge as well as teaching part time at the junior college, I had a letter from one of my Chicago teachers, James Luther Adams. He was doing research on nihilism. Knowing that I was serving in one of the poorest areas of Appalachia, he asked me for illustrations of the workings of nihilism there. I was completely unable to respond.

As a family we were happy at Young Harris. My teaching there was not the sort of college teaching I had anticipated, but it was satisfying all the same. We enjoyed many of the students, and it was a good place for two young children.

Nevertheless, when an invitation came to join the faculty of Candler School of Theology at Emory University, I was excited. This would be a move that Jean would also appreciate. She had attended Emory briefly, and in any case, Atlanta was in the part of Georgia that felt like home to her.

Dr. Ernest Cadman Colwell, whom I had known slightly when he was president of the University of Chicago, was looking for faculty for a new interdisciplinary (I prefer "transdisciplinary") graduate program, the Graduate Institute for Liberal Arts. At that time Emory had no graduate study of religion, and Colwell wanted to include that in his Institute. Coming to Emory from Chicago, he wanted something of the Chicago perspective represented. He consulted with Loomer, who recommended me. Of course, I was delighted by the invitation. Jean was happy to go to Atlanta. We moved to Emory in the summer of 1953.

CHAPTER SEVEN

Emory University

Colwell became an increasingly important person in my life. Years earlier he had gone to Chicago to teach New Testament, but he had soon become dean of the Divinity School. Robert Maynard Hutchins, the university chancellor, called Colwell to be president, and Colwell had made Loomer his successor as dean of the Divinity School. Hutchins groomed Colwell to be his successor. During World War II one of his responsibilities was supervision of the university laboratories which played an important role in the development of the atomic bomb.

Jean and I had met him and his wife soon after Jean joined me at Chicago. The university held a social event for students, a rare phenomenon there, and it was structured around the states from which students came. Jean and I went to the Georgia meeting place and there our hosts were the Colwells. We were the only students there. I was a bit overawed at being with the president of the university, but the Colwells put us at ease and we had an enjoyable visit. Later I audited a class in New Testament he taught in the Divinity School. I admired him greatly.

Colwell probably did not remember these contacts, and they had nothing to do with the invitation to Emory. When Hutchins resigned to organize the Institute for the Study of Democratic Institutions in Santa Barbara, the University of Chicago trustees decided to draw the university back from Hutchins' radical experimentation toward the mainstream of American higher education. Accordingly, they passed over Colwell. Emory University, where he had studied earlier, invited him back to be vice-president and dean of faculties, and heir apparent to the presidency. Colwell accepted.

Hutchins while at Chicago had struggled against the takeover of university teaching by departments organized by academic disciplines. This organization of knowledge was designed to promote specialized research and was, he believed, detrimental to authentic graduate education. Colwell had appreciated his point, and the Divinity School education I received was an excellent example of the alternative. It aimed to stimulate creative thinking rather than scholarly specialization.

One of the many objections to the disciplinary organization of knowledge was that it produced scholars unprepared to teach in liberal arts colleges. Hutchins and Colwell rightly foresaw that without places where students could prepare to teach the liberal arts, there would be an inevitable decline. When Colwell came to Emory a major goal was to prepare graduate students for teaching in these colleges. For this purpose he created a new kind of transdisciplinary graduate program, the Graduate Institute of Liberal Arts. It was to participate in this program that Colwell invited me to join the Emory faculty.

Emory was highly receptive to Colwell's proposal. At the time it had no PhD programs in the humanities, and many faculty members were eager to take part in instruction at that level. Colwell selected the faculty chiefly from classics, literature, philosophy, and religion. It consisted more of younger scholars than of senior ones. He wanted to move the teaching of the humanities away from a collection of separate disciplines to a sense of the cultural heritage as a whole. For example, the students and faculty might all take part in a course on Greek civilization. Obviously this would be different from the sorts of courses given in any one of the several department where aspects of Greek culture were studied. Yet what was studied was relevant to all.

I did not fully understand what Colwell was doing, and I doubt that many of the other professors did either. Certainly I did not really appreciate the struggle that he and Hutchins had so valiantly waged at Chicago. But over the years I have come more and more to admire their far-reaching insights and the efforts they made to stem the destructive tide. I am retroactively proud to have been a part of their efforts, even though they failed, and I wish that I had, at the time, understood better what was at stake.

The quest to identify courses that would be of value across disciplinary lines led me to propose one on the analysis of arguments. I assumed that in all the humanities there are articles and books that argue for particular theses. In the field of literature I had in mind not poems and novels but the writings of critics.

I assumed that it is possible for the student of one of these writings to state a thesis upheld therein and then formulate the argument made for this thesis in a rigorous, logical form. Traditional syllogisms worked well for this purpose. Presented in this form it often becomes clear where the most dubious steps in support of a thesis are located and what its unargued assumptions seem to be. This is often most interesting where the theses of two thinkers are clearly opposed.

I developed a course in which students could take their material from any field but share with the class a syllogistic formulation of the arguments and the conclusions that could be drawn from these. All of us could read the essay being analyzed and discuss whether the argument represented accurately the thought of the writer who put the thesis in question forward. We could often see the points at which writers who defended opposing theses most fundamentally disagreed. I continued teaching this course at Claremont, but I stopped after being told by a mathematical logician that there are far more powerful forms of logic than the syllogism. Of course, in an abstract way I knew that, but it had not seemed to matter. This time I was intimidated. I now regret giving up the course. If someone develops a better course in the analysis of arguments based on more modern logic, I am happy to yield, but I think I should have continued with an effective method until a better one was demonstrated.

The ILA gave me the opportunity to supervise my first two dissertations. One of them was written by Colwell's son, Carter, in the field of literary criticism. He showed how several literary critics who seemed to be in conflict with one another could be seen instead to be complementary when one employed a Whiteheadian hermeneutic. The other student was Jimmy Jordan. He had been an all-American football player at Georgia Tech. He wrote on philosophy of education, partly influenced by Whitehead. Of course, in both cases, scholars with much more knowledge of the fields were on the committees.

In my view, Colwell's idea is still well worth pursuing. The nature of graduate education works for specialized disciplines and against the liberal arts. Liberal arts colleges have to work with faculty trained to introduce students to disciplines rather than to enrich the students' lives by introducing them critically to their heritage.

However, ILA's success was also its downfall. Once this PhD program was established, each department began thinking of having a PhD program of its own. I was myself involved in such thinking both in philosophy and in religion. As new programs developed, the role of the ILA in relation to those fields faded. Its scope became much narrower.

At the time that Colwell invited me to Emory to take part in the ILA, administrators had much more freedom than now in making appointments. On the other hand, no appointments were made primarily to the new Institute. Accordingly, Colwell had negotiated with the retiring dean of Candler School of Theology to place me on his faculty. Much of this happened during the summer. When the professors of theology returned from summer vacation and found that they had a colleague, one of them was very upset—with considerable justification. Part of the upset was about the procedure, but more basically for him, the problem was that I came from Chicago and represented the neo-naturalist tradition of that school. For him this was anathema.

The new dean was the same Bill Cannon I had known at Young Harris and who helped me gain admission to the annual conference. He worked with the president of the university, who happened to be a cousin of my mother, to achieve a compromise. I signed a statement promising never to teach systematic theology at Emory. I was allowed to teach theology only in historical terms. Cannon taught the basic sequence in the history of theology, but as dean he expected to be away much of the time. I would co-teach these courses. I undertook to teach the history of American theology, much of which was new to me. Arrangements were made for me to teach courses also in the philosophy department and a great books course in addition to participation in the Graduate Institute of Liberal Arts. Of course, I was disappointed to be excluded from teaching in my own field, but basically I rejoiced at the new context and opportunities.

The move to Emory was a happy one for Jean and the boys. It worked out well for my ecclesiastical status. Teaching on a Methodist theological faculty was of course an acceptable appointment from the point of view of the North Georgia Annual Conference. I was still in the process of taking courses in the course of study required for those who sought ordination without getting a professional degree, but the Candler faculty was also grading papers of students in this program; so I was drawn into that second relation to it. Both roles were tedious but necessary and unobjectionable.

I was finally ready for ordination as elder and for full membership in the annual conference in the summer of 1955. Jean was expecting another child when I went to Athens for the annual conference meeting at which my status would be changed. While there I received a call informing me that the baby was coming early and imminently. Fortunately, Jean's mother was staying with her in my absence and we lived very close to the Emory University hospital. When I got home I learned that we had twin boys. We decided that we were not destined to have a daughter and that our family was complete.

Emory University at that time was still a regional rather than a national university. Nevertheless, it was a good school and an excellent place for me to be. There was a lively intellectual life, much of it centering on theological questions. The philosophy department was already fully inclusive of Whitehead. Richard Hocking was the son of William Ernest Hocking who had been a colleague of Whitehead at Harvard. The chair, Loemker, was a specialist in Leibniz and appreciative of Whitehead. Ivor Leclerc taught Whitehead, and Hartshorne came from Chicago to join the department while I was there, Accordingly, I did not have the opportunity to give courses in process thought, but no department in the country would have been more congenial.

I was welcomed there as a colleague. I taught introductory courses in logic, ethics, and aesthetics. Because of my extensive work with Richard McKeon, who considered himself a kind of Aristotelian, I was reasonably well equipped to teach Greek philosophy, and I gave a seminar in Aristotle. I had still not identified myself exclusively as a Whiteheadian, but would answer questions by referring both to Aristotle and to Whitehead as my major philosophical interests. Nevertheless, the more intensive work on Aristotle did not lead to his gaining a stronger hold on my thought. Whitehead's thought became more and more convincing to me even though I was teaching on other topics. I left Emory a full-fledged Whiteheadian.

My roles in historical theology and philosophy as well as in the great books program continued to expand my all-too-limited education. I became much better versed in the overall history of Christian thought, and I learned for the first time about American theology. My philosophy teaching, in addition to covering some topics for which I had background, also included courses in material that was quite new to me. Many of the great books that I discussed with students in that program were ones I had previously only heard of. And the work in the graduate institute was always fresh and challenging. I am grateful for all of it.

Unlike Young Harris, Emory offered many excellent discussion partners on matters of central importance to me. Two who were there when I came have been important parts of my life ever since: James Robinson and Will Beardslee. Robinson and I later went from Emory to Claremont together. Beardslee visited Claremont a number of times and eventually retired here. In some ways he became my closest colleague.

At Chicago we knew that there were theological worlds other than ours, but it was only when I came to Emory that I was seriously drawn into one of these. In those days there was a happy union of biblical scholarship and theology. Rudolph Bultmann was the central figure in this conjunction. His use of a version of Heideggerian categories to interpret New Testament texts led to a distinctive Christology and, less explicitly, a way of thinking of the human relation to God. This proposal became central to discussions both among New Testament scholars and among theologians. More remarkably it brought members of the two groups into intensive interaction.

Emory was one of the places where this discussion was most alive. Robinson was already an international leader in this work, having doctoral degrees in both New Testament and theology and giving international leadership to the post-Bultmannian quest for the historical Jesus. Beardslee knew Bultmann well, but was a student of Amos Wilder, when he taught at Chicago. His acceptance of existential thinking was modified by an interest in narrative, in culture, and in history. I found that much existential thought could be assimilated into Whiteheadian cosmology. This may have been one reason that by the time I left Emory I was more fully committed to Whitehead than when I arrived.

One theologian, not at Emory, became important to me during this period. Schubert Ogden attended the Chicago Divinity School after I left, but he moved quickly to stardom. At Chicago our names were often coupled as promising alumni of the program there, whose theology was now being called "process theology." However, he was far ahead of me in significant publications and in public recognition. He went directly from Chicago to Perkins School of Theology and soon published his dissertation, *Christ without Myth*. This proved a major contribution to the discussion of Bultmann, while connecting it with the metaphysics of

Hartshorne. He helped to give respectability to process thinking within the wider theological community.

The discussion of Bultmann drew me into the then-current German theological world. Whereas it had seemed distant and only mildly interesting from the perspective of Chicago, I came to understand at Emory that even after World War II, German theology not only retained global hegemony but also deserved that hegemony. German scholarship was the world's best. Even if one chose to go in a different direction from that of German theology, one could not do so responsibly without wrestling with it seriously.

While I was at Emory, Tom Altizer joined the faculty of the department of religion in the college. I had known him slightly at Chicago, and I was always stimulated by our occasional exchanges. Altizer belonged to the Chicago climate in that he was immersed in ideas and their discussion. But he viewed the thought forms of Chicago from a great distance. He was immersed in the world of the sacred, whereas the Chicago school of theology was the most profane in Christendom. He once explained to me that for some time he sought to recover the sacred roots of Christianity and to revitalize them. That had made him an enemy of the thinking of the modern world. But finally he recognized that the World Spirit was expressing itself in the long process of secularization. For the sake of the sacred he must will its self-destruction and find it again in its opposite. But the profane to which this led was very different from the profane forms and ideas of the Chicago school. It was expressed much less in theology and philosophy than in the arts and especially the writers of the great epics. They were wrestling with the power of the sacred and its transmutations, whereas all this was simply ignored by most of the Chicago faculty. The great exceptions there were the teachers of history of religion, Joachim Wach and, subsequently, especially, Mircea Eliade, who probably understood Altizer better than anyone else.

Altizer has always had the power to draw me into a world that is otherwise strange to me. His authenticity is palpable. What he sees is there to be seen even if it is not what I see. I sense that his insight is more profound than mine. I am left with an uncomfortable feeling of the superficiality of my own thought and work. Yet at the same time I find myself called to deal more with the practical questions that present themselves at my more superficial level than with the deeper level of reflection about the history and death of the sacred. For me to write about that as Altizer has would never be authentic.

Through Altizer I gained a far deeper sense of the way in which God, identified as the sacred, could be, and had been, oppressive. That had not been my youthful experience of God, and hence the ending of my sense of God's intimate presence was not a liberation but an impoverishment. However, I could see that much of traditional theology had led to the experience of God as oppressor. If human beings were to be free and responsible, to become adults in Bonhoeffer's sense, this God must be overthrown. I gained a fuller appreciation of Hartshorne's and Whitehead's rejection of divine omnipotence, and whereas some process theologians want to keep that language and redefine it, I do not. I think the accent upon God's control has done enormous harm. More than anything else, I think, it has been responsible for turning God into Satan for such visionaries as Blake.

Engagement with Altizer forced me to think through my own view of history. His was basically Hegelian in the sense that the movement of the World Spirit can be discerned in the cutting edge of thought and imagination in each generation. This movement of the spirit is far deeper than rational analysis or argument. This is largely convincing; that is, intellectuals give expression to their cultural situation at least as much as they shape it. Nevertheless, it seems to me that very particular beliefs or conceptual moves that could have been otherwise have had fateful consequences. The mechanistic vision might not have gained such an overwhelming hold on the mind of the West. If it had not, that history, including the movement of the Spirit, would have been different. Even today, empirical and rational considerations may weaken the hold of the mechanistic vision and allow for movements of the Spirit of a more promising sort. This view of the contingent character of intellectual and cultural history makes place for a kind of reflection and argument that is virtually irrelevant for Altizer. It certainly does not make his analyses false or irrelevant. These reflections also reinforced my break with the lingering influence of McKeon and Aristotle and strengthened my commitment to Whitehead.

When Altizer published *The Gospel of Christian Atheism,* I was not surprised by the content. But I was amazed at the national and even international response. I had not thought of Altizer as rejoicing in the limelight as in fact he did. I admired him for it. For a brief period theology became a topic of popular discussion. Much of the façade that was, by then, most of what was left of the great movement we call neo-orthodoxy, crumbled before the assertion of the "the death of God." Barthian fideism was no longer widely convincing. The theological climate in the United States was permanently changed.

On the other hand, what Altizer meant by atheism and the death of God was poles removed from the general understanding. Altizer is the embodiment of *Homo religiosus.*

He was proclaiming a historical transformation at a deeply religious level. He emphasized the coincidence of opposites so that through the death of the sacred, the sacred appeared in some new form. I'm sure Altizer was disappointed by the level of the response, but he was pleased that it brought doubts and disbeliefs to the surface and displayed the depth of the unbelief that, he was convinced, actually characterized our culture.

In my case, however, my Whiteheadian theism was only strengthened. Whereas the "death-of-God" writers implied that as long as we affirmed God we could not affirm the world, I gave lectures on "God *and* the World" and published them in a little book that continues to have some readers. I feared that instead of infusing the world with deeper meaning, the absence of God would move society toward a narrowing of horizons of concern and a nihilistic attitude toward life in general. What Altizer saw as bringing about the death of God had long since been strongly rejected by Whitehead. It was in the absence of that God that Whitehead had found reason to affirm God anew, a God much more like Jesus than like the omnipotent deity who was so hard to distinguish from Satan. For a while after my move to Claremont we engaged in an intensive correspondence. He evoked from me deep self-reflection and openness about how I really felt about many matters, especially theological ones. By temperament and habit I took people's beliefs and ideas seriously, whatever they might be. But at another level, I often felt that in discussing them, we spent much of our time dealing with trivial issues or just spinning our wheels. We fiddled while Rome burned. I tended to keep this dimension of my feelings and beliefs suppressed. Altizer drew them out.

My admiration and appreciation continued, but we went our separate ways, and our communication declined. Our separate ways have been similar in that we both continued to talk a lot about God in a theological context that no longer favored doing so. On the other hand, our ways diverged in that what we have had to say has been radically different.

Altizer was grateful to Emory and proud of the university because it in no way inhibited his freedom to speak and write. It is estimated that Emory lost a couple of million dollars in support from those who called for firing Altizer. But no one within the university asked him to tone down what he said. In the long run this academically responsible stance paid off handsomely. Emory ceased being a regional university and became a nationally competitive one. I have seen it ranked fifteenth or sixteenth among all the universities in the nation.

Teaching in diverse fields and involvement in graduate work kept me busy. This was compounded by my financial need to teach in the summer as well. Nevertheless, I did do a little writing.

None of the intellectual stimulus and turmoil I enjoyed in my five years at Emory had much effect on my writing at the time. I was not ready to express new ideas. I published a few articles, more philosophical than theological. Most of these consolidated thinking that I had been doing as a student at Chicago. One was an essay on aesthetics that I wrote after teaching a college course on that topic for the philosophy department. This essay expressed my increasing appreciation for Whitehead as providing a way of incorporating many seemingly dissimilar insights in a unified system

When I found time, I began working on a book of a very different sort. My teaching in historical theology led me to wrestle with the differences among the several Protestant traditions. I thought that, deeper than specific doctrinal differences among Protestants, was a basic sense of what was religiously importance. In order to clarify this for myself, and hopefully for others as well, I worked on a book that I called "Types of Protestant Piety."

That was its actual topic. I finished the book only after moving to Claremont and sent if off first to Harper and then to Abingdon. Both turned it down. Westminster Press accepted it, but rejected the idea of putting "piety" into a title. It eventually appeared under the title *Varieties of Protestantism*. I have never felt comfortable with that title, since my approach was more narrowly focused.

If something like that book had appeared twenty years later under the title "Types of Protestant Spirituality," it might have found a significant market. But there was little attention to such matters in 1960. Its publication was an important event only for me, and chiefly because it initiated a relationship with Westminster Press that helped me a great deal. Roland Tapp toured the country annually, I think, and would talk to his authors about our future plans. It was a wonderfully supportive relationship for a young writer who was not yet sure that he had much to say.

My time at Emory coincided with the civil rights struggle. Retrospectively, I am surprised that it did not have a larger effect on my life and thought there. To some degree, of course, it affected us all. Many Emory faculty members objected to the segregationist policies of the university. Occasionally we could flout them by inviting black professors to campus anonymously or without announcing the race in advance. Of course, we were free to state our views. There was a considerable audience within the churches, especially among the women, for opposition to segregation, and I used what opportunities I had to address the issue.

Such acts made me feel a little better, but were, I fear, otherwise quite useless. I regretfully acknowledge that I was not seriously involved in the civil rights movement and in fact contributed next to nothing to the cause.

The most important effect of the civil rights struggle on me personally was through its effect on Colwell. At Emory, once again, he was cheated of the leadership role for which he was being prepared. The trustees were maintaining that as a church institution, Emory did not have to integrate. They knew that if Colwell were president, he would not stand for such foolishness. Hence they brought in a "good Southerner" who would work with them. This ruse was not effective long, and Emory not only integrated but has given good leadership in race relations.

Meanwhile the trustees compounded their offense by refusing to invite presidents of black colleges to the inauguration of the new president. This provided an opportunity for a symbolic protest. Hocking and I decided to boycott the inauguration and instead, while it was taking place, visited with Benjamin Mays, the president of one of the black colleges in Atlanta, to express our personal apologies.

When word that Colwell had been denied the presidency of Emory got out, he was courted vigorously by the trustees of a new Methodist seminary in southern California. This new seminary consisted of the former graduate faculty and students in religion of the University of Southern California, which had previously been recognized as a seminary by the Methodist church. USC had been founded by the Methodist church but had lost all connection except through the graduate School of Religion. The trustees wanted to cut this remaining tie. The faculty was given the choice of remaining as a graduate school of religion without a professional dimension or leaving. All chose to leave to become the core faculty of a new Methodist seminary.

In those days the "mainline" denominations were growing and prosperous and could dream great dreams. As the former dean of the University of Chicago Divinity School and, later, president of the University, Colwell was well known among theological educators and in higher education circles generally. For him to be the first president of the new school would signal its ambition to become a major seminary. Meanwhile the trustees sought the best location and settled on Claremont.

Eventually Colwell was persuaded. His departure left a large hole at Emory. When the next year he invited Robinson and me to join him in the Claremont seminary, we were both pleased with the invitation. Colwell created an excitement about what he was doing that was almost irresistible. In my case, it was also my chance, at last, to teach theology, which was, after all, my personal preoccupation and my professional field of specialization.

There were, nevertheless, reasons for hesitation. The family was not eager to leave Atlanta. My wife was an only child and her parents lived very much for her and our children. Having her parents nearby was of great practical help to us. Professionally, Emory was a fine institution, far more secure than a new seminary in California.

One reason for leaving was that, although I had many excellent contacts at Emory, I was never fully accepted by my official home institution, the Candler School of Theology. I was much more comfortable in the Department of Philosophy. I was welcome there and had enjoyed my teaching in philosophy. Of my few publications, the more scholarly had been in philosophical journals. Despite my lack of any degree in philosophy, I was offered a full-time appointment in that department. I deeply appreciated this invitation.

If the American philosophical scene had generally been like the Emory philosophical faculty, I might well have accepted. But the national scene was very different from the Emory one. If I were to be a professional philosopher in the second half of the twentieth century, I would have to enter knowledgably into the conversations within the community of analytic philosophers. I had dipped by toes in those waters and did not think that would be particularly difficult, but I also did not find such a career enticing.

My sense of vocation as a theologian pulled me strongly toward Claremont. So when my family agreed to the move, I happily accepted Colwell's invitation. It meant that Jean's parents also eventually retired to California. All this so that in my ninth year of teaching I could offer courses in my own field—theology!

CHAPTER EIGHT

Claremont and the German Connection

Despite his somewhat awkward situation at Emory, Colwell would not have returned to theological education had he not had some visionary ideas for that as well. He was convinced that the church needed highly educated leadership and that in fact seminaries were not able to meet this need. The students they admitted were college graduates, but that did not mean that seminaries could build on any particular knowledge that they brought with them. At the same time, the range of knowledge needed by a minister was very broad. This meant that most of a student's three-year program was taken up with introductions to Old Testament, New Testament, church history, the history of theology, systematic theology, Christian ethics, missions, ecumenism, history of religions, psychology of religion, sociology of religion, philosophy of religion, religion and the arts, media and communications, preaching, Christian education, pastoral counseling, church administration, denominational studies, urban ministry, rural ministry, and so forth. After three years of being introduced to many of these fields, students were graduated, awarded a second bachelor's degree, and declared ready for leadership in the church.

What to do? Other professions prescribed a great deal of college work as prerequisite. Departments of religion with highly qualified teachers were developing in many colleges and universities. The tendency at the time was to discourage students planning on ministry from majoring in religion. If they would have to repeat all that in seminary, such discouragement made sense. But if a religion major became the norm, then theological seminaries could offer genuinely graduate level study.

Colwell's dream went beyond that. He thought that the church needed leaders with great breadth but also with the experience of mastery in some field. This would not be an academic discipline, where specialization is oriented to the advancement of a discipline, but something relevant to the life of the church. Each student should write a substantial paper, different from, but not inferior to, the dissertations required for the PhD. This would require considerably more than the traditional three years even when introduction to some fields could be presupposed—about four and a half years, as it turned out.

Colwell thought that the requirements for ministerial leadership in the church were just as great as for college teaching—but different. Accreditation for college teaching was the PhD. A different doctorate was appropriate for ministry. He decided on a Doctor of Religion degree, a RelD.

Colwell sold his dream to the faculty, and Claremont developed a program along these lines. The practical problems were enormous. A prospective student had to be persuaded to take much more time to prepare for ministry than the church required or even favored. The school was poor; so students had to go heavily into debt. In addition, most applicants did not have the prerequisites; so these had to be provided without academic credit. Meanwhile the mainstream churches were beginning to decline. Ministry became a less attractive option. Most students came to seminary in adulthood having decided on a change of vocation. They wanted to complete their preparation as quickly as possible. Adapting to these changing situations required compromise after compromise.

Nevertheless, the experiment did influence modest changes in theological education. The debates about the Claremont program and a somewhat similar one at Chicago led to giving up the Bachelor of Divinity label in favor of the Master of Divinity. Also many schools now give a Doctor of Ministry degree for work beyond the MDiv. Perhaps, if something like Colwell's vision had been in place in the years immediately after World War II, there could have been a generation of leaders who would have prevented the decline that in fact undermined any realization of the bold vision. We will never know.

In 1958 there was not much to come to in Claremont except a dream that we called the School of Theology at Claremont or, more usually, STC. There were nine faculty who had moved from Los Angeles to Claremont. There were perhaps a hundred students, some finishing up work they had begun with this faculty at the University of Southern California and some entering the school *de novo*. There were a few books that USC allowed STC to have because they had clearly been bought with money given by the Methodist church. There was a vacant piece of land, and there were a couple of Quonset huts and a little rented space for classes.

Mainly, there was Colwell. No sooner had he announced his acceptance of this position than he was elected president of the Association of American Theological Schools. His personal status with the Claremont College faculties had made them accept this school, albeit reluctantly, as a neighbor. He told everyone who would listen that we would become a great center of theological education. And we believed him.

In fact our progress in that direction was remarkable. An attractive campus began to appear. Student enrollment increased. Morale was high.

Colwell knew that the faculty that came from USC, while consisting of highly qualified and capable people, was not at the forefront of theological education. His task was to persuade them to add to their numbers younger scholars who thought in ways different from theirs and had more promise of future leadership. Partly because of his skills and partly because of the personal maturity of the older faculty, he succeeded. Robinson and I were the first fruits of this effort.

The major success was in bringing promising young scholars from Germany. Robinson had a degree in theology from Karl Barth and had worked extensively in New Testament studies with Bultmann. He was intimately familiar with the German scene. Germany was still recovering from World War II, and even Claremont's modest salaries were competitive. Robinson's presence in Claremont made it a respectable place for a young German scholar to consider.

It was easy in those days to bring German scholars with PhDs to the United States. In Germany the PhD only qualified one to teach in the gymnasia. Those who had procured a doctorate and who wished to be university professors had to "habilitate." This required that a university professor take one on as an assistant, that one teach in the university, and that one publish another book. Robinson was sufficiently oriented to the German scene that his interest was in bringing habilitated German scholars to Claremont.

Two early appointments were Hans Dieter Betz in New Testament and Rolf Knierim in Old Testament. Later we brought Ekkehard Muehlenberg in church history. It is my impression that at that time Claremont may have had half of the habilitated German theological scholars teaching in the United States. All three made enormous contributions to the school and its teaching. Betz eventually went on to become the senior New Testament scholar at Chicago. Muehlenberg returned to Germany to head up the leading center of Luther research there. Only Knierim retired in Claremont.

These appointments quickly made Claremont well known in Germany. We were able to bring distinguished German scholars, such as Herbert Braun, Gerhard Ebeling, and Wolfhart Pannenberg as visiting professors. For a West Coast school pursuing a distinctively American style of thought to become an active part of the German theological scene in just a few years was a remarkable transformation. It was also remarkable that the German scholars fitted into the still dominantly American context so well.

Robinson was clearly the key player, but I worked with him on the local politics. I had discovered recent German scholarship while at Emory and was fully convinced that it was an essential part of what was needed in the United States as well. Of course, I knew that my own attachment to Whitehead placed me in a quite different world. I think Colwell's understanding was similar. That the older faculty went along with this process was remarkable.

What was perhaps most remarkable was that the school grew in this way when it was very poor. It brought no endowment from USC. The Methodist annual conference raised the money for the first buildings and General Conference contributed to the annual budget, but even survival without an endowment was a questionable matter. We lived a hand--to-mouth existence. We negotiated with Bay Area seminaries and with Fuller Theological Seminary in Pasadena to share the modest costs of our visiting scholars. Colwell had a system of having a fiscal year begin in July but inviting a new professor to come in September to reduce the burden on the budget he presented to the trustees.

We made strong appointments of young American scholars as well. Tom Trotter joined us at what the church called "minimum salary." He went on to become dean, then Executive Secretary of the Commission of Higher Education and Ministry of the denomination, and finally a university president. Joe Hough took a cut from his scholarship income at Yale when he joined the Claremont faculty. He succeeded Tom as dean here, then became dean of the Vanderbilt Divinity School, and finally president of Union Theological Seminary. On retiring to Claremont he was persuaded to serve as interim president of Claremont Graduate University. Howard Clinebell played a leading role in organizing pastoral counselors nationally and internationally. Over the years our PhD program in pastoral counseling was internationally the most attractive. It gives me considerable satisfaction to recall how we built the faculty in those early years.

Obviously money was not the drawing card, and in fact Colwell was not good at raising it. He hated asking for it himself, and he thought that few professionals in the field raised more than enough to pay their own salaries. Before he retired, the faculty was becoming restive at their low salaries. Much as I admire him, I recognize that he could only take the school so far. He left to his successors the very difficult job of undergirding his dream. The School's financial situation has always been precarious.

An amusing feature of the financial hopes of the school were the speculations about the name it would eventually receive. Many seminaries bear the name of a major donor. We badly needed one and expected to be renamed if a really significant gift were made to the school. There were three Methodist families in California capable of making this kind of gift. One was the Mudd family. One institution in Claremont is named Harvey Mudd College, and the inclusion of the first name overcomes the connotations of simply being Mudd College. So that was tolerable, and indeed our auditorium is named "Mudd." The other two were more problematic. The chair of our trustees, from whom all hoped for a major gift was named Dumm. His full name was John Wesley Dumm, but even so we would end up being the Dumm School of Theology. That was not an attractive prospect. The third family was named Crummy. It was hard to decide whether we would prefer to be the Dumm School of Theology or the Crummy School of Theology. In the event, Mr. Dumm, partly because of failing fortunes never gave much. The Crummy family gave the library but anonymously. So we do not have the Crummy Library in the Dumm School of Theology. The school bears only the geographical name and has done without the badly needed endowment.

I offer one more story about Colwell before my reminiscences move back more directly to theology. He had been an advisor to the Danforth

Foundation for many years. In recognition of his services and his leadership, this Foundation gave him a grant of $350,000 for a chair, which was a lot of money in those days. Despite the poverty of the seminary, Colwell used this as a basis for negotiation with the Claremont Graduate School (now renamed Claremont Graduate University). He gave CGS the Danforth chair in exchange for starting a PhD program in religion in which faculty from STC could participate. The chair was defined as philosophy of religion and gave a prod to the establishment of doctoral work in philosophy as well. Colwell knew that without opportunity to teach graduate students, he could not attract and hold top scholars. But how many administrators, operating schools with virtually no endowment, would give away their first significant grant? Jack Hutchison came from the Columbia/Union program to be the first occupant of the Danforth Chair and ran the graduate program in religion until his retirement. His successors were John Hick and D.Z. Philips, both internationally distinguished philosophers of religion.

Since Robinson and I came together from Emory to Claremont in 1958, our friendship from Emory days became a serious collaboration. We were the "young Turks" on the faculty, with considerable support from the president. We talked a lot about how to shape the school. But we also discussed larger theological questions. We agreed that American theology had been too long a side-show of continental European theology. Especially from the perspective of the continent, acceptable American theologians were classified chiefly in terms of which German theologian they followed. There was more justification for this than we hoped would characterize the future.

We thought that the group of American theologians emerging after World War II showed that this subordinate role did not need to continue forever. Nevertheless, the debates about Bultmann and his successors that had grasped me at Emory continued to have this character. The central debates occurred in Germany. The Americans most conversant with the German scene were those who had the advantage in the United States. The Germans paid virtually no attention to what the Americans had to say, with the exception of Robinson, who had done much of his work in the midst of the German discussions and had published his books in German. We thought it was time to bring the German and American discussions together in such a way that American scholars and theologians could participate in the ongoing theological discussion.

In view of the actual course of events beginning in the mid-sixties, our understanding of our historical situation does not now look far-sighted. In fact German scholarship has ceased to dominate the global theological discussion because radical voices from other places raised questions about that whole style of scholarship and thinking. The death of God controversy, to which Altizer contributed so much, began this process. It was succeeded by Latin American, black, and feminist forms of liberation theology and subsequently by many others. Interest of students of religion in the United States shifted from Germany to France, with its leadership in deconstructive postmodern thinking.

Nevertheless, the relation between American and German-language theology has retained some importance, and the more equal relationship between them has moved both forward. Our project may have contributed a little. In any case, it advanced my own theological education and made some further contribution to cementing relations between Claremont and the German-language world.

Our idea was to identify an emerging topic at the frontier of German theology and bring leading American theologians in touch with it at an early stage in its development. To do this, we planned a series of volumes we called "New Frontiers in Theology."

Martin Heidegger remained the most influential philosopher in Germany. His influence on Bultmann gave him great importance in theology as well. But Bultmann was no longer a "new frontier." I was excited that a young scholar by the name of Heinrich Ott had proposed a quite different use of Heidegger in theology, one that involved a way of thinking about God. Whereas Bultmann's use of Heidegger was based on the earlier, more existential Heidegger, Ott used the later Heidegger. We agreed that our first volume would focus on Ott's proposal, and we entitled it *The Later Heidegger and Theology*. We invited several American theologians to write in response to Ott and held a meeting at San Anselmo to hone our work. Robinson wrote an extended, and very scholarly introduction. My role was limited to an analysis of the argument. Ott wrote a reply.

The book was modestly successful. It was translated into German and read in Germany as well as in the United States, thus contributing to the goal of integrating the two theological communities. Unfortunately, we had misjudged the amount of interest in Ott's proposal in Germany. I still think it was a systematically important one, but the real interest in Germany was elsewhere.

Well before publication of the first volume in 1963 we were hard at work on the second. It was entitled *The New Hermeneutic* and dealt with the proposals of Gerhard Ebeling and Ernst Fuchs. They also appealed to Heidegger, this time to his understanding of language. This book was a far greater success in that there was an extensive discussion on both sides of the Atlantic about the hermeneutical issues it discussed. The conference held to advance the interaction took place at Drew and was a rather strange affair. When it turned out that Heidegger himself could not accept the invitation to speak because of his advancing years and health, we invited Hans Jonas, one of Heidegger's most famous pupils. Jonas chose this occasion to break his silence about Heidegger's relation to Nazism. Heidegger had made no effort to save Jonas' mother from death at the hands of the Nazis, and Jonas had waited for years after the war for some sign of regret or apology on Heidegger's part. It had not come. He had come to the conclusion that Heidegger's behavior was all too consistent with his philosophy. He warned us against it.

The third volume was about Wolfhart Pannenberg. He was still a junior figure in the German scene and regarded as somewhat out of the mainstream there. But he was too powerful a thinker to be ignored. He was a philosophical theologian in a sense that was rare in Germany, and he had a serious interest in Whitehead. The relationship I developed with him was of great importance to me.

Pannenberg had been a visiting professor at the Divinity School at Chicago, and because Whitehead was still important there in the early sixties, he did his usual systematic study of this quite non-Germanic thinker. Alone among German theologians of that time, he was genuinely interested. We shared the conviction of the importance of metaphysics for theology. Both of us thought that theology should be closely interrelated with the rest of the scholarly and intellectual enterprise rather than separated from it as one discipline among others. These views and attitudes gave us much in common.

Already in his student days he had led a group in developing a quite distinctive theological school. It had published an important book explaining its understanding of history as revelation. The history in question was the actual course of events. Of course the interpretation of these events was important, but the focus should be on what in fact occurred. What occurred most decisively was the resurrection of Jesus from the dead. Pannenberg followed up on this with many original and insightful

essays and, in the early sixties, a massive Christology reflecting a kind
of scholarship I have never approximated. In the astonishing German
way, he examined the history of scholarship in the field and worked
through that in order to establish his own views. At the age of thirty-five,
I published my first book. By that age he was a major player in the global
theological scene.

I shared his concern to develop a comprehensive vision to replace
the fragments we encountered in the university and in our cultures. But I
could only marvel at the way he went about this. He undertook to do his
own thinking in every field. Where I turned to Whitehead, he turned to
Hegel, but he was not a Hegelian in the way I was a Whiteheadian. He
was his own philosopher who made use of Hegel only where he judged
Hegel to be correct. He was his own biblical scholar and historian and
social scientist as well. He was even his own physicist.

The major difference between us was his vast superiority as a scholar
and thinker, and the confidence he had in his original conclusions that
enabled him to propose new theological directions while still a quite
young man. I remain in awe of his accomplishments. However, even if
I had more nearly approximated his gifts, I think I would have followed
a different path. Instead of trying to be my own philosopher, historian,
biblical scholar, and scientist, I have tried to enlist as many as I can in
working together on the vast project of change. I think that in the long
run collaborative work of people whose individual gifts are more modest
than Pannenberg's may prove more sustainable and influential.

Pannenberg arranged for me to be invited to the University of Mainz
as a Fulbright Professor. I was delighted and accepted with alacrity.
But there was one very serious problem. My knowledge of the German
language was, to put it charitably, minimal. At Chicago in order to earn
a PhD one had to pass an exam in German. I studied on my own and
passed the exam. But I treated it as simply meeting a requirement. I
was not required or motivated to read anything in German in connection with my studies or dissertation; so I forgot most of what little I
had learned. I had come to regret my inability to read German while at
Emory, but I had done nothing about it. Now I must pay the price for
my negligence!

To my sorrow I quickly discovered that studying German on my
own I had invented my own way of pronouncing it, which turned out
to be quite different from the German way. I rather liked my own way,

but recognized that at least in this case I must yield authority to others. Crystol Betz assisted me, and by the time our family got to Germany, I could communicate a little. Our sons also studied a little, and they managed to survive the plunge into German schools. Indeed, they all did better than I.

Thanks to the Pannenbergs, I spent a memorable year in Mainz 1965-66. My German improved a little during the year but never became really adequate. Knowing my severe limitation in this respect, Pannenberg arranged for us to co-teach one seminar each semester. I gave a one-hour lecture course as well. This consisted in my reading German translations of my lectures. The translator was a quite remarkable woman around eighty years of age who had her own ideas about theology. I had to work carefully with her to make sure that I did not end up reading her lectures instead of mine. By the second semester I was able to have a kind of informal seminar with his assistants, who were wonderfully tolerant of my faltering efforts to speak German. I was also able to follow Pannenberg's lectures reasonably well.

Central to Pannenberg's thinking was the power of the future in forming the present. This was not simply the power of our present imaging or envisioning of the future. Of that I have no doubt. Pannenberg spoke of the future that would in fact be. That future had already appeared in Jesus' resurrection. That future is the God who is revealed in history. My admiration for Pannenberg was such that I tried hard to understand how this could be true. But it has never been convincing to me. In a very pedestrian way, I understand causality as moving from past to present and present to future. Much of what will happen in the future is already determined, but much is not. Even if Jesus' rose from the dead as literally as Pannenberg taught, that does not settle for me the question of the final outcome of history.

Pannenberg found in Whitehead's *Adventures of Ideas* a discussion of anticipatory feelings. He thought he might, through them, make a connection. To this date I regret my flat denial that Whitehead meant anything of the sort that Pannenberg sought. I think I was accurate, but there is something of a mystery about how to explain these feelings in Whitehead. In later years Lewis Ford developed a version of Whiteheadian speculation that sees God as coming into the present from the future. I should have welcomed Pannenberg's inquiries. By slamming the door on this line of inquiry, I probably slammed the door also on Pannenberg's

serious interest in Whitehead, an interest from which my own study of
Whitehead would certainly have profited.

The German students found Whitehead worth serious study, but
there was a deep obstacle to accepting him. The question in their mind
was whether Whitehead was "pre-critical." When that question was
unpacked, it meant, did Whitehead take into account what Kant had
shown in his first critique. That Kant's work was a watershed for human
thinking, such that it determined the boundaries of all future thought,
was an unquestioned assumption for many of them. I realized more
clearly than before that virtually all continental thinking was Kantian
in this sense. Since Whitehead proposed a position that avoided both
Hume's and Kant's conclusions, getting a hearing for his philosophy on
the Kantian European continent would be as difficult as getting a hearing
in the Humean English-language world.

Intellectual disagreements did not harm our friendship. Sadly, later,
political ones did. Although during the year I spent at Mainz our discussions were rarely political, insofar as they were, we seemed to be in
general agreement. But our responses to events a few years later were
quite different. Pannenberg was deeply shaken by the student revolts, the
strength of socialist parties in Europe, and the rise of liberation theology.
He saw all this in the light of a profoundly threatening Marxism. His
new political conservatism was accompanied by a conservative shift in
his theology. His formulations were too emphatic and his feelings were
too intense to allow for enjoyable argument. A wide range of topics was
closed to us. For this and other reasons, our communications declined.
My personal gratitude for what he did for me, my appreciation for his
friendship, and my admiration for his scholarship have not, and though
our contacts in later years were rare, they remained cordial.

We planned a fourth volume in the "New Frontiers" series. This
would be in the reverse format. Instead of American theologians responding to a German, the German theologians would respond to an American. The American we chose was Schubert Ogden. Ogden was a fine
scholar of Bultmann, and of Heidegger as well. He could enter effectively
into the German debates. But he also participated in the distinctively
American tradition. He was deeply influenced by the philosophy of
religion of Hartshorne. In the previous chapter I mentioned the importance of his *Christ without Myth*. In 1964 this was followed by *The Reality
of God*, quickly recognized as another major work. This book was more

distinctively American than the first. His excellence and leadership were widely recognized in the United States and he had published also in Germany. No one questioned his originality or rigor. We were pleased that he agreed to contribute an essay to which the German theologians we had treated in the other volumes all agreed to respond. In 1966, during my year in Mainz, we held a meeting there, where all were present.

I continue to regret that Ogden withdrew from this effort and the fourth volume never materialized. Ogden has a kind of theological integrity that is rare. I certainly do not share it. He will not publish anything unless he believes he has something to say that will advance the discussion. Accordingly, if he was invited to speak or write when he did not have something new to say, he declined. I understand that he declined the Gifford Lectures for that reason. In the case of our volume, all that was needed was a fresh formulation of the ideas he had already published. But he was not willing to provide that. I greatly respect his decision, but I greatly regret it as well. A volume of German responses to his theses would have been very rich. Ogden has written other important books since the two mentioned above, but to a considerable extent the first two books presented his overall thesis well. On the topics there discussed he seems quite satisfied to leave matters at that.

CHAPTER NINE

My Own Theological Development

What I have written about Chicago and my early years of teaching indicates, I think, the deep need I felt to shape and express my own theology in ways that took account of the thinking of others. I felt I had made progress in this respect by the time I reached Claremont. I continued that progress here. Especially my familiarity with contemporary German scholarship and creative thinking was enhanced by the events described in the previous chapter.

I came to Claremont with a reasonable grasp of the history of Western philosophy and of the major contemporary options. My work in the great books course at Emory and also in the Institute of Liberal Arts had broadened my knowledge of great literature to which I had first been introduced in the Army. I gained a smattering of knowledge of the history of art, especially painting.

I do not want to be misunderstood. I am in all these matters no more than an amateur. When I am with specialized historians or scholars in any of these fields, I realize how superficial my knowledge is. Nevertheless, that I have some acquaintance has been important to me, and it usually suffices to enable me to follow the lectures and arguments among the authorities. I can usually tell whether any beliefs or convictions really important to me are stake. Although the limited amount of time I spent in Chicago in specifically theological studies and the long delay in teaching theology have been a handicap to me in my own chosen field, I am grateful for the broader education that I did receive, the variety of courses I was asked to teach, and the discussion partners from whom I learned.

I became aware through all of this of the connections among these various expressions of human experience and how the culture is something deeper than any of its expressions. This seemed especially important for theology. I wanted to understand the experience, or faith, or assumptions, or basic way of being that gave rise to particular theological emphases and convictions. I noted above that the book I was finishing when I moved to Claremont was about types of Protestant piety rather than a comparison of systematic beliefs and creeds. As I began to teach courses in systematic theology for the first time, my reflection led me to think in terms of alternative "visions of reality." By that I referred to different ways of seeing or experiencing reality that were largely unarticulated and even unconscious. I saw consciously articulated beliefs as playing some role in shaping these, but also as being expressions of them. Changes at this level provided the cultural context in which intellectual systems are developed. This was a further break with the influence of McKeon.

For me, however, this did not reduce the importance of explicit metaphysics. The unthematized vision of reality that explains much about what seemed reasonable to people at different historical epochs includes elements that can and should be expressed as metaphysical ideas. We are limited by our culturally determined visions of reality if we do not bring to consciousness the beliefs implicit in them. Whitehead enabled me, I thought then and continue to think now, to bring to consciousness many of the basic beliefs that had been formed in my Christian piety and experience of modernity. He enabled me to bring them into a kind of synthesis that withstood criticism well from a variety of directions. By this time I unhesitatingly identified myself as his disciple.

Although I rejoiced in being able to introduce students to systematic theology, and even to Whitehead, the size of the faculty initially required that I continued to teach broadly. During my first few years at Claremont, I taught year-long surveys of the history of theology. This never turned me into a good historian. In those days Claremont still had separate sequences in church history and historical theology. Partly for this reason, despite my burgeoning historical consciousness, I taught the survey primarily as a study of a series of thinkers, with only secondary concern for their total historical context. I knew the students deserved better, and I am proud of my role in bringing Jane Douglass and, later, Ekkehard Muehlenberg, one of Pannenberg's students whom I had known in Mainz, to the faculty. They are true scholars in the

wider history in which the history of the church and of its teaching are
fully embedded.

I always thought it important that any student seeking a PhD in
theology or philosophy of religion be seriously exposed to the teaching
of these historians. Further, my awareness of the central importance of
nineteenth-century German theology for all that has happened since
then gave me great appreciation for the contribution of my colleague,
Jack Verheyden. I had recognized the importance of this recent history
only late in my formation. I wanted to be sure that our graduate students
encountered and internalized it much earlier.

The ventures I described in the previous chapter gave me some
confidence that I understood enough about the historical grounds of
contemporary American Protestantism, on the one side, and the continental theological situation, on the other, that I could begin to find my
own voice. I was still conscious of one large gap. Since I had just begun
to have the opportunity to teach systematic theology, I did not have an
adequate grasp of the major systematic theological options.

I was now quite sure that I wanted to develop a Whiteheadian theology, but I did not want to do so without some confidence that I understood the strengths and weaknesses of other systems. One question of
central importance for me was the role of metaphysics. I was convinced
that this was important and even inescapable. But I was living in an
extended period during which the word "metaphysics" was being used
only pejoratively by most philosophers and theologians. Philosophers
mostly rejected the systematic and constructive tasks of philosophy in
favor of phenomenological description or the analysis of language. But
theologians still seemed to have systematic ambitions. I did not see how
they could make affirmative statements about God, human beings, or
the world without involving metaphysical ideas. Before working on my
own metaphysically grounded theology, I thought I should examine what
other theologians had been doing, especially those who claimed to have
no metaphysical commitments.

Accordingly, I returned to the project of my dissertation. I took
as my first fresh writing project after moving to Claremont a survey of
Protestant theologies. I tried out early versions of my survey in a lecture
series to pastors. I marvel now that in those days Methodist pastors were
still sufficiently interested in theology to attend such a series. Certainly
nothing like that could occur today.

After ten years of teaching, including just two at Claremont, I had a one-year sabbatical. I chose to spend it at Drew Theological Seminary, which at that time had one of the strongest theological faculties in the nation. During that year I wrote *Living Options in Protestant Theology*. Its focused attention on the question of the role of philosophy in these theologies was grounds for the subtitle added by the publisher: "a study in method." The book was basically new, although it incorporated some material from my dissertation.

I argued in ways persuasive to me that assumptions of some kind about the nature of reality were present in all these theologies. I felt confirmed in my judgment that this presence is inescapable and that it is best to make these assumptions fully explicit. At the same time I remained convinced that no philosophy can be presented as *the* answer to philosophical questions. As a Christian I was drawn to philosophies that fit with my perception of the world. For example, I see the world as containing subjects as well as objects, subjects who play an active causal role in what goes on. I experience myself as both profoundly affected by my context and heritage and as still having some choice with respect to what I do. Philosophies that deny all of this are not as persuasive to me as those that affirm it. Of course, I am supposing that in purely objective, rational terms they are more or less equal.

I recognized that I was drawn to Whitehead in part because he provides a rigorous way of thinking that accommodates my deepest intuitions and assumptions. It seems proper and desirable to me that Christian theologians employ a philosophy that enables them to articulate their convictions richly, as long as, measured in strictly philosophical terms, no other philosophies are superior. Such a philosophy can function for theologians as a natural theology, but we should recognize that it is a *Christian* natural theology. Its arguments and analyses may not be convincing to people who perceive reality differently. If such people point out philosophical flaws in this natural theology, the theologian must certainly take their criticisms seriously. But if they simply express distaste for it, or preference for another style of philosophy, this should be taken as reflecting the ultimate pluralism of visions of reality and the philosophies that express them, not as a reason to abandon this one.

Accordingly, I entitled my next book *A Christian Natural Theology*. The subtitle went on to say, quite accurately, "based on the thought of Alfred North Whitehead." Although like my previous books it was largely descriptive of what others had done, it nevertheless took the form of a direct contribution to constructive theology, my first. The contribution included the realization of the idea of a "Christian natural theology," a third option alongside the traditional views of natural theology as embodying what reason can tell us about the final truth, on the one side, and the rejection of the use of metaphysical philosophy altogether, on the other. I say my contribution was the *realization* of the idea, since the idea of a Christian natural theology was present in Emil Brunner but, so far as I could see, it was not realized in his writings.

The second contribution was the introduction into the theological community of Whitehead's anthropology. A common reason for dismissing him for theological use was that he did not contribute to anthropology. Since, for more than a century, anthropology, or analysis of the human condition, had been central to theology, theologians turned much more readily to the existentialist philosophers than to Whitehead. I wanted to show that Whitehead's philosophy provided a basic anthropology congenial to Christian experience and that it provided a context for the appropriation of the insights of those who worked in much greater detail on anthropological questions.

I intended my third contribution to be a combination of exposition of Whitehead's doctrine of God and a critical development of it for theological use. I believe that my expositions of Whitehead throughout the book were basically accurate and can continue to be helpful to those who are interested in his teaching on the topics I discussed. However, my efforts to criticize and develop Whitehead's doctrine of God were confused by the continuing influence of Hartshorne. I was just beginning to sort out the differences between Whitehead and Hartshorne and was not really ready to write that part of the book. On questions that I consider very important, I came subsequently to a much deeper appreciation of Whitehead's distinctive insights and more and more uncomfortable about being understood in terms of what I published in 1965.

The book has long been out of print, but recently the question of bringing it back into print arose. About the same time a French publisher inquired about my interest in having it translated. This last inquiry pushed me to think seriously about a revised edition, and Westminster John Knox agreed to that. The revised edition is not a rewrite of the whole book from my present perspective. That would be simply a new book on similar topics. But I have rewritten the chapter in which I put forward my largely Hartshornian modifications of Whitehead's doctrine of God in order to express some of the insights about God I have found in Whitehead in the forty years since I wrote the book. I noted that I was particularly indebted here to Marjorie Suchocki. There is nothing in the revised chapter that I have not written elsewhere, but the points are scattered in often obscure places. I feel much better to have them integrated into the revised version of this book.

My fourth intended contribution was of a quite different sort. It would not appear in a book I wrote today, but I still think it has intrinsic interest and importance. Whitehead wrote at length about values, but he made only passing references to ethical theory. During my years at Chicago I had wrestled quite seriously with the question of the "is" and the "ought," and I had subsequently published one article on the topic. The question is whether normative statements can be derived from descriptive ones. If not, can they be justified at all? Or are those positivists who regard normative ethics as simply emotive correct? Do we simply express our feelings when we say that something is right or wrong? Or can such statements, after all, be true and false?

It seemed to me then that some response to these questions belonged in a natural theology. I thought that Whitehead's conceptuality provided a context for discussing them even if he did not treat them himself. Accordingly I used that book to publish the conclusions to which I had come on this topic. I argued that the "ought" can be derived from the "is," and I articulated what I thought the "is" and the "ought" in question could be. I also argued against the legalism to which a deontological ethics can easily give rise. I still think that what I did there deserves consideration, but I am not aware that anyone else has found my solution to the problem of much interest. Still, I have not removed this from the revised edition.

Although the idea shows up very little in this book, by the time I was writing it I was preoccupied with another type of question. I was deeply impressed by the analyses of human existence in Heidegger and Sartre, but they seemed to me ahistorical. It seemed that, whereas they generally seemed to claim to be describing human existence universally, they were actually describing just one form, the form that existence took in post-Christian Europe. I wanted to set this into a wider context of multiple modes of existence. I began to talk about "structures of existence" as perhaps more fundamental than "visions of reality." Every couple of years I taught a course on this topic and progressively honed my thinking.

I have ambivalent feelings about this project today. On the one side, I have never felt myself to be engaged more creatively and originally in imaginative thinking than I did when writing this book. I would read the writings of people from another culture and try to put myself in the shoes of the authors. What vision of reality and what structure of existence would lead one to write in that way? I made a lot of the axial period and the various new structures of existence that emerged at that time. I read in the literature on the history of consciousness, especially that influenced by Carl Jung. But I was too much influenced by existentialism to follow those accounts closely. My most daring speculations were those about the successive structures of existence that led to the diverse visions of reality. I still take some pride in what I accomplished.

On the other hand, I have become dissatisfied with the overall picture. I had not thought of myself as a great believer in progress, but the picture that I presented in that book is certainly one of progress. It depicts "primitive existence" as giving way to "civilized existence" and that in turn to "axial existence." Within axial existence it presents "Homeric existence" as giving way to "Socratic existence," and "prophetic existence," to "Christian existence." The earlier forms are not described pejoratively, but I clearly had a sense that there was advance in these transitions. At the time I took this pretty much for granted.

The one place where I was conscious even then of some difficulty was in the discussion of Christian existence as in some way going beyond Jewish existence. I introduced a bit more nuance and ambiguity there, but the basic pattern remained. It is surprising that as late as the early sixties, when I was working on this, I could write without a sharp consciousness of the problem of Christian supersessionism.

However, my real shock on this topic of supersession came from another source: Paul Shepard. I think it was in the early seventies that I began to become aware of his quite opposite picture of the course of human events. He argued that human beings evolved as hunters and gatherers. The vast majority of people gave up that mode of existence within the past ten thousand years. In hunting and gathering cultures, the body and the psyche were in sync. Human relations were healthy. Shepard showed that even today in the remaining cultures of this sort children are brought up in a much healthier way, and there is far less dysfunction psychologically and socially.

He went on to show in great detail how every step of what we ordinarily call progress has forced human beings to behave in less natural ways. He showed the results of this in the growing alienation from society and from nature that has characterized humanity. What I celebrated as the prophetic tradition of social criticism and commitment to justice, he saw as the deepest form of alienation. On this, as on many points, we agreed in our description of phenomena and on their historical importance. We both saw the prophetic tradition of criticism as central to Christianity. But our evaluations were quite opposite. I saw it as the great accomplishment of Christian existence. He saw it as the greatest threat to human and social, as well as ecological, health.

On two occasions we taught a joint seminar. I presented my ideas, and he presented his. He supported his with vast anthropological data. He treated me graciously and my ideas respectfully. Some of my criticisms of his views had some effect on him. But in this relation I never felt myself to be his equal. I could never again see in the course of human events a fundamental progress. Hence I don't know what to do with a book that describes that progress, even if much of the detailed account still seems to me insightful. I acknowledged my concern in the preface to a reprint of the book, but of course the reason for the concern remains.

One other book belongs to this theological series. It is *Christ in a Pluralistic Age*. It was not published until 1975, but it reflects a process of thinking that began much earlier. Clearly, for a Christian theologian Christ is a central topic. Christians may share a natural theology with others. That is, the same natural theology that Christians employ may prove useful to Jews or Muslims. But Christology is the heart of what is distinctive about Christian faith.

Nevertheless, my approach did not make the difference quite as sharp as this might imply. I did not want to say things about Jesus or about Christ that other theists would have to deny in order to affirm their own views. The title intended to point to that goal. I would not expect Jews or Muslims to devote so much attention to Christology, but I tried to make statements that were historically accurate and could be acknowledged as such apart from any sort of fideism. Of course, that meant the complete exclusion of supernaturalism, but I was strongly opposed to supernaturalist theology anyway. For me, learning from Whitehead, the exclusion of supernaturalism was by no means the exclusion of God's activity in the world and specifically in Jesus. From a Whiteheadian perspective, the exclusion of God's secular or natural role in all things, and the practical acceptance of this exclusion even by many theologians, is one of the great calamities of modern thought.

By the time I wrote this book I was convinced that in a Christology one must distinguish between Jesus and Christ. "Christ" should not be use as a proper name for Jesus, nor should we try to restrict its application to him. On the other hand, going back to the original meaning of "Messiah" does not help. Arguing with Jews as to whether Jesus was the expected Messiah is not a fruitful exercise. He fulfilled some expectations but certainly did not fulfill all or even most. Christian faith for me does not depend on claiming that those he did not fulfill on first coming he will fulfill when he returns. I simply do not believe anything of that sort.

What is central to Christian faith has much more to do with the idea of the incarnation of God. If Jesus is still properly called "Christ" it is because God was present in him or incarnate in him. But from a Whiteheadian perspective, in some way God is present in everything. That this is so has become manifest to us through Jesus, so that God's immanence in the world is far more emphasized in Christianity than in most other theistic traditions. The nature of that immanence and its expression in creative transformation is a major part of the book. Another topic is the way in which God's role in the world is enhanced in the field of force generated by Jesus' ministry and by the spread of Christian faith. Another is speculation about the distinctive structure of Jesus' own existence, especially about the unusual role played in this structure by the presence of God. I devoted Part Three of the book to discussing what we could hope for and how our hopes are also related to Jesus and to that form of God's presence in the world that I labeled Christ.

In this book I think I showed that strong affirmations of God's creative and redemptive presence in Jesus do not require fideism or supernaturalism or stand in opposition to strong affirmations of other religious traditions. Since it is Whitehead's metaphysics that makes this possible, I definitely consider this a Whiteheadian Christology. However, this does not mean that one must first adopt Whitehead's metaphysics before one can accept the ideas.

In the prologue of the Gospel of John we are told that the Word was with God and was God, that nothing came into being apart from it, that it is especially manifest as life and as the light of all people. The last phrase suggests human mentality. Students of Whitehead have often noted how closely this resembles what, with great systematic rigor and detail, Whitehead says about the primordial nature of God. John goes on to say that this Word was enfleshed in Jesus. This Christian confession and claim can certainly be made without in any way conflicting with Whitehead's thought or with the central affirmations of other communities. My point is that the role of Whitehead's conceptuality here is to enable me to articulate, expand, and develop the biblical text. Most of the ways I do this are formulated without explicit reference to Whitehead and can stand on their own merits.

I continue to take pride in the book, but of course I have long since become aware of its limitations. By the time it was published, feminist scholars had shown that Sophia (or Wisdom) is a better name for God as present in the world than Logos, and actually much more common in the New Testament. Wisdom is a richer idea than Word. Furthermore, in conformity with John's prologue and the doctrinal formulations of the early church, I restricted the incarnation to the second person of the Trinity. I came later to the conclusion that the church would have been wiser to remove the restriction. In every other act of God, the church later decided, all three Persons participated. Why exclude the other Persons from this one? In Whiteheadian terms this means that the consequent nature of God is also enfleshed in Jesus. I believe that to be true. To shift from Logos to Sophia also suggests the shift to a more inclusive notion of the divine that is incarnate.

I made some gestures in the direction of a Trinitarian doctrine. I acknowledge their weakness. Apart from the gender language, I like the terms Father, Son, and Spirit, and if it were not for the excessive masculinity of the language I would strongly support the continued use of these terms. They are biblical, traditional, and still richly suggestive. I also strongly affirm the doctrine of the incarnation with its important distinction between the divine that is incarnate and the creature in which it is incarnate. Nevertheless, I find the doctrinal formulations of the Trinity unbiblical, unintelligible, or incredible.

The truth of these negative judgments is often recognized and then obscured by naming the doctrine "a mystery." There are, indeed, mysteries aplenty. Indeed, the more we know about our universe and about ourselves the more mysterious reality appears. There are many mysteries in Christian experience. But the doctrine of the Trinity as developed in different ways in both the East and the West turns inescapable mystery into unnecessary mystification.

I would have no serious objection to having a variety of speculations about the relation of the Father, the Son, and the Holy Spirit if these were recognized as such. But the situation in the church has been quite otherwise. It is often held that the doctrine of the Trinity is the essential teaching of the church. It is this that is put forward to distinguish Christians from Jews and Muslims. There is little agreement as to just what this doctrine affirms beyond the claim that God is at once three and one. When one asks for an explanation, the impossibility of an intelligible explanation that can also pass the tests of orthodoxy brings quickly into play the category of mystery. On pain of exclusion from the church, one must believe this mystery without expecting either to understand it or to learn why it is so important. This has done great harm to the very idea of church doctrine and of its role. Indeed it has done great harm to the church and to millions of its members.

Centuries ago the insistence on belief in the Trinity understandably, even rightly, alienated Mohammed. Since then the Gentile appropriation of Israel's wisdom has been split into two great factions that have spent far too much of their energy opposing each other. A few centuries later differences in the formulation of Trinitarian doctrine in the East and the West destroyed the unity of Christendom.

The doctrine of the Trinity still leads to pointless speculations. Today, new, attractive reasons are thought up for affirming the Trinity. As we realize the tendency during the Enlightenment of becoming too individualistic and now reaffirm the importance of community, we can claim that Trinitarian doctrine shows that the God in whose image we are made is eternally a community. There is a tendency to ignore the fact that to affirm God as a community emphatically requires an emphasis on three distinct persons in the modern sense and that no one has shown how that can avoid tri-theism.

Of course, these implications can be softened by emphasizing that all language about God is analogical, or symbolic. If this means that strictly speaking we do not mean what we seem to be saying and are only claiming that there are positive uses of certain traditional images, there need be no argument. We can then say that to be part of the Christian community is to use its traditional symbolism, and that this is the reason for affirming the "Trinity." One is not thereby making any claim about what an objective reality referred to by the word "God" is actually like. But for me this is no solution to the needs of the church. It only serves to increase the tendency to suppose that the word "God" has no reference beyond itself. I believe the lack of realistic teaching about God is a major reason for the decline of the old-line churches.

When Trinitarian teaching is regarded as a central feature of how Christians should understand a real God, masses of people develop a negative attitude toward theology as a whole. Theology is something they will leave to a handful of specialists. What they conclude as to the correct formulation of the doctrine makes little difference to the faithful. If that is theology, then the real interests of believers lie elsewhere. This means that few are encouraged to bring the insights of the Bible and tradition to bear on the truly critical issues of our day.

Let me emphasize two things. I am not opposing Trinitarian think-ing as long as it remains fluid, does not pretend to be describing objec-tive metaphysical reality, and is recognized as optional for Christians. As a Whiteheadian I affirm complexity in God. Whitehead speaks of three natures of God, and it would be easy enough to say that what he means by "natures" is close to what the church meant by "persons." If my goal was to assure readers that as a Whiteheadian I am quite orthodox, I could easily do so. But I cannot bring myself to play this game. Any connec-tions I would establish between the three "natures" of the Whiteheadian God and the New Testament uses of Father, Son, and Spirit, would be artificial and arbitrary. Such artificiality and arbitrariness has character-ized the tradition and continues to characterize most Trinitarian teaching. I prefer to call the church to repentance for allowing this game to play so large a role in its life when matters of authentic personal faith and of global importance are neglected.

Let us encourage biblical scholars to tell us more about the meaning of the many terms used to indicate God in the Bible. Let us celebrate this diversity and make use of many of these terms in our liturgies. Let us make unequivocally clear that all these terms and images refer to one God who works in the world in many ways. Let us cease to suppose that from this whole list three names represent the ultimate metaphysical truth, and let us abandon efforts to explain their supposed metaphysical connections. Let us stop using any language that suggests to the hearers that we affirm three Gods. If this makes me a heretic, so be it. At least I will be in the company with Jesus, Paul, and the other apostles.

John B. Cobb, Jr.

I have noted before that my publications were often on topics about which I had been thinking a long time, even when the cutting edge of my thought and passion had moved on to other topics. This was true of this book as well. It was for me a kind of completion, the end of a trajectory. By the time I had finished it, I felt that I knew where I stood in relation to the central questions of the faith. I had articulated for myself the beliefs that formed me as a Christian. Of course, there were many topics to develop further, and new ones to which I could attend. If I had not been drawn to a quite different kind of inquiry, I might well have pursued them and thus stayed closer to a standard theological trajectory. But that was not to be.

CHAPTER TEN

The Sixties and Seventies

The Vietnam War changed the character of academic life in the United States. In terms of its scale and actual effects on the American economy, it was not remotely comparable to World War II. It was not much greater in these respects than the Korean War. But its effects on the American psyche were of an entirely different order, and this was certainly true in my own case.

The deepest difference was that the vast majority of us Americans thought the American role in World War II, and also in Korea, was basically righteous. At the outset, most of us supported some involvement in Vietnam as well. But as time went on more and more of us began to oppose an ever more destructive war.

My own ambivalence turned to clear opposition through an event at my church, the Claremont UMC. Our pastor, Pierce Johnson, organized an evening in which there would be speakers on both sides chosen by those members of the church who stood most articulately on each side. I thought that the policy of containment of Communism was a necessary evil, and, despite my increasing doubts, I was open to taking seriously the argument that involvement in Vietnam was a needed part of Cold War global strategy. But the defenders of our involvement were not able to make such a case, so far as I could tell, whereas the opponents of the war were highly convincing. The Vietnamese Communists were strong nationalists whose victory would not mean an extension of either Soviet or Chinese power. Instead of fighting them, there were possibilities of developing a positive relation with them that would end our continuation of the terrible history of Euro-American imperialism, avoid the horrible destruction of which we were part, and advance any legitimate Cold War objectives far better than what we were doing. After that day I did not waver in my opposition.

The strong opposition to what our nation was doing led to reappraisals of U.S. foreign policy generally. During the sixties we were also given deeper insight into the conquest and near genocide of the indigenous population. The sense of American exceptionalism that I had imbibed as a child and that had not been shaken by World War II and its aftermath collapsed. The mixed feelings of loyalty and guilt I had previously felt toward the South have, since then, characterized my feelings toward my nation as well. Whereas I had been shocked when President Eisenhower was caught in a lie about American U-2 spying on the Soviet Union, I have now ceased to expect truth from our political leaders.

Actually, my life experience had prepared me for this recognition that I had been naïvely misled by American propaganda after the war. In chapter 1, I explained this in some detail. Nevertheless, the full realization of the role that the United States adopted was a profoundly painful experience.

The war and the accompanying draft had effects on my family. My two older sons decided they were pacifists. Although I never became an absolute pacifist, I certainly sympathized with them and supported them. I could not have fought in *that* war. To participate in unspeakable evil for a cause that was, at best, misguided and, at worst, an expression of a fundamentally bad national policy was simply not a possibility for a Christian as I understood Christian faith. I had no interest at all in persuading my sons that there were some occasions when war might be the least evil choice.

The changed attitude toward American history and foreign policy affected also changes in my attitude toward the church. Growing up on the mission field, I had always felt that the program of spreading Christianity around the world was a fully positive one. I do not mean that I was completely ignorant of its dark side, but I did not experience it in Japan or think much about it. I only gradually became aware of the close connections between missions and colonialism. That their connection in Japan during my lifetime was minimal had impeded my recognition of the extent to which missions had served the purposes of colonialism.

Retrospectively, it seems strange that it took American Christians so long, even after World War II, to recognize Christian responsibility for Hitler's anti-Jewish policies and especially for at least tacit support of many of them by the majority of Christians in Germany. So far as I can recall, I did not hear the connection made before the sixties. And it was only then that awareness of the long history of Christian anti-Judaism became part of the normal consciousness of most Christian thinkers. I was myself slow to appreciate the importance of this history. I wonder now why my Jewish friends in the Army did not force me to look at this side of Christianity. Eventually I educated myself by teaching courses on Christian anti-Judaism and how Christian theology should change to overcome its supersessionism. But I was too slow in realization of the importance of this matter for it to have affected my major theological writings.

The war had a silver lining. Its effect on the Claremont School of Theology was positive. Young men could often be exempted from the draft if they enrolled in a school of theology. Some very capable and sensitive students who came to the school during those years would not have done so apart from this advantage. I am not cynical about this. Those motivated in part by this advantage were deeply sincere people, keenly interested in their studies. They contributed greatly to the community. Some actually ended up in Christian ministry. Others, like many of our graduates, entered other service careers, not all church related. Some went on to doctoral programs and careers in teaching.

The sixties were a heady time for theologians in other respects. Deeply entrenched habits of mind were shaken in other ways as well, and in many cases permanently changed. I will describe the effects very personally. But my experience simply represents that of a considerable community. I will begin with the Second Vatican Council.

I grew up absorbing from my parents a mildly anti-Catholic attitude, and although my experience with Catholics during World War II led me to great appreciation for Catholic theology, the earlier suspicions were not entirely allayed. In childhood these concerns were partly because some of the do's and don'ts of our Methodist piety were flouted by Catholics. I refer to our emphasis on abstaining from alcohol, tobacco, and gambling. By our behavioral standards, the Catholics seemed to be only halfway Christians. In addition the use of statues and rosary beads and even the mass with its supposed transubstantiation all seemed vaguely superstitious or even idolatrous. It is interesting that to this day there are parts of Asia where governments distinguish between "Christians," which means Protestants, and "Catholics," treating these as distinct "religions."

But the more important reasons for distrust of Catholics were social and political. The separate school system was offensive to our Protestant sense of what was needed for a good democracy. And most important, we saw an authoritarian system that told people what they could do and think, and we suspected that the Catholic ideal for the United States was a Catholic nation with ties to the Vatican. The fact that in Boston the Catholic hierarchy was able to prevent the showing of films of which it disapproved supported our fears. Our picture of what Catholic success would mean was antithetical to our democratic ideals.

The Second Vatican Council seemed to us to come into being out of nothing. Of course, it did not. But most of us had not followed the course of events within the Catholic Church in such a way as to be aware of the emergence of a climate that made this event possible. I think many Catholics were hardly less surprised.

This event called for radical rethinking of who we were as Protestants. It was no longer enough to be Christians who rejected the authoritarianism of the Catholic Church. Further, the ancient debates about justification did not provide a reason for separation. In recent years Lutherans and Catholics have been able to come to virtual agreement on this topic, and the World Methodist Council has associated itself with the joint formulation. We found in the new exchange of views with real live Catholic thinkers that they were as open minded and honest in their thinking as were Protestants, and often better informed. Perhaps the vision of a reunited Christian church was not simply a chimera! Perhaps in the meantime as individuals we should consider a return to the mother church! The attraction I felt toward Catholicism for a while in my Army years revived.

Becoming a Catholic was for me only a vague idea of possibility, and I think that was true for many Protestants. We were in no hurry to abandon our present communions. We would prefer any return to be as denominations rather than as individuals. The post-Vatican II church reached out to us as denominations to discuss our differences, and I was for a few years a member of the United Methodist team that engaged in such discussions. The conversations were friendly and fruitful and represented a wholly different relation from any that had existed before Vatican II. But they did not move far in the direction of institutional reunion.

Even earlier I had thought that, in the long run, Whitehead's philosophy might find a better home in the Catholic than in the Protestant world. This was because Catholics took metaphysics seriously and most Protestants did not. I had spent a lot of time arguing with my Protestant colleagues that they could not really escape metaphysical questions and should deal with them openly. But my efforts had very modest success. With Catholics no such extended prolegomenon was needed. Even before Vatican II, Thomism had been a conversation partner with process philosophy, and some Thomists had made adjustments in their formulations to take account of our criticisms. They were often especially sensitive to the point that if God were completely immutable, as official theology asserted, what happens in the world would make no difference to God. That did not conform with their real piety any more than with mine.

In the aftermath of Vatican II, Catholic theologians were open to exploring alternative philosophies with great freedom. There was an explosion of interest in Teilhard de Chardin, whose thought in many ways overlapped that of Whitehead. Some of those excited by Teilhard recognized the connection and joined the community of process theologians. The first book with the title, *Process Theology,* was an anthology edited by the Catholic theologian, Ewert Cousins. It contained articles by Teilhardians, but was mostly from the Whiteheadian side. David Tracy, who was certainly a major star among American Catholic theologians, began his career with *Blessed Rage for Order*, a definitely process book.

Perhaps the greatest fruit of Vatican II was the change in Latin America. I was slow to learn about this, but the meeting of the Latin American bishops in Medellín gave a social and political concreteness to the implications of Vatican II that I later realized was of enormous importance. Within the church there had long been those who were appalled by the close alliance of the Catholic hierarchy and the economic and political elite. At Medellín, in 1968, the bishops announced that the church was on the side of the people. The church's theologians began to develop the implications of this profound shift. Gustavo Gutiérrez published his master work in Spanish in 1971. Orbis Press published an English translation, *A Theology of Liberation,* in 1973. It was only after that that I began to learn a little about what was going on.

Since I was preoccupied with other matters, my learning curve would have been even slower had it not been for Ignacio Castuera. He had been a brilliant student at the seminary, and we established a friendship that has endured to the present. He was born in Mexico, and at that time, I think, he was still a Mexican citizen. In any case, he kept up closely with

Latin American developments, maintaining a personal relationship with many of the leaders of liberation theology.

Retrospectively I am embarrassed by the conversation with Castuera that first made me realize something really different was going on. We were living together in a commune at that time. As late as the mid-seventies I took for granted that, with all its limitations, the program of Third World development was going in the right direction. When Castuera told me that liberation theologians opposed "development," I was shocked. Surely, I said, what was needed was both development and liberation.

Fortunately, I was at least sufficiently shocked to realize that something important was going on and being said, and that I needed to pay attention. It was the beginning of my education about the global economy. Through that I was led to reflect about the economic theory that was used to justify it. This became an important part of my further development.

Liberation theology also showed me the importance of one's social situation for writing theology. I had not previously reflected on how my social location affected my choice of topics and the way I treated them. It became clear to me that there was much I had to learn from these Latin American thinkers. The more I studied them the more I was convinced that they were right.

The leader of liberation theology in the American Academy of Religion was Frederick Herzog of Duke. He gave himself to liberation movements unstintingly and at great personal cost. He is one of my saints. The first process theologian to join him was Del Brown who wrote a book, *To Set At Liberty*, that made the connections clear. He had been my student some years earlier, but by this time, I gladly followed where he led, and for some years supported Herzog's projects as well as I could. I was never a leader in this field.

The Latin American liberation theologians were very suspicious of North American theological movements, including process theology. They saw that our thinking came out of the university context and had little to do with struggles for justice in society. Our work represented the interest of middle-class Christians in resolving our intellectual questions rather than the interest of the poor in survival and justice. The liberation theologians were convinced that the Bible should be read from the perspective of the poor, and they were clear that we were not engaged in anything of that sort.

My initial reaction was that they were only partly correct. Process theology had a background in the Social Gospel with its concern for social justice. On the other hand, however, the great emphasis on existentialism as the context in which we were working in the fifties and sixties had directed theological formulations away from social concerns. And as I thought more fully about this, I recognized that even the Social Gospel failed to satisfy the legitimate demands of the liberationists. It rightly called on those in power to recognize that the Christian faith calls for justice to the powerless. But it did not give voice to the powerless themselves.

Some liberation theologians organized a conference in Mexico to which they invited me. I was not able to go, and David Griffin represented process theology. He was treated roughly. The major guest was Jürgen Moltmann, and he was treated equally roughly. It was a good learning experience for both process theologians and for Moltmann. Years later we planned a major conference of process theologians and liberation theologians in São Paulo. Regrettably, after we had spent a great deal of time in planning and organizing and spent a lot of irrecoverable money, the Latin American hosts had to cancel their invitation.

Only later did I understand that much of the anger toward Moltmann was due to his dismissal of the work of the Brazilian liberation theologian, Rubem Alves. At the time of the conference the Latin Americans assumed that process theologians were in the same camp as Moltmann. Griffin did not understand the issues well enough to disabuse them. Later Castuera intervened and explained that Moltmann's insensitivity did not reflect the real position of process theologians at all. In particular he talked extensively with Hugo Assmann. Gradually Assmann and others became more open to interaction with us.

By far the most important connection between process theology and liberation theology was through the person of George Pixley. Pixley was the son of a Baptist medical missionary in Nicaragua, studied in Nicaraguan schools, and was thoroughly bilingual and bi-cultural. He studied Bible at the University of Chicago, where he was influenced by process thought. After completing his PhD he devoted his career to teaching in Latin America. He became a highly regarded biblical scholar in the liberation movement. He brought process theology explicitly into the mix.

Sadly, this aspect of his work was not appreciated at the time. Since his writings were all in Spanish, English-speaking process thinkers knew little about him. Liberation theologians who knew and admired him paid little attention to this side of his work. Although some friendly contacts took place, and a few people in addition to Pixley understood themselves to be parts of both communities, the ties between the two groups that might have benefited both were not forged.

Nevertheless, I was deeply affected by what the liberation theologians taught. I have indicated some of the ways. I was definitely shaken out of my preoccupation with existential thought. However, I never thought that I could or should become a liberation theologian. I was not a member of an oppressed group, and my identification with such groups would always be partial. I have mentioned my admiration for Frederick Herzog who did in fact effect such an identification. But I did not feel called in that direction.

I decided that my role was more like that of the political theologians in Europe whose work was, in my view, basically complementary to liberation theology. What are we middle-class, university-oriented, First World males called to do in response to the truth we recognize in the voices calling for liberation? The answer for most of us, I thought then, and still think, is to engage in criticism of features of our nations' policies and practices that make liberation so difficult for those who are oppressed by them. Accordingly, my only serious publication in this field is *Process Theology as a Political Theology*. It is an appreciative but, also critical, dialogue with Dorothee Sölle, Johann Baptist Metz, and Jürgen Moltmann.

I also believe that a strength of the Whiteheadian perspective is that it leads to both/and answers rather than either/or ones. The liberation theologians often presented their approach as the only genuinely Christian one. As a process theologian I was persuaded of its authenticity and importance and of the need of most of us for repentance. I was not persuaded that the questions with which I had heretofore been preoccupied were unreal, unimportant, or limited in their relevance to a small segment of the Christian community. Although I noted in the previous chapter that I ended my more narrowly traditional theological trajectory in 1975, I by no means repudiate what I did in those books. They provide an important part of the basis on which I continue to operate, and I think they can be helpful to others in the church.

Sadly, from my point of view, within a few years all this possibility of involvement with Catholics and especially with liberation theologians was ended. I was most affected personally by the change in the graduate student body and the placement of Protestant graduates. For a few years half of my doctoral students were Roman Catholic monks and some of my Protestant students got jobs in Catholic universities. The possibility that process theology might come to play a large role in the Catholic Church seemed real. To play a part in that change seemed to me a wonderful possibility. But, quite abruptly, Catholic students stopped coming. Protestants were squeezed out of teaching religion in Catholic universities. And even Catholic theologians such as Tracy, who continued to befriend us, dropped references to process thought from his publications. A door that had been wonderfully open slammed shut.

I do not mean by this to condemn those in the Roman Church who tightened the reigns. That Church is authentically global as is no other. That is an achievement to be greatly prized. I marvel again and again at the quality of devotion, sensitivity, and personal spirit cultivated among Catholics in all parts of the world. Also, some of the excesses and distortions produced in the Protestant context are largely avoided in the Catholic one.

Maintaining unity in an institution of that sort is no easy task. The Pope must have ultimate control. There must be limits to the variety of teachings and practices that are allowed. The rejection of ideas and practices that I also find unacceptable is inevitably, I suppose, accompanied by rejection of some that I find promising. I myself am typically Protestant in that I have never been willing to accept anyone else's authority over what I believe and say. I am certainly glad that I did not become a Catholic. But I can understand that for the sake of the unity of the Church, people of great integrity are willing to conform to the requirements of the hierarchy. I respect that decision. I also understand that the church often allows them to continue to work quietly for changes in which they believe. Catholics can think of such changes taking centuries, and accept that with patience. That attitude is almost impossible for Protestants.

There are even signs that despite the crackdown, here and there a process voice can be heard in the Catholic context. Also four successive International Whitehead Conferences were held in Catholic universities in Austria, India, Japan, and Poland. I believe that if the door opened again, there would be many Catholics willing to consider a shift of philosophical basis toward Whitehead.

Much more serious was the church's closing the door on liberation theology. I have expressed my effort to understand the tightening of the reins that came some years after Vatican II, and obviously there were

expressions of liberation theology that challenged the hierarchical authority of the church. Nevertheless, I find it hard to forgive the Church for
closing so great an epoch in its history at such cost to so many. I hope
that some of the shift of church teaching to support of the common
people has been a permanent change, even if the church could not con-
tain the full import of the new theology and its accompanying practice.

Despite the crackdown on liberation theology in Latin America,
there remained some remnants. I am glad to say that the close relationship process theology failed to achieve with liberation theology in the
days of its flourishing has been realized in the days of its decline with
those who are now dong the most to continue its spirit. We belong
together. Our unity was expressed in a small gathering in Claremont of
some of the authors of two books, one by process thinkers and the other
by the heirs of liberation theology: *American Empire and the Commonwealth of God* by Richard Falk, David Griffin, Catherine Keller, and me,
and *Beyond the Spirit of Empire* by Néstor Miguez, Joerg Rieger, and Jung
Mo Sung. Also, around George Pixley, events have taken place in Colom-
bia and Nicaragua.

Most important, today the Roman Catholic Church has a new pope
whose deep background is in the spirit of liberation theology. I think the
depth of his commitments was not appreciated by many of those who
voted for him. He has an enormous task in recovering what has been
lost in recent decades, but he offers just the vision that is most needed
today. There is no leader on the global scene to whom I now look with
greater hope. If he truly succeeds, if he opens the door once again, the
question will arise for me, and I think for many Christians, will I still
wish to "protest?"

During the same period when Latin Americans were developing a
new theology in light of Vatican II, American blacks were developing
a new theology in light of the civil rights struggle and the subsequent
black power movement. What they told us was harder to endure than
the more distant challenge of the Latin Americans. Accordingly, they
rightly complain that there was far less response to them by the dominant white community.

Black theologians made it clear that the Social Gospel movement,
of which Protestant progressives, including process theologians, were so
proud, had continued the tradition of white American theology of simply
ignoring the fact that the United States has always been a racist society

built on slavery and exploitation. Niebuhr's correction and deepening of the Social Gospel had been no improvement in this regard. The plain, sad fact is that the suffering of black people in the United States had been virtually invisible in American theological writings, even those of the Social Gospel. I was one of many who were certainly guilty as charged.

This was not because I was indifferent to the evils of slavery and seg-regation. Indeed, as a white Southerner and descendant of slaveholders, as explained in Chapter 1, I was particularly sensitive to these matters. Nevertheless, when I wrote theologically I ignored them. I am certainly not proud of this.

We were all aware that the shift from King's call for integration to the black power movement was affecting the tone and content of black activ-ism within the church. I belonged to a large segment of progressive Prot-estants who sympathized with the work and the demand of the various black caucuses. But I still did not see how any of this should affect my work as a theologian. I assumed that any discussion of the racial problem belonged in courses in Christian social ethics. Since I did not teach that, there seemed to be no place for such questions in my teaching or my writing. My colleague, Joe Hough, later president of Union Theologi-cal Seminary, taught social ethics and had written his dissertation about racism. He did an excellent job of teaching about racism, and although I fully agreed and supported him, I left that topic to him.

Gradually the writings of James Cone opened my eyes to how theol-ogy might be different when it was informed by the black experience. His earlier writings, antedating my acquaintance with Latin American theolo-gians, were so closely tied to description of the history of black suffering, the character of black church life, and the current movement that I was not able to see that they were seriously calling for a new theology on the part of whites. But by the publication of *God of the Oppressed* in 1975, I was beginning to understand the depths of the theological challenge.

Looking back I try to understand why, despite excellent reasons to prioritize black theology over its Latin American cousin, I did not do so. One reason was the difference between the discussions of the two topics at the AAR (American Academy of Religion). Discussions of Latin American liberation theology were chiefly among sympathetic North American whites. That made for easy entrance. But the black theology group was composed of black theologians. It was not clear that whites were really welcome.

In the political struggle, the role of whites had been highly circumscribed, rightly so. The struggle was to be led by blacks. Whites were told to go back to their churches and work there. In response, at Claremont, Joe Hough led the faculty and students in an intensive program on racism in the white churches. We sent teams of students to spend as much as a year in a local congregation helping it to come to terms with the often unconscious racism that pervaded even the most liberal white churches. Part of the training for participation in this project was to expose ourselves to black rage. We did this in somewhat artificial ways, and were certainly not expected to respond. I think I was not alone in finding this a painful confrontation of a sort that I did not seek out or to which I did not willingly expose myself.

I judged at the time, in part no doubt as a cop-out, that whites should not try to participate in the discussions through which black theology was being shaped. We should only try to teach our students what we learned from it. And we should try to influence our churches to understand and respond to the accusations of racism.

I had one opportunity to do the latter. Our bishop was black, and on one occasion at our Annual Conference he lost his cool and, after accusing the whole conference of racism, he walked out. Many in attendance were furious, believing themselves to be entirely innocent. I was invited to address the conference. I did not know just what the bishop had suffered at our hands, but I tried to encourage everyone to begin with the recognition that we, at least we white Americans, are all racists. Our whole culture through the centuries has been so deeply racist that one cannot be socialized into it, even by those who are trying to overcome it, without imbibing its racism to some degree. For many of us progressive Christians, this is unconscious and directly contrary to our espoused beliefs. I could testify that being called racist myself had made me quite angry, but that I tried to acknowledge the truth. I hope my address helped in the healing process.

I fear that the difficulty I had, and have continued to have, in engaging the issue of race theologically may itself express a kind of racism. I fear that even the form of these reminiscences about why I did not engage black theology more seriously as a theologian is too defensive. In any case, I must simply acknowledge that this has been, and is, a difficult topic for me to address.

Retrospectively I have realized that this was not enough. I realize that in my case, I felt defensive, on the one hand, and too guilty to make any criticism, on the other. But not engaging with black theology critically meant that I did not integrate it into my own thinking. I should have risked criticism so as to be corrected and to learn more. But I did not engage the topic systematically in writing until much later as half a chapter in a book called *Postmodernism and Public Policy.* I was finally helped to do so by the work of Thandeka, to whom I owe much, but with whom I disagree a little. This is too little and too late to contribute to any serious discussion of black theology.

Through the Center for Process Studies, we Whiteheadians did organize a couple of small conferences. There were a few black theologians, such as Henry Young, who found process theology useful and a few others who were willing to talk with us. The number has grown over the years. As a percentage of total numbers process theology today probably plays a larger role among blacks teaching theology than among whites.

CHAPTER ELEVEN

Gender

The third great liberation movement was feminism. Of the three it touches us all most immediately. Gender is part of our being in a way that race and class are not. I will write in this chapter extensively in a very personal way.

I first learned of the new feminist movement from a thoughtful mothers' day sermon by Pierce Johnson, probably in 1969. That I remember it indicates that it made a deep impression. But nothing much followed from that. I found it interesting, but thought of it as someone else's concern. I had no idea how important this movement would prove for me personally, for the school where I taught, for my congregation and denomination, and for the world as a whole. Feminism proved successful far beyond the other liberation movements.

Before this new wave of feminism took place, my denomination officially allowed the ordination of women. Georgia Harkness, who had led the church in adopting this policy, retired in Claremont and attended our congregation; so I had the chance to know her. She did not herself seek ordination, and indeed few women did. Our local bishop, despite his reputation for progressive leadership, had long opposed ordaining women, and made it almost impossible in southern California.

Despite the lack of progress in actualizing equality in the Protestant churches in the early 1970s, a decade later half of the students attending our seminary and a good many others were women. It took longer to equalize women's participation in faculties, but that, too, has now occurred in Claremont and at a good many other places. Locally, my pastor for the past decade has been a woman, and both our current

114

bishop and her predecessor are women. Women bishops are by no means rare in the United Methodist Church. Indeed, many of us believe that already, women are the progressive leaders of the church. At this level, the feminist movement has been remarkably successful in the churches as also in much of society.

But feminism was and is about far more than full participation of women in the institutions of society. It was, and is, about changing the way we think. A major expression of this change is in theology. From an early date it was much clearer to me that feminism involved theological change than that the other theologies of liberation did so.

The side of early feminism to which I personally found it difficult to respond was the rage. Black rage I experienced chiefly at a distance, but feminist rage came at me and other men from friends and students. Generally it was directed against males in general, but if one were the male who was present, it felt quite personal. The result was that, I now recognize, some of my early response to feminists was seriously distorted by defensiveness.

Understanding my response to the first encounter but also my total response drives me to reflect about how I thought about gender before this encounter, or perhaps better, what were my assumptions and attitudes. The truth is that I had hardly *thought* about it at all.

Whereas the oppression of blacks had been obvious to me from childhood, and I had no difficulty in understanding black rage, I had never thought of women as oppressed. In my own family, my mother seemed to me the stronger of my parents. That does not mean that my father was weak. He was not. My parents made decisions in discussion without any sense of hierarchy. But it was, and is, my impression that they usually ended by agreeing on what my mother thought. This seemed to me then, and seems now, perfectly correct, since I think my mother was, in a deep sense, the wiser of the two. But my point here is that I have difficulty thinking of her as oppressed even though it was obvious that my father was the more public figure.

At my school, Canadian Academy, my experience was that the girls were, on the whole, better students than the boys. The women teachers were certainly not inferior to the men. No doubt there was discrimination in some respects, but it was not visible to a child studying there.

On the mission field in Japan there were many single women who had positions of great influence and importance. I have come to see later that this was a phenomenon of the mission field that resulted from exclusion from leadership positions back in the U.S. In any case, the context it created in Japan was that the American women I knew were heads of institutions and missionary entrepreneurs. The board that sent them was composed of women. If they were oppressed by men, this was very indirect and invisible to me. On average they were, almost certainly, psychologically stronger and more independent than the male missionaries. Because the women raised more money than did the general board, the institutions they created and operated were better funded even through the Depression years.

I cannot forbear from telling about one woman who made a great impression on me as a youth. We called her "cousin" Mary Culler White, but the exact relationship was vague. She had gone to China as a missionary, probably in the 1890s, from a small town in Georgia. When she went and where, there was no established work; so she was a true missionary pioneer. It took a strong person to undertake such work alone. And she was strong. We spent six weeks with her in the summer of 1936 travelling in China with her as our guide, and the forcefulness of her character was palpable. It was my impression that she got up early every morning to give God his orders for the day.

That others recognized her strength is illustrated by one of my favorite stories. A couple of years later, Japanese armies had taken Shanghai and were moving up the Yangtze. There was a summer resort on a mountain not far from Shanghai. The Southern Methodist bishop responsible for the denomination's work in East Asia, Arthur J. Moore, was in the International Settlement in Shanghai with church leaders. A messenger came to him saying that Mary Culler White was on the mountain with a hundred Chinese women church workers. Japanese troops had surrounded the mountain and were taking it. What should they do?

Bishop Moore responded: "I'm sorry; there is nothing we can do. The Japanese will just have to look out for themselves." It was his judgment that the Japanese army was no match for Mary Culler White. I think he was right.

I am certainly no authority about the white Georgia culture from which my family and some of these women came. No doubt there are many true horror stories about how men dominated and abused women. But my sense of the common relationships even on the home turf is somewhat different. It was certainly the case that public leadership roles were all in the hands of men, and that the women who wanted such roles did much better on the mission field. But it is not my impression that the public roles were always the location of real power.

Consider the churches that were typically the most important institutions in Georgia towns. The pastors and the official leaders, the ones who debated and voted, were men. But the heart and soul of most of these congregations were the women. I think of my mother's mother who for decades headed the primary department of the Newnan Methodist church. This was for her a serious job. She studied educational theory and made sure it was applied. A child growing up in Newnan might have better teaching on Sunday than during the week. Certainly Sunday School, even for adults, played a larger role in spiritual formation than the church and its preachers, who came and went. The women were glad when men would help, but the education of children was in their hands. Any pastor who alienated the women of his congregation would accomplish nothing.

Women had their own organizations in the church. They sent their own missionaries around the world. The women seriously studied what was going on in the world and did so from an authentically Christian perspective. Men did not. The women were ready for racial integration. The men were not. Politically this showed up in Atlanta when the women squelched a boycott of integrated restaurants planned by the men.

Everybody understood this arrangement. If it is depicted as the men giving the orders while the women did the work, one would expect a lot of resentment. That was rare. The women who wanted to play a public role could do so through their own institutions. They were willing for the men who supported them to fight it out in the competitive world of business and politics, while they could shape the lives of their children and their communities around more cooperative principles. They were distressed when their men carried their competitiveness into war, but they maintained what humanity was possible and provided the basis for reconstruction afterward.

Many years ago I delighted in finding a report of a sociological study about who is happiest. It confirmed my view that the males of the species lived with significant illusions. They typically spoke of "old maids" as women to be pitied if not ridiculed and despised. But the study concluded that unmarried women were the happiest group. Next came married men, then married women, and last, least happy, single men. This confirmed my sense that women were the stronger sex. If men needed to bolster their egos by public recognition and competitive success, let them.

That was, at any rate, the view of the family in which my wife grew up. Her case was unusual because her household was thoroughly matriarchal. The home was owned first by her grandmother and then by her mother. Her great aunt lived with them. Her father had moved into the home when he married, but he remained something of a guest who did odd jobs around the house and spent most of his time elsewhere. He doted on his daughter, but the women raised her. The women who constituted the household thought that significant decisions are best made by women and that men usually mess things up. Jean naturally absorbed these views.

Jean's attitudes have been reflected throughout her life. She went to a women's college, named LaGrange, after the town in Georgia in which it is located. There she was a recognized leader, being elected head of a number of organizations including the student body. She also graduated with highest academic honors. Her name was included in the national *Who's Who among Students in American Colleges and Universities*. After we married, I expected that she would want to continue in leadership roles; but no, she had had enough of that. She was glad for others to play that game. She felt no need of public recognition.

Years later she enjoyed working first as a church office manager and later as a librarian at the Claremont School of Theology, but she had no professional ambitions. On one occasion the library lacked a director, and she and Elsie Freudenberger managed it for a year. They did this so well, that they were invited to continue on a permanent basis. Jean was not interested.

We married in a conventional ceremony with Jean's father "giving" her to me and with Jean promising to obey me. But neither of us had the slightest idea what that was all about. Jean had not experienced any oppression by men, and she had no intention whatsoever of being obedient to me or any other man. She was only slightly less opposed to obeying women. But the concerns of feminists never interested her despite occasional efforts on my part to get her involved.

I had never been told that men were supposed to be bosses. Because of the difference of our upbringing, I did hope for a more participatory relationship than the one Jean's family had modeled for her. In later years my admiring sons gave me a card with a picture of a man wearing unfashionable pants. It was inscribed, I wear the pants in my family, and my family makes fun of me. They certainly did not picture me as a successful dominator.

I did not recognize how discriminatory was the university world. No doubt the overwhelming preponderance of male faculty at the University of Chicago should have awakened me, but, since nondiscrimination was written into the founding documents of the university in the 1890s, discrimination may have been less determinative there than in some other schools.

Similarly, the faculty I joined in Claremont was all male, but I failed to see that as a result of discrimination. And, in a direct sense, events proved me right. I think the story of the appointment of Jane Douglass is worth reporting. Two years after moving to Claremont I spent a sabbatical year at Drew Theological Seminary in Madison, New Jersey. While there I had a call from President Colwell asking me to interview some East Coast candidates for a position in historical theology. I did so.

There were several excellent candidates, but the one I interviewed at Harvard was clearly the best. The faculty agreed with me, and she was hired. She was the first woman on the faculty. The point of the story, however, is simply that the fact she was a woman was never brought up in the discussion. We simply agreed that she was a superb candidate and that we were lucky to have the chance to bring her to the faculty. After the vote, for the first time, one professor, Harvey Seifert, commented that it would be good to have a woman colleague.

Our judgment of her excellence was confirmed in a variety of ways. She was a fine teacher, colleague, and scholar. She was also an outstanding leader in the Presbyterian Church, and this was a major reason for her leaving us to go to Princeton. We jokingly, but still half meaning it, called her our missionary to Princeton. Among the services she performed was leading the World Council of Reformed Churches.

In the interest of full disclosure, I should add that, although I do not think Douglass felt any discrimination from colleagues, she did experience problems with the administration. She objected to the fact that so many forms assumed the maleness of those who filled them out, and encountered resistance to making the needed adjustments. But I was not awakened to this discrimination until years later.

My comments are not intended to question the truth of feminist theory or to challenge the importance of the feminist movement. I want only to say that some women have always found ways to use objectively hierarchical structures in ways that have taken the sting out of them. In taking distinctive gender roles for granted, while seeing women in general as the stronger sex, I was reflecting views shared by a good many women. It was not simply a male perspective. I think my life experience may explain why it took me a while to realize how many women had experienced the limits of the roles assigned them as highly oppressive.

I happened to have had some personal acquaintance with the two women who were, in the early days, the key leaders in feminist theology. Rosemary Ruether earned one of the first PhDs from the new Department of Religion at Claremont Graduate School. We knew her as a splendid student with a deep passion for justice. But in the early sixties gender issues were not central for her.

A decade later I had a very different encounter with Mary Daly. This was at the Portland Christian Lecture series. Each year the Catholics and Protestants each chose a speaker. The Catholics had chosen Mary Daly before she had left the church. Since she had accepted, she came on. But she enforced her rule that she would only take questions from women. She had also decided to limit her conversation to other women; so our exchanges were very brief.

Nevertheless, the experience was important for me. For example, I discovered the importance of limiting her questioners to women. When she finished speaking a forest of hands went up, mostly men. When she refused to answer them, women began asking questions that, I felt sure, were better nuanced and more authentic than would have been those of the men. Another memorable experience was my introduction. One of Daly's disciples had been chosen to introduce me. She read a quite powerful poem depicting men as "Monsters," and then said that John Cobb would speak.

The most important event was the concluding one. Each of us spoke twice and then we were to have a joint session in which we addressed the same topic. The only way we could address the same topic would be to address one she chose. This was "androgyny," a topic on which I really had little to say. Obviously, the real interest was what Daly had to say. After both of us had spoken, men could not be prevented from asking questions. The result was that I spent the time answering questions that were obviously about her views. I am proud to say that I handled the situation well enough, that Daly has in some measure trusted me since then, or at least, I have been one of those to whom she has turned when she needed professional support from men.

Actually, with respect to the development of feminist theology, despite my slowness really to understand, I was extremely fortunate. I was privileged to be adviser to some excellent women students in Claremont in the middle to late seventies. Even before women came to study in large numbers I was gently introduced to feminist issues by one male student and two women. Ignacio Castuera wrote a RelD dissertation showing how in Mexico worship of the feminine divine was combined with oppression of women. He became a lifelong friend and companion.

Marjorie Suchocki wrote rigorous and insightful process theology in a way that I later recognized as subtly but significantly feminist. After successful teaching elsewhere she came back to Claremont and was, for some years, dean. In retirement, in my view, she has succeeded James Wall as the leading theological voice in film criticism.

Mary Elizabeth Moore worked on the boundary of theology and the one theological seminary field in which women had all along given leadership, religious education. This made her a "practical theologian," and, at least in my opinion, the leading woman in that field, both as a mode of theological reflection that came to have considerable academic importance and in relating her impressive theological thinking to the actual structures and institutions of the church. She is now dean of the United Methodist School of Theology at Boston University.

As the feminist movement intensified, a larger group of women students arrived eager to do more explicitly feminist theology. Their work was nurtured in discussions with Nelle Morton, Anne Bennett, and Charlotte Clinebell, who dropped her husband's and father's names to become Charlotte Ellen. Around 1979 the students organized a group in which they read papers to one another. They called it "Thiasos." I am sure that this was as important for them as their class work, perhaps more so. Their work was thoroughly responsible and truly imaginative and constructive. They educated me without making me too defensive to learn.

Most of these women were committed to the development of feminist theology. Among existing forms of theology, they often favored process. Bernard Loomer spent a year in Claremont and interacted in a very positive way with them. For such reasons as these, I had the great privilege of working with a number of them on their dissertations. Their projects were highly varied but all were existentially and even historically significant. I could be confident that from Morton, Bennett, and Ellen they were getting the help they needed to be responsible to the cutting edge of feminist thought. It was a great epoch in Claremont's history. During a time when there was much doubt among feminists as to the possibility of remaining in the church, most of our students did so and went on to serve the church with distinction. Claremont's contribution to the development of Christian feminism may prove to be its greatest.

I will mention four of those who were shaped by their experience in "Thiasos." Rebecca Parker and Rita Nakashima Brock have jointly written two major theological books: *Proverbs of Ashes* and *Saving Paradise*. Parker studied only in the seminary and went from here to serve a church. From there she was called to be president of Starr King School for Ministry. Brock took a PhD degree at the Graduate School. She first approached me with a proposal to write her dissertation on "Christ the Rapist." That proposal obviously expressed a great deal of anger against Christian support of patriarchy. However, she worked through that anger and ended up writing *Journeys by Heart: a Christology of Erotic Power*. It remains a standard text in feminist Christology. She has successfully taken on a succession of innovative tasks, currently giving leadership in the field of "moral injury" especially as it leads to the suicide of soldiers and veterans.

Sue Nelson wrote her dissertation on sin from the point of view of women's experience. She thought that the focus on pride clearly reflected the male perspective and that women in our culture were more inclined to the "sin of hiding." After years of teaching at Pittsburgh Theological Seminary and giving significant leadership in the Presbyterian Church, she returned to Claremont to be dean of the Claremont School of Theology. Sadly, cancer has taken her from us.

Catherine Keller worked on the question of relationality. This was much emphasized by feminists in a positive way, but it could take forms that inhibited the personal freedom they also prized. Her dissertation was published as *From a Broken Web*. She has gone on to a great career of teaching, publishing, and holding conferences at Drew Theological Seminary integrating process thought with European postmodernism. Some consider her the leading progressive theologian in the United States. I concur. Certainly she is doing more than anyone else to nurture an impressive new generation of process theologians.

There have been other fine women students from whom I have learned (and of course some fine men students as well). I have identified a particular cluster because they were here at a time when feminist theology was taking shape and have been able to participate in its development. It was a time of transition, when a supportive male could help. In subsequent years, women faculty became numerous and could serve as mentors to women students in almost all fields of study.

I became convinced that feminism has few objections to make to process thought as far as it goes. Even Mary Daly had a relatively positive view of Whitehead. But feminism has a great deal to teach process theologians. Prior to the emergence of feminism, process theology had almost nothing to say about gender, and its criticisms of dualism and its affirmation of the centrality of relations were, for the most part, highly abstract. For feminists these were fully concrete and historically important issues. Eco-feminists also gave a much richer account than process theologians had done of the way human beings are part of nature. For example, Nancy Howell, who was part of the group in Claremont at the height of the development of feminist theology, has given special attention to the kinship between human beings and such other species as chimpanzees.

It was clear that women who studied process and feminist theologies together could connect them fruitfully. My belief is that eco-feminism, wherever it develops, has many of the same teachings as process thought. The process community has promoted Rosemary Ruether and her writings despite her lack of interest in process philosophy. My sense of a rich congeniality between eco-feminist religious thinking and process theology was confirmed in recent years through the writings of Carol Christ, a leader of the Goddess movement. In some of her earlier writings she mentioned process thought in a favorable way. Her full commitment to process thought is expressed explicitly in *She Who Changes*. This book unabashedly recommends Hartshorne's philosophy of religion to her feminist followers.

I entitled the chapter "Gender" instead of "feminism" in order to include a brief note about homosexuality. Like the other topics, it was one about which I had some knowledge and general opinions. I certainly did not share the harsh condemnations and contempt that were so widespread. But I did not take it up as my cause or think of it as a proper topic for theology.

In the late sixties one of our students, Ed Hansen, took an internship in the tenderloin area of San Francisco working extensively with gay men. He wrote a thesis about this work. Ed had a brother who was out of the closet and had suffered for it. Working with him gave me a sense of the moral issues and social and personal importance of the topic. Some years later Ed himself came out of the closet. He has become a leader in the gay community in Los Angeles, while maintaining his leadership in the church.

Although I was certainly alerted to the issue, it still did not become a high priority for me. I recall early in the seventies that Ignacio Castuera, my teacher on so many points, announced that he was giving priority to justice for homosexuals. I expressed my surprise and, I fear, objection. He was probably the leading interpreter of Latin American liberation theology in the United States, and I thought he should stick to that role. He replied that in the United States gays were the most oppressed people. Liberation theologians should direct their attention to those who are most oppressed.

This was for me a true wake-up call. Never again did I belittle this issue in comparison with others. Some have suggested that a black woman lesbian is the most oppressed of all. The competition for that place is fierce, and we should consider matters case by case. But homosexuals, far more than the poor and those of despised races are likely to be rejected even by their own parents. Even in prison they sometimes suffer abuse from fellow inmates. There is little doubt that their liberation is of great urgency and importance. We may celebrate the quite remarkable improvements that have recently occurred in the United States and many other countries as well.

These changes occurred in the church as well. My denomination continues to have difficulty changing its official position because of the alliance of conservatives in the United States (especially from my beloved South) with the large group of voters from Africa. But in Southern California and much of the country, change occurred fairly quickly. My own congregation, like many, had openly gay members long before this became an issue in the church. It delayed formal action to become a "reconciling church" until it could be taken almost unanimously. It has taken this move very seriously, and the now retiring pastor, Sharon Rhodes-Wicket, has become a regional leader. She has joined the growing group of clergy who refuse to be bound by the rule against marrying gay couples. Bishop Carcano, our second woman bishop in a row, gives moral support.

The leading woman theologian of Methodism, of whom I wrote at the beginning of this chapter, was denied admission to my present retirement community, Pilgrim Place, because she would not come in without her female companion. The only couples allowed were legally married heterosexuals. Today, this story is a source of embarrassment. Pilgrim Place now has several homosexual couples of both genders. The ancient prejudice now seems ludicrous as well as vicious. This is surely progress in both my church and my retirement community. I wish I could claim to have contributed significantly to the change, but I cannot. At most I can hope that I gave some moral support to those who were working effectively on this very important matter. At any rate I rejoice in the weakening of one more injustice.

CHAPTER TWELVE

My Conversion

I have described in the previous chapters a period of many deep changes in my thinking and understanding of the world. I would identify them as creative transformations. But one creative transformation affected me so deeply and so pervasively that I call it "my conversion." It came before the full impact of most of the others. If it had not already changed me in this more fundamental way, perhaps the others would have. But in the actual course of events, it both prepared me for the others and affected the way I incorporated them into my ongoing vocation.

My conversion occurred in the summer of 1969. It came about through reading a little book by the ecologist, Paul Ehrlich, that my son, Cliff, wanted me to read. The book was a potboiler and a bestseller that made a considerable impact on a number of people. It was called *The Population Bomb*. It was wrong on many details and in almost all its specific predictions. It was alarmist in the worst sense. I remain deeply grateful to Ehrlich for writing it.

Despite its numerous errors, the book was profoundly prophetic. Perhaps the errors and exaggerations were necessary to make its point sufficiently powerful to grab the attention of a somnolent public. I was part of that public. The basic message of the book was that humanity is on a collision course with disaster. As the title indicates it gave central attention to an issue that I had barely considered and that so many liberals still try so hard to avoid, the rapid growth of population. The basic message was not only true but of utmost importance. Once it broke through to me I could not again doubt it.

126

I call this a "conversion" because it was not simply a recognition of a heretofore unnoticed fact that I needed to integrate with what I had known before. It gave a new center to my sense of vocation. The previous center was the service of Christian community through theological reflection and writing. I thought that the church was in a theological crisis and that I could in some ways be helpful. That seemed eminently worth doing. Teaching theology in a seminary gave me a great opportunity to do it. I assumed that would be my life's work and was quite content to pursue it.

I had always wanted to do my work in a wide horizon, but that had been largely an intellectual horizon. I have described the ways in which that was broadened at Chicago, at Emory, and in Claremont. Throughout this period I had strong convictions about social ethical matters that occasionally prodded me into action. I contributed a little money to a good many causes. I brought social issues into my preaching and gladly addressed them when invited to speak. Social issues played a much larger role in conversation around the family dinner table than did theology!

In California as well as in Georgia there were opportunities to work against racial segregation. At election time I sometimes volunteered to help get out the vote. In the late sixties I had become bitterly opposed to the war in Vietnam and spent one night in jail as part of a protest in Washington, D.C. But I had arranged my trip there so as to miss only one class, for which I made adequate arrangements.

It is clear that this was all peripheral. My vocational priorities were not in question. My involvement in such issues was important as an expression of my Christian faith and conviction. I greatly appreciated the leadership of those who gave it priority. But I saw my role as only supportive of their work. The faith of the church was relevant to responding to these questions. It would be relevant to responding to other questions for generations to come. To focus on the theology rather than on relevant social action did not seem to be a cop-out.

Being awakened to the threat to the future of humanity and even to that of other living things was different. If humanity did not awaken and change its ways, a few improvements in the way Christians thought did not seem so very important. I had to rethink what I was called to do. What role could I play as a Christian theologian?

The answer was made easier by my discovery of the important essay by Lynn White, Jr., "The Historical Roots of Our Ecological Crisis." He had given a lecture to the American Association for the Advancement of Science that was published in a 1967 issue of *Science*. White traced the roots of the crisis to the anthropocentric reading of the Bible in the West. This had liberated Western Europeans to exploit nature and paved the way for both science and technology. When these came together in the chemical revolution, the erosion of the natural world was greatly accelerated.

His thesis was not popular. Scientists and technicians do not like being told that there are theological grounds for their actions, and Christians do not like being told that their historic teachings are responsible for something as terrible as a threat to the future of life on the Earth. Furthermore, there is much more to be said about the causes of the crisis. But I found White's argument persuasive. I felt then, and continue to believe now, that White was essentially correct.

One of the best consequences of White's essay was its effect on biblical scholars. Many of them decided that it was important to show that the Bible was not responsible for the kind of anthropocentrism that paved the way to destructive exploitation of the natural world. They may have exaggerated the innocence of the Bible in this respect, but at least they began teaching the Bible in a different way. Prior to that time, the dualism of nature and history had played a large role in biblical exegesis. Sometimes the distinctively historical motifs were taken to be authentically Hebrew, whereas the talk about nature was regarded as the pagan background. This obviously reflected just that anthropocentrism that White attributed to the Western use of the Bible. It rather quickly disappeared from mainstream biblical scholarship to be replaced by a far more balanced reading of the texts.

The Bible in fact provides many reasons for caring for the Earth rather than exploiting it. White never denied that. His point was about the way it had been read in the West, and on this he was quite correct. We can be grateful to him for having, at least to some extent, changed the standard Western exegesis.

I was not a biblical scholar; so my theoretical engagement was philosophical and theological. I could point out that the anthropocentric tendencies in the early church and medieval Christian theology were greatly intensified as philosophy reestablished its independence from theology. St. Thomas may be accused of anthropocentrism, but it is mild in comparison with René Descartes. Immanuel Kant went further still. These philosophies in turn influenced modern theology, especially modern Protestant theology, and even more particularly, its most liberal and progressive forms—the theology in which I had immersed myself. No form of thought could be more anthropocentric than the existentialism that had been my conversation partner. In the summer of 1970, I wrote a little book aimed at a popular audience to tell some of this story. I called it *Is It Too Late? A Theology of Ecology.* It had very little immediate effect, but it has had a longer shelf life than most of my books. In 1995 a slightly revised edition was brought out by Environmental Ethics Books, and it has been in print since then.

Working on this book made me keenly aware of two things. First, I had myself been sucked into anthropocentric thinking and writing. My *Christian Natural Theology* had very little to say about nature. Its topics were humanity and God. *The Structure of Christian Existence* was even more glaringly limited to the human in its discussion. The question of how human beings are related to the natural world did not enter into the horizons of my thinking. How right White was!

Second, I had far less excuse than most theologians. Most of them had been socialized into the view, so explicit on the European continent, that theology must be done in the context allowed by Kant's first critique. According to that critique the human *Geist* is the creator of the world. Given that starting pointing, there is no escape from anthropocentrism. My philosophical teachers, on the other hand, broke drastically out of this anthropocentric world. I took for granted the independent reality of the natural world. Yet in my effort to participate in the ongoing theological discussion, I had allowed those who were inescapably anthropocentric to determine my theological agenda as well as theirs. Even after I realized this, I continued to be affected in much that I wrote by this deep-seated anthropocentrism of the Western intellectual tradition.

The abruptness of my conversion was expressed in a way that I mildly regret. One of the many limitations on the Whiteheadian influence was that, on the whole, those few of us who had been deeply affected by Whitehead's thought tended to cut ourselves off from the dominant analytic tradition. One exercise that had seemed worthwhile to me was to engage that tradition directly. I had chosen as the topic for such engagement the question of explanation in history. There was an extensive, but not overwhelming, body of literature on that topic written by people in the mainstream of analytic philosophy. I undertook to read that literature and engage it.

I developed a typology of positions, each of which, I thought, had merit. They were generally presented by their proponents as mutually exclusive. I wrote chapters on each and undertook to show that when carefully formulated and placed in a wider context, they could be seen as complementary. The wider context was, of course, offered by Whitehead's conceptuality. I avoided pressing Whitehead into the discussion heavy handedly. I had spent a lot of time on this and had almost completed a manuscript. But when I was awakened to the ecological crisis, I set this project aside in order to write the little book on ecology, and I never returned to it. So little in the real world, or even in the world inhabited by historians, seemed to be at stake in this exercise. I do not know what if anything was lost by this. As an outsider to the philosophical discussion I might never have found a publisher for a purely philosophical book. Even if it had been published, the book would probably have been ignored by mainstream analytic philosophers. Nevertheless, it could have been a test of the possibility that bridges could be built between process philosophers and the mainstream.

One reason for not completing the book was that I turned for a while from writing to "activism" of a sort. I took the lead in organizing two conferences, in 1971 and 1972. The first we called "A Theology of Survival." It was not very good, but the topic was sufficiently current to attract some attention in the press.

The second was a much larger conference on "Alternatives to Catastrophe." After the first conference, a small group of students worked with me to survey the literature. We were looking for people who agreed about the crisis and then went on to propose solutions. We got the support of the Southern California Council of Churches and worked closely with Al Cohen. In some ways the conference built on the work of the USA Task Force on the Future of Mankind and the Role of Church, and Edward Carothers of the National Division of the Board of Missions of the United Methodist Church came to report on that. We ended up with some interesting people, with two of whom I continued relations. One of these was Herman Daly, who had just published an essay on a steady-state economy. Our continuing collaboration since that conference has been an important part of my life. I will return to it in Chapter 18.

The other was Paolo Soleri, who died recently. He had shifted from his earlier experimentation with houses dug into the earth to a vision of great architectural ecologies, or "arcologies," that could accommodate large populations on a small piece of land without dependence on motor transportation. I continue to believe that Soleri's vision of how to build cities points in the right and necessary direction, and I deeply regret that no one ever gave him the money to begin the long process of needed experimentation.

After the conference, I organized an Arcology Development Center to promote Soleri's proposals. Through this organization, we introduced Soleri to the Los Angeles City Manager, Anne Houk, who invited him to present his ideas. Also, we arranged some visits to Arcosanti. But our dream of producing a film to promote his work fizzled, and, in general, the ADC puttered along for a few years and expired.

I have done what I could to increase interest in his work by my writings. More recently I had the chance to involve him in conferences in China, where so many huge cities are being built, to talk about arcologies there. The direction he pointed characterizes some of the construction in China, whether under his influence or simply as a response to the obvious problems I do not know. I still have some hope that the Chinese will see the need to incorporate more of Soleri's insights and proposals. But thus far neither my help nor that of any of his other admirers has paid off. I marvel at his persistence and maintenance of an optimistic spirit, through thick and thin, mostly thin, until his death in April 2013.

I marvel, in quite another way, at a society that pays so little attention to the few promising proposals that are available. We prefer business as usual, or very slightly modified, even when this leads us onward to the precipice. How could the Greeks have considered us to be "rational" animals?

I also chaired a small "eco-justice" task force for the Southern California Ecumenical Council. This task force was the official sponsor of the "Alternatives to Catastrophe" conference. We also organized students to make speeches in local churches.

I established relations with colleagues in the colleges who shared my concern, especially with John Rodman, a political theorist at Pitzer, who participated in the Alternatives conference. His great potential as a national leader was cut short by health problems and an untimely death. I gave occasional lectures around the country.

My environmental concern led to reconnecting with Jitsuo Morikawa, who for a while had been my pastor at the First Baptist Church in Chicago. I attended that church because during World War II it had

opened its doors to Japanese Americans and invited Morikawa to be
associate pastor. While I was there, he became senior pastor. At the time
we reconnected, he was head of the American Baptist Home Mission
Board. I have never met a church bureaucrat with more creative imagination or greater commitment to do what needed to be done for the deeper
mission of the church.

Morikawa shared with me the conviction that contributing to the
redirection of human activity on the planet was now central to the
church's mission. I worked with him in organizing several conferences.
He promoted what he called an "evangelical life style" which was, at its
heart, also an ecological lifestyle, and he got his generally conservative
denomination to adopt it. How much effect that really had I do not
know, but under his leadership the American Baptists were far ahead of
any other denomination in this respect.

Morikawa visited me from time to time in Claremont, and he often
talked with me about the need for a theology of institutions. I hardly
understood what he meant. Years later, after his retirement, he became
the unpaid and unofficial Christian minister to the University of Michigan. He arranged for Hans Küng and Gutiérrez to be visiting professors
at the university. He persuaded key figures in the administration and
senior faculty that they ought from time to time to discuss the goals and
purposes and values of the university. He remained very much in the
background, but he arranged to have me invited to lead one of these
discussions. I finally understood what would be involved in a theology of
the university. It has been an important topic for me since then.

Morikawa was farsighted in other respects as well. He saw that the
center of world political and economic life was shifting from the Atlantic
to the Pacific. He thought that Christian theology, which has been so
Eurocentric, needed to be re-thought in terms of this change. When he
died, one of his disciples, Paul Nagano, organized a group to promote
Asia-Pacific theology. I helped with an initial conference.

More important for me personally was that Jean and I joined an
experiment in communal living with Heidi and Joseph Hough and Judy
and Loren Fisher. Joe Hough taught ethics and served as academic dean
of our school. Loren Fisher taught Old Testament. We three couples had
been for some years a couple support group along with Charlotte and
Howard Clinebell, our professor of pastoral counseling. The Clinebells
decided not to join the communal living experiment.

Ours was a very bourgeois commune, with each couple having its quite private space. Chiefly it meant sharing the kitchen and dining area, eating the evening meal together, and taking joint responsibility for the property. There were many rewards but also many problems. After a couple of years, the Fishers left for a farm in northern California. The Houghs bought a house in Claremont and moved out. We stayed for four years with changing companions, including Ignacio Castuera, whom I introduced in earlier chapters, and his family.

There was extensive response to the new understanding of the ecological crisis that emerged around 1970. Earth Day that year marked the beginning of a new epoch. The United Nations responded with remarkable speed, holding a conference on the topic in 1972. Regrettably, the World Council of Churches held back from supporting the movement because the initial response of much of the Third World was that ecological matters were a concern of the First World bourgeoisie and distracted attention from the profound injustices from which the Third World suffered. The slogan of the World Council, "a just and participatory society," reflected this concern.

A few years later, however, the situation had changed. Third World peoples realized that much of the environmental problem focused on the devastation of their lands, forests, and fisheries by the exploitative practices of First World businesses. Ecological concerns were not primarily a matter of the beautification of highways or increasing the number of city parks. The WCC meeting in Nairobi in 1975 changed the slogan to "a just, participatory, and sustainable society." Charles Birch gave the main speech on the topic of sustainability.

Birch had studied in Australia with a biologist, Wilfred Agar, who already in 1943 had published *A Contribution to the Theory of the Living Organism*, clearly influenced by Whitehead. Birch had made contact with Hartshorne while on sabbatical in Chicago. Process thinking had helped him integrate his science and his faith. He had been working with the ecumenical movement for some time and had given leadership in the move to add "sustainability" to the concerns of the WCC. His work with the ecumenical movement as well as in biology caused him to travel around the world. In 1966, on one of his travels he had stopped by Mainz to see me.

Having added "sustainability" to its concerns, the WCC organized discussions around the world with regard to what this meant.

It also organized in 1979 a major international conference at MIT on the subject of "Faith, Science, and Technology." The main work of the conference was to be done in working groups, and most of these were on specific topics such as atomic energy and education. One section was planned to provide the theological grounds, and this was called "Faith and Science." This name reflected the epistemological bias of Protestant theologians, a bias that prevents any real escape from anthropocentrism.

Charles Birch and Bishop Gregorias of the Syrian Orthodox Church of India persuaded the organizers to add a second theological section that would discuss "Nature, Humanity, and God." This reflected the continuing ontological approach of the Eastern Church that had not been reshaped in its thinking by Descartes and Kant. I was a United Methodist delegate to this conference and ended up chairing that section. It was my only opportunity to give leadership in the WCC. I think the statement we came up with was a good one. I think the positions developed in the other working groups were also good.

My contacts with Charles Birch became increasingly important. In 1976 he had visited me in Washington, D.C., where I was spending six months as a Woodrow Wilson Fellow. He suggested that we write a book together on ecology. I gladly agreed. That was before the days of e-mail, and working together was a challenge. We were helped by the fact that he traveled a lot in connection both with the WCC and with international biology conferences. He came by Claremont several times. In 1981 we published *The Liberation of Life: From the Cell to the Community*.

It was genuinely co-authored. Although we divided up responsibility for initial drafts of chapters, every chapter includes contributions from both of us. It is a book that neither of us could have written alone. It provides a Whiteheadian vision of the nature and role of life that cannot be contained in any academic discipline and is quite different from that provided by any such discipline. It provides a way of looking at the world that, if adopted, would change not only what is taught in universities but what is practiced in global economics and politics. Yet there is little in it that is factually controversial. Both of us have written other books dealing with ecological issues, but I think this is our best work. Subsequently Birch won a Templeton Prize for his life work in the area of science and religion. I like to think that our work together contributed to his being thus honored.

Looking back I am impressed by the speed of the initial changes in response to the environmental crisis both in the United Nations and in the church. Important legislation was also enacted in Washington. It was satisfying to be part of a movement that was having some effect. However, it was frustrating that so much of the positive change was obviously too little too late.

Much of the agitation for change took place on university campuses. Many professors were involved. Yet the actual change in the functioning of universities was trivial. The deeply entrenched disciplines continued on their way. The dualism of the natural sciences and the study of human beings in the social sciences and the humanities was not reduced. The study of human beings in the latter disciplines remained radically anthropocentric. The growing competitor in shaping the universities was not the ecological crisis but capitalism. Economic considerations have come to dominate higher education as a whole. They, too, are purely anthropocentric.

In the church, by contrast, there were real changes. Not only the World Council of Churches but the Roman Catholic Church, the Eastern Orthodox Church and many Protestant denominations made excellent statements. There was real repentance for the long acceptance of dualism and anthropocentrism and for the disregard of the natural world. I noted that in the church also, what changed least was the teaching of the several academic disciplines in seminaries, although there was more change in them than in most other parts of higher education. In these respects, I was proud that my own seminary gave significant leadership.

However, I noted two other matters that were not so encouraging. First, even though the church spoke well, and even acted well when its attention was directed to the global environmental crisis, most of the time it thought about other things and, when doing so, acted in ways that ignored the natural world. I found this was often true of me as well.

Second, even though the teaching of the church had, at an earlier point given shape to societies' styles of thought and action, today it does not have much influence. The church could repent without effecting any of the changes needed in public policies or even generating a public discussion of these policies. The real theology that now governs the world is taught in departments of economics, not in schools of theology. This conclusion led to new directions in my study and reflection to which I will turn in later chapters.

There was one issue related to, perhaps part of, the new environmental concern that was important to me but ignored by the church even in its improved statements. This was the question of animals, sometimes formulated in terms of animal rights. On this topic there was more writing among analytic philosophers than in the church. Whitehead-ians generally take an intermediate position between those who treated nonhuman animals as having value only for humans and those who gave equal value or rights to all. We affirm gradations of value according to the capacity to integrate greater variety into the unity of an experience. The implications are that, at least in our society, human beings sin egregiously against other animals, and we Whiteheadians believe that the church should speak out against these crimes. However, the newfound emphasis on the respect that should be shown to God's total creation rarely led to critical reflection or moral criticism on this topic.

Two Whiteheadians, active in the WCC, Charles Birch and Jay McDaniel, organized a small WCC conference at Annecy, France, in 1988, specifically designed to integrate the discussion of nonhuman animals into the broader topic of the natural world. I was glad to take part. We came up with a fine statement. It turned out that the higher echelons of the WCC wanted nothing to do with it. However, it was much in demand by segments of the public. Many of the papers were published in a book edited by Birch and McDaniel along with William Eakin, *Liberating Life: Contemporary Approaches to Ecological Theol-ogy.* The door to this topic in the church was cracked open. Later Birch co-authored a small book that was published by the WCC press. A few denominations have dealt with the issue. But clearly Christian anthro-pocentrism has not died altogether.

In this chapter I have traced the effects of my conversion in terms generating efforts to raise concern and encourage reflection, chiefly in the church, about ecological issues. But the effects were broader than this. I realized with a shock how my acceptance of disciplinary boundaries had limited my theological work. I had occasionally dealt academically with social ethical issues, but only when I was asked to teach a course on ethics. Those issues in turn were defined anthropocentrically, so that it had not occurred to me to consider the relation of human beings to the natural world. I saw that it was not only I, but the academic community as a whole that was limited in the topics it could treat and the way it could treat them by the definitions of academic disciplines.

It seemed profoundly wrong to me that Christian thinkers should allow themselves to be controlled and limited in this way. My sense of wrongness was only heightened when I learned that at the Chicago Divinity School ethics had been separated from theology as a discipline only a few years before I arrived. How arbitrary these boundaries were! In this case I was quickly convinced that both theology and Christian ethics suffered from the disciplinary and departmental separation and ceased to respect it.

More broadly, I redefined theology in nondisciplinary terms. The great classical theologians knew nothing of disciplinary boundaries. They felt free to address as Christians any problem facing the church or individuals or society as a whole. Their theologies dealt with economic and political issues routinely. I defined theology as "intentional Christian thinking about important matters." By that definition I was doing my work as a theologian when I pursued ecological issues. *The Liberation of Life* was a theological book, and it would still have been theological even if we had not included a chapter on God.

Birch and I had wanted to make that clear. In the introduction we had explained what we shared that enabled us to work together. We wrote that we were both Christian believers. It was interesting, and sad, that the one change that Cambridge University Press required us to make was at that point. They did not want to publish a book on a broad topic of this sort by "Christian believers." They said few would read past that statement. Perhaps they were correct. We settled for saying only that we subscribed to Christian values. I was reminded, if I needed reminding, of how alienated the scholarly and even the ethical community has become from the church and from "believing" Christians. How far can one compromise in articulating who one is before it becomes betrayal of the faith on the one side or deception of the "cultured despisers" on the other?

I wish that I could simply condemn the cultured despisers for their attitude. Sadly, when Christians formulate their beliefs in a fideistic way, we invite this kind of rejection. If we present our views as if they were beyond rational criticism because they are vouchsafed us in revelation, we deserve to be ignored by those who do not share this notion of revelation. On the other hand, I wish that the cultured despisers could recognize that other Christians are acknowledging that their understanding of reality has been shaped in a long tradition centering in Jesus and Paul. That this tradition contains some distinctive wisdom is surely a claim that can be argued in a public context with no special pleading. Reinhold Niebuhr is an example of this kind of theological work. He is certainly not alone.

To dismiss his insights *a priori* because he was a Christian believer would be irrational. People of intellect and culture should be able to make this distinction. I have certainly not tried to conceal the fact that I write as a Christian believer, and I do not intend to do so.

I continued to teach courses in theology that fit the normal disciplinary scheme. But from the time of my conversion I have felt no hesitation to deal with bodies of literature that come from other disciplines. For me, a course is authentically theological if we are dealing with an important issue and if we examine the literature in any field from a Christian point of view.

Another dimension of my change was the ending of a deep-seated assumption about progress. If one had asked me in the sixties whether I believed in progress, I would probably have said No. I would have understood the question to be whether progress was inevitable, whereas I thought the future was genuinely open. Nevertheless, as I noted in an earlier chapter, before my encounter with Shepard, I supposed that over the past hundred thousand years human beings had definitely progressed. And I also thought that in the years after World War II, we were making progress. We had the United Nations, and this time the United States had joined. Europe and Japan were being rebuilt. The colonial age had been replaced by the age of Third World development. There were breakthroughs in race relations in the United States. There was some progress in the reduction of poverty. Higher education was open to almost everyone. I felt that we were moving, too slowly, of course, in the right direction.

Suddenly, all such improvements seemed secondary. If we were destroying the habitability of the planet, then improving relationships among people was almost like rearranging the deck chairs on the Titanic. I found in myself a tendency to withdraw energy from the social causes to which I was committed.

Fortunately, working in the context of the church soon corrected that tendency. Church statements always tied justice and ecology together. The Task Force I served was called "eco-justice," and this term was widely used in Christian circles. The World Council called for a "just, participatory, and sustainable society." We had previously emphasized that there could be no peace without justice. We now emphasized that there could be no sustainability without justice. I was quickly convinced. But I understand how those committed to justice could fear that those focused on environmental issues could withdraw support. I have seen it happen with people whom I greatly admire for their ecological commitment. Thomas Berry rightly saw the fate of the Earth as *the* decisive issue. Some of his followers, rightly agreeing with this judgment, give less attention to issues of justice.

I am grateful for the Christian milieu that saved me from this separation of the one issue from all the others. But that milieu has not prevented me from viewing decay as the deeper trend of this historical epoch. The shift from the view that we humans collectively are moving toward a better world to the view that we are satisfying our present wants at the expense of our children is not a minor one. That change occurred for me in the summer of 1969.

CHAPTER THIRTEEN

The Center for Process Studies

When I was a student and for some years thereafter, the Divinity School of the University of Chicago was the place that kept serious study of Whitehead alive in an otherwise inhospitable climate. I took this for granted. My decision was simply about how to relate to this established situation.

When the faculty under which I had studied began to break up, I assumed that they would take with them their interest in Whitehead. This might be seen as an occasion for extending Whitehead's influence. This was true to a limited extent. Daniel Day Williams certainly increased interest in Whitehead at Union Theological Seminary. Charles Hartshorne made Emory University a mecca for philosophy students interested in process thought, and later he played the same role at the University of Texas. Bernard Loomer had some effect at Berkeley. But all of these depended on single individuals and faded with their retirement. The decline of interest at Chicago continued.

Furthermore, even at the height of Chicago interest, when a good number of dissertations were being written in which Whitehead played a significant role, the interest remained relatively narrow. Whitehead's relevance extended in many directions, but his influence was largely limited to a small coterie of philosophers and theologians, with some attention also in departments of education. There was no sustained cultivation of the wider application.

In the late sixties Lewis Ford spent a sabbatical semester in Claremont. He had taken an MA in philosophy at Emory before completing his graduate work at Yale. I had been his advisor at Emory. We shared both an interest in promoting Whitehead studies and a concern about their future.

Ford deplored the difficulty of publishing technical material on Whitehead's philosophy. I was concerned that there was no place to publish discussions of Whitehead's wider relevance. We decided to test the possibility of launching a quarterly journal that would respond to these two needs.

We decided that we would go ahead if we could get two hundred people to agree to subscribe. With great help from Norman Pittenger, among others, we succeeded. We found a family printing operation that was inexpensive. The School of Theology gave us a small subsidy. Ford agreed to be editor, while I agreed to be responsible for business matters to be handled at Claremont. Robert Hutton, a Claremont student who had been a professional printer, took over most of the work here. After many difficulties and delays the first issue of the new journal, *Process Studies,* appeared, dated Spring 1971. I believe it was actually later than that. We have had great difficulty over the years publishing in a timely fashion. Nevertheless, the journal has been successfully published for more than forty years.

Editing the journal was a labor of love for Ford, and with no compensation he gave unstintingly of his time and talent. For many years *Process Studies* was not technically a refereed journal because Ford did most of the actual refereeing himself. Although he sought help when he needed it, when articles were within the scope of his primary competence as a Whitehead scholar, he felt free to accept or reject. The quality of the journal did not suffer. Actually, articles received more careful attention under this system than occurs generally in refereed journals.

Indeed, if there was a complaint, it was of a different sort. Often an author would receive from Ford a detailed critical commentary as long as the original article. Ford delighted in the resulting interchange, and when the writer was willing to participate in it, the resulting article was certainly strengthened. On the other hand, some would-be contributors found this process unduly time consuming.

The main policy issue was rooted in the double interest that we brought to the journal from the beginning. Ford's focus was philosophy and philosophical theology. I certainly had no objection to emphasizing these topics, but I saw that he was accepting very few articles relating

Whitehead's thought to other fields. His problem was that those who wrote on other topics were rarely as philosophically sophisticated as Ford wanted. Eventually we developed "focus sections," edited by others, which broadened the range of topics published in the journal.

When eventually we succumbed to the required standards for an officially refereed journal, Ford found his role less satisfying. He was succeeded by Barry Whitney. The workload Whitney inherited was enormous, and his recognition for this work by his university was even less than Ford received. Nevertheless, the journal flourished under his editorship and became far more international as process thought has become important in other parts of the world. The success of the journal in surviving and growing over the years was due to the selfless generosity and capable efforts of these two men. Sadly, Barry was not well and had to give up the editorship. He recommended Dan Dombrowski to succeed him, and we are extremely fortunate that Dombrowski agreed.

Even before we launched the journal I had been fantasizing about having a center in Claremont that could promote the study and the use of Whitehead's concepts. On a visit to Emory, I was asked whether I would consider returning to the theological faculty there. I replied that I was very happy where I was, but that the possibility of establishing a center for process studies might attract me. I exchanged ideas about such a center with David Griffin, a Claremont graduate, who was teaching in Ohio. The possibility of actually having such an institution seemed remote.

While I was on sabbatical in Hawaii in the fall of 1972 I received an invitation from Emory complete with the possibility of a center for process studies. This entailed the agreement to hire David Griffin to teach part time and run the center. I would receive a faculty chair that included an extra stipend that could be used for operations. The dean, Jim Laney, made a trip to Hawaii to discuss this with me. I was flattered and excited. The great respect in which I held Laney at that time has only grown since then, as he became president of Emory University and then ambassador to South Korea. In that capacity he brought former president Jimmy Carter to Korea to talk with the North Koreans and ward off a threatening military crisis. He continued to work with Carter and played an important role in establishing the Carter Center at Emory.

Emory with Laney's leadership was an attractive place to teach, but by then I was deeply rooted in Claremont and had no desire to leave. In any case, before accepting the Emory offer it seemed only right to explain the situation to colleagues and administration at Claremont. I had previously participated in faculty efforts to keep colleagues who were invited elsewhere, but even so the responses from colleagues were such that I felt that no eulogy would be needed when I died. It was wonderfully gratifying for one, who not many years earlier had lacked any secure home in academia, to be strongly wanted in two places.

Still, my interest in establishing a center for Whiteheadian studies was strong. Although Jean was happy in Claremont, she was willing to return to Atlanta. Emory had developed a strong, well-funded graduate program in religion that offered full scholarships and stipends to the students it admitted, whereas almost none of our students received comparable help. I was ready to accept the Emory offer despite my great appreciation for the letters of my colleagues.

I was truly astonished when it turned out that Claremont made a remarkably similar offer to Emory's. Griffin would become Professor of Philosophy of Religion succeeding Don Rhoades who was near retirement. I would be made Avery professor at the graduate school, with an extra stipend of $10,000 a year that I could use for the operations of the center. And the school of theology would pay an assistant $3000. The school also supplied a room. I stayed in Claremont. I remain deeply indebted to Laney.

Griffin and I began right away to plan two conferences. The second conference was held at the University of Hawaii and dealt with Whitehead and Buddhism. It initiated most of the discussion that will be treated in Chapter 14.

The first conference of the Center for Process Studies was also, in many ways, the most impressive. Charles Birch arranged for it to take place at the Rockefeller Center in the Italian Alps at Bellagio. It focused on a question in Western thought that had been central, especially since Descartes: the status of the subjective and mental in a nature conceived objectively and mechanically. Its papers were published in *Mind in Nature*.

This conference approached these questions chiefly from the biological perspective. Thanks to Birch's connections and reputation, the attendees constituted an illustrious group including Theodosius Dobzhansky, C.H. Waddington, Sewall Wright, and Arthur Koestler, together with such leading process philosophers as Milič Čapek, Ivor Leclerc, and Charles Hartshorne. I recall that a picture was made of the group and that, because I was director of the center that organized the conference, I was seated in the middle of this distinguished group, with others standing around me. I am not sure whether I was more proud or embarrassed.

Waddington brought with him a then still little-known physicist, a student of Einstein, David Bohm. Bohm's presentation was the most riveting of the conference. The center worked intensively with him in later years. He participated in several conferences and spent several weeks with us. His vision of a "holographic" world was remarkably similar to Whitehead's understanding of concrescence. I am proud of a tape we made in which the similarities come out very strongly. Nevertheless, he never identified himself as Whiteheadian.

David Griffin, as director of the center, proved to be a brilliant conference organizer. One incident that says a lot about his thoroughness and insight is somewhat amusing. We wanted to do something in honor of Charles Birch. His choice was a conference on the mind-body question, and we agreed. David's custom, once we had settled on a topic, was to familiarize himself thoroughly with the literature so that he could select the best people for the conference. In this case he read both philosophers and scientists as well as persons involved with animal behavior and artificial intelligence. Although very few were close to process thought in their approach, he invited those who he thought might be open-minded.

David often wrote a paper introducing the process perspective to those who were wholly uninformed about it, to be read in advance of the conference. He did so in this case as well. However, this time the paper was three hundred pages in length! I doubt that any of the participants read it. And partly for this reason, this conference, as such, was not a great success. However, David sent his introductory paper to the University of California Press, and it was published as *Unsnarling the World Knot*, probably the most important process book on the mind/body problem.

The way books have developed out of conferences has been quite diverse. Of the two I have mentioned, one was simply a collection of the papers presented and the second was a paper prepared for study in advance of the conference. A third pattern has been more common.

We received modest support from the Templeton Foundation for a series of three conferences on science and religion. They dealt with evolution, quantum theory, and cosmology. I was responsible for the first. Lynn Margulis was our most exciting participant, and the conference led to a continuing relation with her until her untimely death. There were other fine papers, but they did not add up to a book. I was authorized by participants to take a strong hand as editor and make a book growing out of the conference. The book, *Back to Darwin,* included a good deal of material not delivered at the conference. Indeed, I made it into a book with a thesis by imposing my views upon it and writing a good part of it. The book made of the papers a coherent critique of the standard neo-Darwinian account of evolution, an exploration of better scientific options, and an introduction to a Whiteheadian one. Happily, none of the contributors objected to being included in the volume thus structured.

The examples mentioned indicate that many of our conferences dealt with the physical sciences. Other conferences have dealt with professional concerns, such as education, universities, management, and psychotherapy. Still others dealt with social ethical issues and political theory. And some were more narrowly philosophical or consisted in conversations with individual thinkers. Still others have been oriented to the contemporary scene in terms of black theology, feminism, and critiquing economic globalization and American empire. We have given sufficient emphasis to dialogue among religions and religious pluralism that I am devoting a chapter to that topic in Chapter 15.

Perhaps the most important institutional change occurred when we decided to become a membership organization. This increased costs as much as it increased income. We needed a considerably larger staff. We also needed a new publication to share information with our members and keep in touch with them. *Process Perspectives* has developed into a cross between a newsletter and a small magazine, and we are quite proud of its present form. We prize the relationships established through membership. And the generosity of a few members has been very important.

By far the most important of these supporters has been John Buchanan. He had been deeply involved in transpersonal psychology, and at Emory University he had found that he could understand his experience in that community best in Whiteheadian terms. He wrote a dissertation with Will Beardslee. On one occasion he told me that he was considering setting up another center for process thought. I suggested that he partner with us on the Claremont one, and he agreed. We probably would not have survived without his help.

Prior to that time, the journal and the center were formally quite separate, even though some of the same people worked on both. However, largely for the sake of the journal, when we became a membership organization, we made the journal a part of the benefit of membership. Increasingly, we considered the journal an organ of the Center, and later we made that relationship official.

The largest contribution to fixed costs was developing CPS into a significant center for research in process thought. Just as important as holding conferences is providing a place for serious research. Accordingly, a major task of the center has been to make itself the world's leading library for Whitehead studies. Our collection consists not only of books but also of articles, dissertations, and unpublished papers.

Our interest extends to other process thinkers, but for some of these there are other centers. Accordingly, we do not seek comprehensiveness with regard to the writings of William James, John Dewey, C.S Pierce, or Henry Nelson Wieman. On the other hand, we seek as much material as we can get on such people as Charles Hartshorne, Daniel Day Williams, John Spencer, and William Beardslee. I mention the four instances in which we have received collections from their estates.

We are of course interested in reaching the local community as well. We have held hundreds of afternoon seminars, and some community people have come. However, by far the most effective program was initiated by Marjorie Suchocki. She made herself an authority on film, *the* leading authority among process thinkers, and instituted the annual Whitehead Film Festival. This has become a Claremont institution.

In 1998 we marked the 25th anniversary of the Center for Process Studies by holding the Third International Whitehead Conference in Claremont. The first two had been in Bonn, Germany, (1981) and Nagoya, Japan (1984). They were rather small gatherings. In Claremont there were about three hundred participants. Most were from the United States, but a good number joined us from other countries. Whereas prior to that time, such conferences were an occasional matter, with no shared planning, at the end of this one there was a definite sense that there should be others.

An aftermath of the Claremont conference was the decision to gather representatives of various process-oriented groups in order to consider ways of working together. An international group met in Claremont in 2000. Out of that meeting developed the International Process Network. I worked hard to create an initial board, but I was eager that it be fully independent of Claremont and did not myself remain a member. Thanks to the effective leadership of Herman Greene, it has survived and become an important part of the wider Whitehead movement. Its value thus far is as much symbolic as real. Perhaps its most important practical role is now to decide where International Whitehead Conferences will be held and to support the local planners.

One of the most important functions of the center has been to attract visitors from other countries to study here and make use of our library. These international visitors contributed to the founding of the IPN and to its subsequent work. Retrospectively it is clear that they have been an important factor in the growth of interest in Whitehead around the world.

As it turned out the visitor who has been most important for us was Roland Faber from Austria. He is now the Professor of Process Thought at the Claremont School of Theology as well as director of the Center for Process Studies. His book, *God as Poet of the World,* has been an important contribution to the development of process thought in both its German and its English versions. With his European connections he is continuing to build bridges and spread interest in Whitehead in Europe. Indeed, he has made a major contribution to making Whitehead's thought a respected part of the continental philosophical discussion. He has organized the Whitehead Research Project as a project of the Center for Process Studies, and this project has greatly increased the value our library has for research on Whitehead. Even more importantly, it is now producing an exhaustive critical edition of Whitehead's writings.

An early visitor was Jan Van der Veken, who had been appointed professor of natural theology at Leuven. Leuven had been a major center of phenomenological research, and Van der Veken wanted to keep this alive. But he had become interested in Hartshorne as well, and he came to Claremont to pursue that interest. He brought with him a student, Andre Cloots. These two scholars have established a process-oriented center in Leuven. We have been able to help in its development of the strongest library in this field in Europe. The Leuven center has played a significant role in Belgium, but its greatest importance has been for students coming from the Third World. Leuven is the only university on the European continent where one can study exclusively in English. It is Catholic, and Catholic students from English-speaking countries or former British (or American) colonies, who want to study in Europe, often find Leuven their best choice. A number of these wrote dissertations on Hartshorne's thought under the direction of Van der Veken.

Andre Cloots now serves as Van der Veken's successor. Their work has introduced process theology in such countries as the Philippines, India, and Congo.

Another visitor at the Center for Process Studies, Michel Weber, has become the most prolific publisher of process writings in the world, both in French and in English. He has also translated books into French and organized conferences.

Gabor Karsai spent a year in Claremont. Later he was co-translator of *Process and Reality* into Hungarian and played a major role in making Whitehead a center of interest among Hungarian philosophers. He has formed an international organization of leaders interested in compassion and worked with the mayor of Reykjavik to organize the "Spirit of Humanity" and to hold conferences in Iceland.

Helmut Maaßen became the organizer of adherents of process thought in Germany. The German Society of Process Thought owes much to him. It holds an annual summer school that may be the most important gathering of this kind in the world. He is currently chair of the International Process Network.

A more recent visitor was Gorgias Romero from Chile. He was writing his dissertation on Whitehead and Husserl. He encouraged us to do more work in Latin America, and this resulted in the organization of the Latin America project, chaired by George Pixley and Ignacio Castuera. It has built on their connections going back to the halcyon days of liberation theology. Previous connections with Alberto Múnera made possible a significant event in Bogotá, Columbia, and George Pixley's contacts in Nicaragua led to organizing a conference there that included Ernesto Cardenal. This resulted in establishing a center. A later conference was held in Mexico City, and another is planned. Meanwhile, Romero has worked with staff members at the Center to make connections in Spain as well. The conference in Claremont, mentioned in Chapter 10, which brought together persons whose opposition to American empire developed from Latin American experience with opponents from the process tradition, included Lilia Marianno. She has subsequently taken the lead in generating interest in Brazil. We expect a good delegation from Brazil to the tenth IWC in Claremont, and interest there sufficed to issue an invitation for the eleventh IWC to be held in Brazil. In fact, another Portuguese-speaking nation, the Azores, trumped the invitation! Prospects for the future of process thought in the Latin world are bright.

The international visitor who has done by far the most to advance process thought in his own country has been Zhihe Wang. He came to study with David Griffin and while a student initiated the China Project of CPS. He stayed on to make Claremont his center for work in China. He was joined by his wife, Meijun Fan, a leading professor of Chinese art and aesthetic theory. Together they established the Institute for the Postmodern Development of China. Their work has been of such importance that I devote a separate chapter to it.

Here, however, I note that in 2002, they organized in Beijing the Fourth International Whitehead Conference. This drew attention in China to process thought and undergirded its future development there. It ensured that the idea of holding conferences every two or three years would be actualized.

The Fifth International Whitehead Conference was held in Seoul in 2004 by two Koreans who had studied in Claremont: Wangshik Jang and Sangyil Kim. They also organized the Korea Whitehead Society. Jang teaches in the Methodist Theological Seminary in Seoul. Kim returned to the United States and organized and directed the Center's Korea Project. When he found it necessary to spend most of his time in Korea, Kilsang Yoon took leadership.

Two former visiting scholars at the center are now in Salzburg. Their joint presence led to their inviting the Sixth International Whitehead Conference to meet there in 2006. One of them, Hans Joachim Sander, has been approved by the Vatican to teach theology in the small seminary there. The other is Franz Riffert, who works in the fields of psychology and education. He has edited and published impressive collections of process-oriented writings in these fields. He has completed his habilitation and is now a full professor at the University of Salzburg, active in applying process thought to issues in psychology and education.

The Salzburg conference was different from the earlier ones in an important respect. Because much of the leadership in Whitehead studies has been by Claremont theologians, we played a leading role in all the preceding conferences, even the ones in China and Korea. However, the organizers of the Salzburg Conference rightly decided that, for the sake of the future of process thought in Europe, theology and theologians, along with Claremont's role, should be kept in the background. The plenary speakers were for the most part scientists, and none were from Claremont. Isabelle Stengers, whose book *Thinking with Whitehead* had just come out, played an important role. Partly as a result, even though the conference was held in a Catholic seminary, the difficulty of getting Whitehead seriously considered by secular thinkers in Europe has been much less than in the United States. Bruno Latour, a close associate of Stengers has given the Gifford Lectures.

For me, a meeting of those interested in *Process Studies* at the end of that conference had considerable practical importance. When this journal was started, its constituency was almost entirely in North America. Hence, to be the "global" organ for process studies was little more than to serve the North American scene. But the Salzburg conference gave expression to an emerging reality that was quite different. Much earlier, the Japanese had established their own journal and the Australians had their own electronic publication. Nevertheless, *Process Studies* was generally recognized as the major organ for the movement, although most of its articles were still written by North Americans.

This situation seemed to me unstable. We could go either of two ways. We could encourage the Koreans, the Chinese, and the Europeans, for example, to develop their own journals, keep *Process Studies* as the North American journal, and move toward a situation of equality among regional journals. This would be easiest for us. But if we were to be the major global organ of the movement, we needed to find ways to relate more effectively to the international process community. I put this question to the group and, somewhat to my surprise, there was unanimous response that *Process Studies* should be the international expression of process thought. We have worked to realize that goal, although there is still a long way to go.

The Seventh International Whitehead Conference was quite different, reminding us of cultural differences. It was held in Christ University in Bangalore, India, in January 2009. The IPN board was initially concerned about the prominence Kurian Kachapilly, the organizer, proposed to give religion, reminding him of what had been done in Salzburg. However, Kachapilly replied that the Indians would not be interested if religion were not featured. So this time I was invited to give one of the two keynote addresses.

Kachapilly was expecting nearly three hundred attendees before the terrorist incident in Mumbai. The whole contingent from Australia withdrew because of their government's warnings, as did many others. Still there were about 200 participants including about sixty from outside

India. Much more than in any previous conference, the administration, faculty, and students at the university had been involved in planning and contributed to the presentations. Many had actually studied Whitehead in preparation.

Of special interest was that three Congolese delegates, graduates of the Leuven program, announced their intention to establish a center for process thought. This has happened subsequently, giving Whitehead-ian thought a toehold in Africa. The organizers believe that Christianity interpreted in process terms will communicate much better to Africans than the Aristotelian version.

Process thought has had some importance in Japan for a long time. There has been and Japan Whitehead Society for nearly fifty years and it has published its own journal. The conference we now call the Second International Whitehead Conference had been held in Nagoya some years before the one in Claremont. There had been close relations between the Claremont center and the work in Japan. Internationally the most visible leader in Japan has been Tokiyuki Nobuhara, who studied in Claremont. He has written many books and translated others.

The Japanese invited the Eighth International Conference to meet in Tokyo, at Sophia University in 2011. Yutaka Tanaka, whose chief connections with Claremont will be noted in the next chapter, was the chief organizer. Prospects were bright until the Fukushima nuclear accident made many outsiders fearful of going to Japan. Those who did attend reported an excellent event.

The Ninth was in Krakow, Poland, in 2013. It is striking that the earliest and strongest interest in Whitehead in Europe has been in the East. That conference was the fourth in a row held in a Catholic university. Since philosophical theology has a more natural home in Catholicism than elsewhere, we can hope that the suspicions that have marginalized process theology in the Catholic Church are fading. The connections between the organizers of this conference and Claremont had been cordial but only occasional.

The Tenth IWC will be in Claremont in 2015. This has absorbed my time and energy. It is too important for my "theological reminiscences" simply to treat in this chapter. I will devote Chapter 20 to discussion of planning for this.

The official existence of the center was as my faculty project. When I retired in 1990, support from both the School of Theology and

Claremont Graduate School ended as did the special arrangements for
Griffin to give half of his time to the administration of the center. The
subsidy of the journal had already ceased. The normal procedure when
professors retire is to end their faculty projects. Although the center
through becoming a membership organization had gained an independent base, even with help from the schools its finances had always been
hand to mouth. Prospects for continuation were poor.

The practical response seemed to be to negotiate for the school to
take over our library and, with our remaining income, we could fund
further acquisitions. We could thus maintain a good collection so that
Claremont could continue to be a place where research in process
thought was possible. The journal was more or less self-supporting,
given that the editor received no recompense for his work. Membership
and *Process Perspectives* would end, and there would be no more
conferences.

Although this seemed practical, several of us were not happy to see
so drastic a reduction of activities. We considered offering the center to
another seminary, but this did not work out. We thought we would like
to discuss our options with some of our special friends and some former
student leaders in the center. Some thirty people came at their own
expense to consult with us. Although not all of them were personally
committed to Whiteheadian process thought, all expressed strong support for keeping the center going. We resolved to try, and the continuing
support of John Buchanan made it possible. Indeed, the center flourished
as the faculty project of David Griffin.

The next crisis came with Griffin's retirement. That of Marjorie
Suchocki, the other process theologian on the faculty, came around the
same time. For financial reasons, the trustees authorized only one replacement. The faculty wisely said it should be the best theologian they could
find. Given the demographics of theologians in the country, the likelihood that the new appointment would be someone who would continue
the center as her or his faculty project seemed very dim.

I was even more distressed at the prospects of the center's demise this
time than I had been before. For the first time anywhere in the world, it
seemed that process thought had a chance of playing an historical role.
In China it was becoming a player in both universities and governments,
provincial and national. The collapse of the Claremont center, to which
the Chinese process communities looked for leadership and guidance,

would, at the very least, be a major setback. But I did not know anything to do about it.

As a Christian believer, it is hard for me to avoid theological language to describe what happened. There was no process theologian among the top three applicants. All agreed that the strongest was a student of Wolfhart Pannenberg, Philip Clayton. I was delighted that he was invited. Through our shared interest in science and religion, we had become acquainted, and I appreciated his remarkable scholarly and intellectual gifts. Nevertheless, his appointment did not reassure me with respect to the Center's future. In my previous encounters, he had been at some pains to emphasize that he was not a Whiteheadian. Since I had known Pannenberg quite well, and knew his emphasis on a different approach, this was fully understandable. But when I broached the subject of closing the center with him, he said that the existence of the center was for him one of Claremont's attractions. He did not want to see it end, and he would take it on in order to preserve it. What a joy and relief!

The actual developments were even better! We had long been hoping to establish a chair in process theology so that the future would not be so precarious. Philip wanted to have someone else take on the center and be the public figure identified with a position he respected but did not hold; so he strongly supported our efforts. With the generous support of a dear friend and wonderful UCC minister, Mary Ellen Kilsby, a chair was established, and Roland Faber was chosen as its first occupant.

But the developments were even better! During his first years in Claremont, Philip's views changed in two ways. He did not give up the positions that differed from Whitehead, but his appreciation of Whitehead's thought in general grew. Also, he discovered that there is considerable diversity within the Whiteheadian family. No strict orthodoxy obtains. One could be an honored member of the family while retaining one's own distinctive ideas. Philip now identifies himself as part of the community, and indeed a major leader within it.

There is still more! When the faculty sought for someone to teach black theology, the best candidate was Monica Coleman. Monica had studied with Marjorie Suchocki. She was convinced that process theology could be adapted to the needs of the black church. The School of Theology now has three professors who are committed to process thought and are co-directors of the center. Having feared for the extinction of any role for process thought in the faculty and the demise of the center, I trust my readers will forgive me for my belief that God helps us.

To conclude this celebration of good fortune, I might say that the role of process thought in the seminary overall has changed. While I was teaching there it was important to the administration to downplay the place of this theology in the school. The presidents rightly judged that the close association of the school with the process tradition might damage church relations, student recruitment, and fundraising. It would certainly not help in relation to other academic institutions. Recently, in contrast, presidents take pride in the prominence of the Center for Process Studies.

Despite its location at the Claremont School of Theology and the theological commitments of its directors, in the early years little of the work of the center was theological in a narrow and explicit sense. Some of the members of the center were adherents of other faiths or of none at all. We did not want them to think that their membership payments were being used in a "sectarian" way.

Some Claremont graduates, especially William Stegall, asked us to do more for the church. In response we organized the Process and Faith program with a separate membership and budget. The New Testament scholar and theologian, William Beardslee, retired from Emory to Claremont and became director of this program. When he died, Marjorie Suchocki succeeded him. With this leadership, Process and Faith came to rival the center as a whole in membership and program.

Process and Faith is officially a project of the Center for Process Studies. It conducted mini-conferences and classes directed to pastors and lay people. It gathered and produced materials for use in churches. It published a magazine, *Creative Transformation*. It had a small bookstore.

Process and Faith leaders reflected about how they could respond to the decline of the progressive branch of Protestantism to which they were personally committed. We realized that given the anti-metaphysical character of much of Protestantism, process theology could not be the basis of a unifying expression of this movement. So we worked together with George Regas, retiring pastor of All Saints Episcopal Church in Pasadena, the flagship church of progressive Christianity in Southern California, to organize what is now called Progressive Christians Uniting.

Because of significant changes, I have written about Process and Faith thus far in the past tense. Its more recent history has been mixed.

Marjorie brought in Jeanyne Slettom to work with her, and when Marjorie retired, Jeanyne became the director. She did excellent work. She added a publishing arm and produced a number of worthwhile books. She added a monthly FAQ, called "Ask Doctor Cobb." I'm not sure that it is widely read, but Jeanyne arranged publication of some of my pieces in two books. Most important, she added a lectionary that is widely used.

Sadly, due to a serious family illness, she had to resign. Gene Wallace, Ignacio Castuera, Andrew Schwartz, and David Lull have given interim leadership, and soon Monica Coleman will take over. We expect a bright future.

Meanwhile Jeanyne's circumstances have improved and she has redirected her energy and capacity for leadership. Although she left Claremont for a teaching position in Minneapolis, she has created Process Century Press. It is still an infant, but it has the potential of becoming an important part of the process family.

CHAPTER FIFTEEN

Physics and Metaphysics

I started to name this chapter "Science and Theology." That would identify a familiar topic of discussion: how to relate what we learn from the sciences to what we believe as Christians. That is certainly my interest. And issues of this kind crop up here and there throughout this book. I discussed some of them in Chapter 12 where my relation with the ecologist Charles Birch played a large role. In the previous chapter I mentioned the book I edited on evolution, and I will discuss that further in the concluding chapter.

I decided, however, to focus this chapter on a more specific question that has been of central importance to me. In Aristotle, deepening the questions of physics leads to metaphysics, and for the most part metaphysics has continued to be connected especially to physics. Within the sciences, physics has a kind of ultimacy since it studies that of which the objects of study in the other sciences are composed. If we press the question of the composition or nature of these ultimate constituents of all things, we are engaged in metaphysics. And clearly a metaphysics that is not informed by physics is of little value.

My immersion in modernity had led me to fear that my Christian beliefs did not fit well with facts and truths that are well established scientifically. This was wholly unacceptable for me. One of the great attractions of Whitehead's thought for me was the belief that what could be said in consistency with his cosmology and metaphysics would also be compatible with the best of contemporary science. I was pleased to see that a number of writers on issues of science and religion made use of Whitehead for similar purposes. This was true even of those who, like Langdon Gilkey, did not like what Whitehead had to say about God. Most reassuring for me were the writings of Ian Barbour who, over the years, made increasing use of Whitehead.

Nevertheless, I was not completely satisfied. I had sufficient respect for Whitehead that I had little doubt that at the time he wrote he was dealing with such knowledge as was then available to physicists. But physics has grown and changed greatly in subsequent decades. There seemed to be no problem with respect to the special theory of relativity. But the general theory was a different matter. New evidence was available from time to time. Were Whitehead's theories able to encompass the new findings?

General relativity theory was a topic to which Whitehead gave a great deal of study. He greatly admired Einstein but had philosophical objections to Einstein's formulations. He wrote: "My whole course of thought presupposes the magnificent stroke of genius by which Einstein and Minkowski assimilated time and space. It also presupposes the general method of seeking tensor . . . relations as general expressions for the laws of the physical field, a method due to Einstein. But the worst homage we can pay to genius is to accept uncritically formulations of truths which we owe to it" (*The Principle of Relativity,* 88; hereafter, *R*).

In dependence on Einstein's achievement, Whitehead worked out his own formula expressive of his different view of reality, clearly distinguishing the physical from the mathematical and avoiding the idea of the variable curvature of space. This formula occupies much of his book. Its predictions are almost the same as Einstein's and accounted equally well for the empirical data available at the time he wrote. He himself noted the possibility that evidence might not support him at the points where their predictions differed. I wanted to know what had happened.

It turned out that Clifford Will at California Institute of Technology had checked on half a dozen theories put forward as alternatives to Einstein. As new tests were possible, most of these theories were shown to be unsuccessful. However, for some years Whitehead's theory was successful along with Einstein's. However, there was a testable difference between the two in that Whitehead predicted that distant galaxies have some effect on earthly tides, whereas Einstein's theory did not. The effect would be so small that only very refined measures would discern it. The amount and nature of this effect would depend on the distribution of matter throughout the universe. Eventually, based on calculations of this distribution, and the failure to find the predicted effect, Will declared Whitehead's theory refuted.

I considered, and still consider, this to be a matter of importance in the evaluation of Whitehead's metaphysics. I had a graduate student, Dean Fowler, who had a good background in physics. He studied the evidence and showed that the data on the basis of which Cal Tech had made this announcement were actually inconclusive. They made assumptions about the distribution of matter that were questionable. Physicists who have examined Fowler's work think he was correct. But meanwhile still more refined measures were made with no indication of any gravitational influence from outside our galaxy. It was increasingly difficult to rely on the limitations of our knowledge of the cosmic distribution of matter to justify the claim that it made some difference on the tides. Obviously, I was troubled by the possibility that the evidence was incompatible with the conceptuality that underlay Whitehead's physics.

Today, if we introduce dark matter into the equation, no reliable estimate of the distribution of matter is possible; so, even within the dominant conversation, the supposed empirical refutation is problematic. On the other hand, as I will explain below, I am doubtful that there is any dark matter; so this gives me little comfort. If distant galaxies affect the tides, one should finally find some evidence. That the mass of the universe is just so distributed that the effects of the various galaxies completely cancel each other out seems *a priori* doubtful. It is a desperate hypothesis selected to defend an *a priori* assumption. I oppose such moves on the part of others. I did not want to defend Whitehead in this way.

I was comforted by the fact that Whitehead wrote (*R,* 84ff.) that, if empirical data did not support his preferred formula, there were other possible formulae that met his requirements. He called one of them Einstein's Law, presumably because it resulted in the same predictions as Einstein's, but did not violate Whitehead's assumptions. He went on to say that if neither of these was supported by future evidence there were still other possibilities. Clearly he believed that his conceptuality allowed for multiple possibilities and could be adapted to the empirical evidence.

Few had paid much attention to Whitehead's Einstein formula. From the point of view of physicists in general, Einstein was vindicated, and if the predictions based on a different formula were identical with

Einstein's, there was no reason to bother with it. But for me the question of whether Whitehead's conceptuality could account for the scientific facts was very important. Even if I supposed that the apparent superiority of Einstein's physics over Whitehead's preferred formula does not prove the superiority of Einstein's cosmology, it certainly cuts against interest in Whitehead among physicists, and it has supported the widespread acceptance of cosmological ideas that Whitehead rejected.

In 1984, while I was in the midst of these worries, we organized a conference on time. We brought together two physicists who, in quite different ways, were highly congenial to process thought: David Bohm and Ilya Prigogine. I mentioned Bohm in the preceding chapter. We had become acquainted with him at the very first CPS conference, the one at Bellagio, Italy, on "Mind in Nature." Bohm's work focused especially on quantum theory. Although his inspiration came more from India than from any form of Western thought, he agreed with us in rejecting the idea of substance and highlighting relationality. He liked the image of the hologram.

The hologram shows that the whole image is present at every point, however faintly. We need the events at many points in order to reinforce the image. For Whitehead every actual entity is in some way, however trivially, affected by every event in its actual world, that being the entire past of the occasion. The congeniality is apparent.

However, there were other ways in which Bohm presented his view that were less congenial. He reacted against the language of probability waves and other notions that the entities of which the world is composed are indeterminate. For him, "to be" is to be something determinate.

For Whitehead, in the process of concrescence of a single momentary occasion there is indeterminateness as to the outcome. This does not mean that a concrescing occasion can be ontologically understood as a probability wave. It has its own distinctive type of actuality. But that type of actuality, while it leads to a determinate outcome, does not lead to a pre-determined one. Bohm's rhetoric in opposing the idea of indeterminate actuality often seemed to support determinism.

On the subject of temporality we preferred the work of Ilya Prigogine. We hoped that Bohm and Prigogine being together in a conference might stimulate them to generate what would be, from a Whiteheadian perspective, a still more adequate model. That did not happen, but the conference was a rich one.

160 John B. Cobb, Jr.

During the conference, Hank Keeton invited one of the speakers, Henry Stapp, to discuss the possibility of initiating an ongoing group to study Whitehead's theory of relativity. Others joined them and a group formed that met for several years. The three who carried this discussion the furthest were Christoph Wassermann, Robert Russell, and Yutaka Tanaka. We met a number of times over a period of years. Wassermann and Russell finally spent the necessary time to translate Whitehead's "Einstein's Law" and found that indeed its predictions were identical with Einstein's. It achieved these results on the basis of multiple time systems without any use of curved space.

Despite the remaining questions, I was pleased by the results. I knew from *Process and Reality* that Whitehead considered the idea of variably curved space to depend on the fallacy of misplaced concreteness. For anything to be variably curved it would have to have a substantiality that Whitehead could not attribute to space. In his mature doctrine, space is a dimension of the extensive continuum which is a type of potential. Any space that could be dealt with by Euclidean geometry could equally well be dealt with by elliptic or hyperbolic geometry. More broadly, mathematics and physics need to be distinguished. To say that space is locally flat but curved over long distances may be useful for physical approximations, but it is profoundly misleading for philosophical interpretation. Further, explaining the empirical evidence for relativity without any reference to gravity did not resolve the issue of treating gravity as a physical force. Einstein did not regard it as such, but Whitehead did.

The group did not meet further after this conclusion was reached. I regret that Wassermann, who impressed me as an exceedingly promising person to lead in the Whiteheadian study of physics, was not retained at the University of Geneva where he had a short-term position in science and theology. The university decided not to continue this emphasis. Wassermann left the academic world to continue his father's work with Near Eastern languages. I have felt the loss keenly. Russell continued as leader of science and religion studies in the United States, but he did not continue to give sustained attention to Whitehead. Tanaka has continued his multifaceted work with process thought in Japan. As noted in the preceding chapter he was lead organizer of the Eighth International Whitehead Conference.

It turned out that the person who has continued the conversation and leadership in this field has not been one of these three but another participant in the discussions whose work was not directly in relativity theory. This is Tim Eastman, a plasma scientist who has worked for many years in space science, at times with NSA and NASA. He has been the most important person in shaping my views of science. In his quiet and careful way he has radicalized me.

The change has been that I no longer care whether Whitehead's formula can encompass the theories that have developed in the Einsteinian community. I now judge that these theories are themselves not reliable. I will illustrate with respect to the Big Bang. Whitehead's view was that the world is everlasting, evolving gradually from one cosmic epoch into another. The abrupt beginning of our cosmos in a singularity of an utterly unimaginable sort was not part of his vision and fits poorly with his cosmology. I did not think of this as a metaphysical challenge at quite the same level as general relativity theory, but I nevertheless avoided speaking of the Big Bang, and I considered that its acceptance would involve a considerable change in a Whiteheadian cosmology.

On one occasion I confessed my resistance to Eastman, indicating that I supposed it was time to give it up. He surprised me by encouraging me not to do so. Apparently plasma physicists as a group were skeptical, since the theory ignored the effects of electromagnetism and space plasmas, whereas such effects are now well established in the local cosmos. However, Eastman gave me other reasons for doubting as well. His paper, "Cosmic Agnosticism," highlighted the concerns of many famous scientists, the lack of any direct experiments, and how available observations are all model-dependent.

Also it may have been from him that I first learned about the politics of those areas of science that are most removed from human experience and have the least observational and experimental constraints. I learned that in the field of physical cosmology, scientists committed to the standard model controlled the major journals and university departments and effectively silenced the critics. The public, therefore, gets the impression that the consensus of this group about the Big Bang cosmology represents a consensus among physicists.

My earlier experience with economists prepared me to believe that this could well be the case. My suspicions of the guilds had been strengthened by learning from Lynn Margulis how she had been treated by the neo-Darwinian establishment when she demonstrated that evolution could occur, and had occurred, by symbiogenesis. Rupert Sheldrake visited the Center for Process Studies twice and represented a vivid instance of excommunication by the scientific establishment. He called for experiments that would test his hypotheses about "morphic resonance" or "formative causation." The establishment ignored his evidence, refused to discuss his views, and declined to engage in any of the experiments for which he called. It also tried to silence and discredit him.

In the related field of quantum theory, I had long rejected the idea that since two outcomes are possible in every instance there must be separate universes in which each possibility is actualized. I sensed that a simple confusion of mathematics with physical actuality is involved in such speculations. Instead of treating mathematics simply as an immensely useful tool for model making, some appear to read reality directly into the formulae. (See, for example, Max Tegmark, *The Mathematical Universe.*)

Furthermore, such conclusions follow only in a deterministic system. In that system what happens is the only possibility. In reverse, that means that whatever is really possible is actualized. Therefore, if quantum physics shows that there are multiple possibilities and only one is actualized in our universe, the holder of these assumptions must posit other universes in which other possibilities are actualized. The result is a wildly implausible cosmology. But the presentation of such ideas by serious scientists leads the public into believing they must be true. This kind of reasoning from bad metaphysics to judgments of fact does great damage.

The situation seems to me somewhat similar when cosmologists posit that 95% of matter and of energy is "dark," that is, not found by our instruments. They do this, not because of empirical evidence, but in order to save the theoretical structure to which they have become committed. The difference in this case is that they hope to find supporting evidence of some kind. In my judgment, however, the need to introduce not only a singularity but also vast quantities of new entities into the picture suggests that reconsidering assumptions is a better alternative. I had given up using the improbable hypothesis that the Earth is quite near the center of all the masses in the universe to avoid abandoning Whitehead's relativity theory. I thought the dominant community should recognize that when defense of their theory required wildly implausible ones, it was time for serious consideration of alternatives.

When we learned of a physicist in Australia, Reginald Cahill, who was developing a "process physics," we were, of course, interested. We invited him to a conference on quantum theory. One important part of his research has been to re-examine the Michelson-Morley experiment that had been taken as proof that there is no ether. The assumption that there is no ether is one of the bases of Einstein's theory. Cahill found that the original experiment did show that there is very little of what was then called "ether," that is a medium through which light was propagated. The positive figure was so small that it was dismissed as "noise." But it turns out that the same amount of presumed noise is found whenever a similar experiment is conducted. The proper conclusion seems to be the very different one that whatever the "medium" through which light is propagated may be, it has very little effect on light.

Cahill's work seems to point toward something like Whitehead's theory that a "vacuum" is space in which there are no "enduring objects," only a plenum of non-social occasions. Their possible effect on the propagation of light is an empirical question not to be decided by inadequately tested theory.

Cahill is working on new theories that take this different starting point into account. Much of what he says is very congenial to Whitehead. Their understanding of process is remarkably similar, considering the difference in sources. At our meeting he described realistically the obstacles placed in his way by the physicist establishment once he challenged the Einsteinian consensus. He inspired great confidence (at least in me), and he reinforced the skepticism encouraged by Eastman.

Recently, on Eastman's recommendation, I read Hilton Ratcliffe's *The Static Universe: Exploding the Myth of Cosmic Expansion.* I found it quite convincing. The evidence on which the Big Bang theory is based is shaky; the formulations involve inconsistencies; other theories are ignored or suppressed.

In the much more moderate formulation of Jayant Narlikar and Geoffrey Burbidge, *Facts and Speculations in Cosmology,* I learned that among the theories that are largely ignored is the "tired light" hypothesis, the idea that, over great periods of time, photons lose energy. The authors note that there are "severe physical objections" (273), but they do not elaborate. In any case, their main point is that this theory has been too quickly dismissed from consideration.

I am obviously in no position to propose a cosmological theory. I have had no formal study of either mathematics or physics since high school. But even a rank outsider can comment on what might happen if physicists adopted different assumptions. Contemporary cosmology is based on the view of a rapidly expanding universe on the basis of its discovery that the red-shift increases with distance. The standard interpretation is that the cause of this increase is that more distant bodies are moving away from us at greater speeds. This presupposes the constancy of the wavelength of light in a vacuum. It also presupposes that for relevant purposes, the space between us and those distant bodies is a vacuum or at least that whatever fills it has no effect on the speed of light.

I want to question the last of these assumptions. We know that the space between us and distant stars is filled with low-density plasma. Eastman tells me that, by definition, this is an interactive mix of neutrals, ions, electrons, and fields that can carry current and exhibit collective effects. He also tells me that contemporary cosmology ignores its possible contribution to red-shift. Obviously plasma has little effect on light, but "little" need not mean "none." Perhaps the effect is so slight as not to be discernible in relatively short distances. Perhaps, however, over thousands of light years it causes discernible energy loss by light waves. If so, the red-shift would be accounted for without the theory of accelerating expansion together with all the problems that it has raised.

When I put this conclusion before him, Eastman responded: "Indeed, specific models for coherent plasma red-shift have been formulated but not yet adequately tested (Brynjolfsson, 2005); several other coherent red-shift mechanisms also await testing (Ratcliffe, 2009). The real issue is whether there is *any* interference with light in its long journey through the intervening plasma medium between the stars and galaxies. This can only be resolved by careful tests between alternative models, including several 'tired-light models,' some of which enable the preservation of coherent images over very long distances; such is not resolved by a continued focus only on various ways to confirm the 'standard' model" (personal correspondance, 2014). Clearly my journey of speculation has led me into a well-populated terrain. May it soon receive the attention it deserves.

Returning now to the question of gravity models, I noted above that Cahill showed that the Michelson-Morley experiment did not show that there is *no* "ether." However, there are other reasons to deny what was meant by "ether" at that time. "Ether" was conceived as an undifferentiated quasi-material medium analogous to the medium of air molecules that sustains the sound waves that make oral communication possible.

Eastman describes the situation in this way: "Instead the 'ether' of modern field theories is a nexus of events. The kind of nexus of events that occupies the space between the heavenly bodies is plasma, and the underlying quantum field-event nexus enables all physical interactions, including gravity." It is important to replace the old notion of ether with the scientific ideas of quantum fields and plasmas.

My complaint is that alternatives of this sort in both cosmology and gravity theory are not adequately considered. They are not less plausible than the ones now being put forward and investigated at great cost. I am appealing for attention to evidence and for a level playing field in physics to replace one built on taking for granted assumptions that seem to be mistaken.

My earlier experience with economists prepared me to see how far a guild may go in silencing or excluding those who propose basic changes. Most students socialized into a discipline regard at least some of the understanding into which they are socialized as required by the discipline as such, so they consider any challenge to these ideas a threat to their cognitive world. Their reaction to critics is rarely open-minded.

More recently, Ronny Desmet, a young Belgian scholar, is doing remarkable historical work in the early debates about how to understand the phenomena of general relativity. He has clarified the basis of disagreements and spoken wisely about the Whiteheadian type of theory and its advantages. He seems to be able to do this in ways that gain considerable traction. Whether Whitehead's own theory becomes an important contender again would not be especially important to Whitehead or to us, but a theory that does not confuse geometry and physics would.

Desmet studied Whitehead's Einstein theory very carefully in writing his dissertation. He understands it in a different way from what I described as the conclusion of the earlier discussions in which I participated. Russell had concluded that Whitehead was correct that the predictions of his different theory were identical with Einstein's predictions. According to Desmet, Whitehead does not show that a mathematically *different* theory can arrive at the same conclusions as Einstein's. His mathematical proposal is identical with one portion of Einstein's own theory! Only the interpretation is different.

This is even more astonishing. If Desmet is correct, then there is a fundamental question about the interpretation of Einstein's laws. Whitehead's derivation is in the context of his clear distinction of geometry and physics. This means that there is no need for their blending, as in Einstein's interpretation. There is no need to follow Einstein's interpretation in order to get the predictions that have proved so valuable. His interpretations are not supported by his predictive success. The historical implication is that generations of scientists have based their cosmology on unfounded assumptions. Desmet is optimistic that the recent publication of the *Cambridge Companion to Einstein* will help to correct the confused situation.

The fact remains that Whitehead preferred a different theory as better expressing his own cosmology. Explaining the empirical evidence for relativity without any reference to gravity does not resolve the issue of treating gravity as a physical force, as Whitehead affirms and Einstein denies. Whitehead devoted much time and effort to a theory in which gravity does play a physical role. Can that be salvaged by adjusting to the fact that other galaxies have no effect on earthly tides? I have been glad to learn that a lively discussion about Whitehead's theory is continuing, with Hank Keeton and Gary Herstein playing the central role.

Eastman has helped me understand what has happened with respect to gravity. Whereas Einstein was right to reject the older view of gravity, he was wrong to put nothing in its place. In private communication he wrote: "Actually today his followers have reintroduced a type of space-time ether. However, this is distinct from Cahill's recent experiments that appear to reveal a type of space-time 'flow' of space that emerges from an underlying quantum ether of events, which Cahill describes in terms of an information-theoretic model. Recently this and several other 'emergent' theories of gravity have been formulated—clear tests between these models and with standard gravity models are needed to resolve these questions."

Whitehead's conviction that gravity is a real, physical phenomenon seems to be sustained. Still, his assumption that even distant galaxies must have some effect on the Earth is not supported by evidence. What does this mean?

I have a simple suggestion. Whitehead thought of gravity as a field and believed that it interacted with other fields. Perhaps "field" is not the best category for its understanding, but newer findings do not support the idea that it is inherently unaffected by other features of reality. Just as we may conjecture that the effect of plasma on light is so little that it is imperceptible locally but sufficient to be measurable over great distances, so something similar may be true of gravity. Perhaps over great distances it is dissipated so that any remaining gravitational effect of other galaxies is strictly indiscernible.

If we adjust our understanding of gravity, I believe we could adapt and adopt Whitehead's distinctive theory. Considering that gravity may be affected by its relations with the electromagnetic field and plasma seems to me generally congenial to Whitehead's cosmological vision. Of course, it is a factual suggestion that would need empirical validation before being accepted, but the failure to detect any such effect would not count against his theory.

Central to Whitehead's contribution to physics is his calling attention to the "fallacy of misplaced concreteness." There is a widespread tendency to treat abstractions as if they were concrete. For example, we theologians may appeal to love or hope as is they were causes of actual occurrences. Whitehead does not question their importance, but in his view, only some individual embodiment of love or hope can actually function as a cause. The same is true of energy or matter.

Whiteheadians call for renewal of what was once popular among physicists themselves. They claimed to build theories inductively from evidence. Deductively from theory, they could propose hypotheses; but only those hypotheses could be considered scientific that were in principle subject to empirical test. Today cosmologists often make pronouncements about reality that violate these rules. Whiteheadians would like to see the rules reinstated. This would work against the tendency to posit myriads of universes unrelated to this one as an explanation of the peculiar character of this one.

It would also reduce the confidence in theories whose initial justification is only that they are needed to avoid abandoning existing theories. The recent announcement that most of the energy and matter is "dark," would appear, then, as a theory worth investigating rather than a cosmological fact. Even that would require some indication of how it might be tested. In the current situation it has gained credence not because of any direct evidence or inherent plausibility, but simply because it is needed to prop up cosmological orthodoxy. This is not healthy.

I conclude this chapter with a brief history of the relation of modern science to metaphysics. To deal with metaphysics presupposes and employs a realistic understanding of the world.

Whitehead's philosophy of science is a fully realistic one. By "realism," I mean the affirmation that things are what they are independently

of our experience of them, and that they were what they were long before
human beings arrived on the scene. Physics developed as an account of
a fully real world of this sort. However, the science that assumed this
also adopted a philosophy that combined the epistemological primacy of
sense experience with an understanding of nature as composed of bits of
"matter" pushing and pulling each other around.

Hume showed that this combination of beliefs was not possible. If
we begin with sense experience, we end with the data of sense experience,
that is, with appearance or phenomena. Both matter and causality disappear. Kant solved the problem by asserting that all knowledge is limited
to phenomena. Nothing can be known about a reality that appears; that
is, metaphysics must be abandoned. Kant also taught that the human
mind is such that it can only order appearances in the way the current
science, based on Descartes' metaphysics, was doing. He thus supported
what science was doing while closing the door on criticism of its assumptions. The price was the abandonment of realism by the tough-minded.

On the other hand, for most scientists, Cartesian materialism has
remained intact in terms of unexamined assumptions. The refusal to
consider assumptions has allowed materialism to retain its power even
though physics speaks only of "mass" and recognizes that "energy" is
more fundamental to nature than "mass." Regrettably, materialism has
maintained its dominance in the "modern mind" in general despite its
lack of scientific or philosophical support.

Within science, the limitation to phenomena encouraged the focus on
the development of mathematical formula that provided testable results.
These tests determined the acceptance of the formula into physics. Sadly,
now, the need to be testable has declined in importance. Today the idea of
multiple universes is widely regarded as scientific even though it can in no
way be tested. The fallacy of misplaced concreteness is victorious.

The most obvious problem arises from the adoption of this limitation of science to phenomena in the study of human beings. If we
study human behavior "scientifically," we are not allowed to give any
role to human hopes and purposes in its explanation. If scientists would
acknowledge that their explanations are necessarily incomplete and that
much explanation is left to the humanities, there would still be real
problems, but their effects would not be so disastrous. As it is, there is an
implicit claim, sometimes fully explicit, that subjective experience plays
no role in the world.

With respect to human beings, of course, the work of physicists and biologists is supplemented by that of psychology and the social sciences. Although the underlying assumption is that what is studied in these sciences is ultimately explicable by physics, no one demands that these connections actually be made. Accordingly, much is taught in the university that is inconsistent with its assumptions.

This inconsistency saves the situation from complete absurdity. But the same limitation is applied to the study of animals, and in this case there is no widely used supplement. Animal behavior is explained, supposedly exhaustively, with no reference to the feelings and intentions of the animals involved. The evolution of animals is supposedly fully understood by reference only to random mutation of genes and natural selection of the outcomes despite the overwhelming evidence to the contrary.

For a Whiteheadian it seems that, if a science limited to phenomena wishes to be intellectually responsible, it must acknowledge that in principle it can only provide partial explanations. If, as Kant taught, there is no knowledge of any other sort, then we must acknowledge ignorance on an enormous scale. But why should subjective experience not be carefully studied in disciplines such as phenomenology and the results be recognized as knowledge? Why should this knowledge be wholly segregated from the knowledge of phenomena? It is time to reconsider the assumptions that have led us into this quandary.

Whitehead offers an alternative to Descartes, Hume, and Kant that allows for a vast expansion of critical intellectual activity and the liberation of the natural sciences to contribute hugely to this. For him, the unitary, indivisible events that make up most of the world are unconscious throbs of feeling. It is these that exercise causality on subsequent events by being partially included in them. This means that the world of subjectivity and the world of objectivity cannot be divorced from one another. Evolution explains how out of this world life and consciousness emerged. There are enormous differences between human experiences and quanta, but they are not metaphysical. Both quanta and human experiences are both subjective and objective. For Whitehead, they are subjects in the moment of their occurrence and then objects for all future events.

The inclusion of subjects by scientists is not out of the question. Among physiological psychologists a few have taken the causal role of subjective experience seriously. The Center for Process Studies held several small conferences with Roger Sperry, who won a Nobel Prize for his work on the split brain. His experiments led him to conclude that conscious experience plays a causal role in what happens in the brain. He saw this as having profound implications for science and for society. There are individual zoologists who have lived with animals in the wild and whose reports and explanations certainly involve the subjectivity of the animals.

Donald Griffin, who attended one of our conferences, notes how students of animal behavior often cross the line into terminology that involves the subjectivity of animals. Some neuroscientists today are more open to recognizing the interaction between subjective human experience and the behavior of neurons than was earlier characteristic of most physiological psychologists. Indeed, the results of their experiments clearly indicate that cause is bi-directional.

My faculty in the University of Chicago Divinity School hoped for a new science that would take seriously the evolutionary discovery that human beings are part of nature. Instead, the dominant move was to maintain the Cartesian view. The situation became worse as the struggle to keep the university a place of intellectual activity lost out to its restructuring for the sake of specialized research. Even physics was divided into separate disciplines, each with its own assumptions and preferred theories. This has led to ignoring sensible proposals and taking less plausible ones all too seriously. Let us hope that the boundaries will be loosened and evidence will triumph over settled assumptions and received theories. Attention to Whitehead could play a large role in improving the situation.

WORKS CITED

Whitehead, Alfred North. *The Principle of Relativity.* Cambridge: Cambride University Press, 1922.

Brynjofsson, Ari, 2005. "Redshift of photons penetrating a hot plasma," arXiv:astro-ph/0401420v3 (also at http://www.plasmaredshift.org).

Narlikar, Jayant, and Geoffrey Burbidge. *Facts and Speculations in Cosmology.* Cambridge: Cambridge University Press, 2008.

Ratcliffe, Hilton. 2009. "A Review of Anomalous Redshift Data." 2nd Crisis in Cosmology Conference, CCC-2, ASP Conference Series, Vol. 413, F. Potter, ed., 109-15.

CHAPTER FIFTEEN

Buddhism and Religious Pluralism

Growing up in Japan I was, of course, aware that Christianity is only one religious tradition among others. Nevertheless, the others did not seem to me to be quite on the same level. The religiously serious Japanese I knew were all Christian. Shinto and Buddhism appeared as part of a traditional culture that, despite its charm, did not constitute a serious religious alternative to Christian faith.

At Chicago I audited a course on history of religions with Joachim Wach. But even this did not awaken me to religious pluralism in the fuller meaning of the term. More important for this purpose was the high esteem in which Charles Hartshorne and Alfred North Whitehead held Buddhism. My awakening to religious pluralism began with my recognition that Buddhism had a philosophically profound view of reality and powerful spiritual disciplines. I learned that the process philosophy to which I was deeply attracted was closer to Buddhist thinking than to that of the West. Hartshorne emphasized the similarity of the Buddhist doctrine of no-self with the process understanding that there is no underlying, substantial self.

At Emory I found that Tom Altizer also had great appreciation for Buddhism, and conversation with him heightened my interest. But Buddhism remained at the fringes of my interest and concern. It was only at Claremont that my interest in Buddhism and in religious pluralism generally was richly stimulated.

There was in those days the Blaisdell Institute of World Cultures and Religions. It had been founded by a farsighted president of Pomona

College who believed that the center of world history was moving from the Atlantic to the Pacific. He created this institute to build understanding among the peoples of the Pacific Rim. It was not well funded, and eventually what was left of its assets became the endowment for Claremont Graduate School programs related to world religions. But while it existed it affected the climate of the community.

Interest in world religions was also strongly supported in the Dept. of Religion of Claremont Graduate University. Jack Hutchison, the first Danforth Professor and chair of the department, made major contributions to this topic. He was succeeded by John Hick, who gave global leadership in the field.

Indeed, although Hick and I disagreed on many topics, we shared a hope that Claremont might become a center for interreligious dialogue. There seemed no prospect of it ever developing a program in history of religions comparable to that at such schools as Santa Barbara, but it would take much less to develop a distinctive program expanding the work we were both doing in this field. What we mainly needed, we thought, was a strong dialogue partner, preferably Buddhist or Hindu.

At one point it seemed that a chair in one of these fields would be established in Claremont. We were optimistic. We expressed to our colleagues the need for the occupant of the chair to be a believing Buddhist or Hindu. At this point we were reminded of the dominant academic mentality. We were told that such a commitment would be an inappropriate consideration. The only acceptable criterion was scholarly knowledge of those fields. Interfaith dialogue was not an academic activity. We knew this was the attitude of the American Academy of Religion, but we had had higher hopes for Claremont. I saw that the guild in the field of "religious studies" shared the narrowness of focus for which in previous chapters I have criticized economists and natural scientists. My sense of the refusal of the American university to deal with the real needs of the world was further heightened.

Many of the scholars who came to the Blaisdell Institute were Japanese, and of them several were serious exponents of Japanese Buddhism. I encountered committed Buddhists there who fully challenged me. I never engaged in extensive scholarly study of Buddhism; so my historical knowledge remains very limited and my understanding comes chiefly from conversation. Two of these men became especially important in my education.

The one who has been best known in the United States is Masao Abe, who died recently in Kyoto. Soon after World War II he studied at Union Theological Seminary with Reinhold Niebuhr and Paul Tillich to improve his ability to serve as a Zen Buddhist missionary in the United States. He thought of himself as a successor in that role to D.T. Suzuki. He pursued his mission by teaching as a visiting professor at American universities, giving lectures, publishing articles, and participating in conferences. His activity touched many lives.

He spent a term at the Blaisdell Institute in 1965-66, but at the time I was in Germany. I heard many good things about him, and when he returned a few years later, I took advantage of his visit to begin a friendship and co-operation that lasted many years. He taught for several years, successively, at the Claremont Graduate School and the Claremont School of Theology.

The other important contact for me through Blaisdell was Ryusei Takeda. He came to study Christianity and took a couple of courses with me. I was deeply impressed by the depth of his insight and the quality of his thinking. He came from the Pure Land tradition, which in Japan had far more adherents than Zen but, at that time, was far less well known in this country. Indeed, as we learned Buddhism from Zen teachers, we were inclined to view Pure Land as a concession to popular thought and feeling rather than a fully developed understanding of Buddhism in its own terms. Abe may have given that impression even more than other Zen teachers because he had grown up in the Pure Land tradition and been converted to Zen by Hisamatsu. Over the years I gained the impression that even among the scholars of the Pure Land tradition, some had an inferiority complex in relation to Zen and tended to downplay those features of Pure Land that are distinctive or to reinterpret them in ways that reduced their distinctiveness. Takeda, however, was not inclined in this direction. Accordingly, I delighted in three-cornered discussions with Abe and Takeda on those occasions when they were both in Claremont.

For Abe, the complete negation of God was essential. Even in relation to Buddha, negation played an important role. I believe it was his teacher, Hisamatsu, who emphasized: "If you meet the Buddha, kill him." The point was that one should not look outside oneself for help. His emphasis was an expression of what the Pure Land School called the Zen reliance on "self-power." Since the absence of any self is a central

Buddhist teaching, emphasized by Zen, this term can be misleading. This is even more true because the great effort of the Zen practitioner is to get the self out of the way so that enlightenment can happen. But I will not try to press the point further here. The contrast to Pure Land is that any effort to look to another for help expresses an illusory view and distracts from what is needed.

In the Pure Land tradition, on the other hand, one acknowledges one's complete inability to do what is needed and one's complete dependence on that which is not oneself. One can formulate the Pure Land vision in a way quite parallel to Luther. One can move toward enlightenment only through grace apprehended in faith. Faith is directed to Amida, a legendary Buddha, much earlier than Gautama. Amida vowed not to enter into Nirvana except as all sentient beings accompanied him. He established a Pure Land in which all that is required for enlightenment is saying his name in trust. When separated from its mythological features, the message of Pure Land Buddhism is that grace is available to those who call on Amida, trusting in his vow to save all.

The parallels between Pure Land Buddhism and Christianity have been noticed and commented on by many, including Karl Barth. Of course, in traditional Christian formulations, there is a tendency to treat God and Christ and the believer in substantialist ways that place a major barrier between the two traditions. But process theology joins Buddhists in rejecting substance as a category for understanding. Hence faith in Christ and faith in Amida's vow more nearly approximate each other.

Obviously, there are still many differences. The Christian idea of salvation is quite different from the Buddhist goal of enlightenment. Amida's grace expresses itself only in relation to enlightenment, whereas God's grace expressed through Christ relates to believers not only in terms of their ultimate destiny but also in the many dimensions of daily life. Jesus is an historical figure, whereas Amida is not.

Takeda pointed out that the nonsubstantial "other" in which Pure Land believers trusted should not be conceived as a separate self-contained being any more than was true for the believer. Both are to be understood in terms of the fact that everything is what it is only as the coming together of other things. For Abe the "other" and the "self" are not different and neither is properly understood as either "other" or "self." He did not object to the practice of calling on Amida as long as this is a step toward attaining the state of mind that is sought. But there is no "other" properly named "Amida," and therefore no actual vow and nothing in which to place one's faith.

Viewing matters from a Whiteheadian perspective, the vow, which is typically called "primal" can be seen as an aspect of the ordering of pure potentials that constitutes the primordial nature of God, which can also be understood as the Logos of the first chapter of John or the divine Sophia. Zen Buddhists seemed to me to have no interest in such a Logos. They rightly see each event as constituted by dependent origination, which Whitehead described as the concrescence of the many into the one. But Whitehead thought that the many included possibilities as well as actualities, and that these gave an element of directedness to the concrescence. For Whitehead the status of the future is ontologically different from that of the past, whereas Abe denied this. Hence the theological difference between Zen and Pure Land, understood in Whiteheadian terms, connects with a metaphysical one.

Participating in these discussions heightened my understanding of the religious importance of Whitehead's vision even where he was not himself aware of it. Whitehead regarded the ultimate to be "creativity" which is distinct from concrescence only in that it highlights the temporal passage rejected by Abe. It is defined as "the many become one and are increased by one." For Buddhists enlightenment consists in the full realization that everything that is is an instance of concrescence. Nothing underlies concrescence. Realizing this liberates one from guilt and anxiety and opens one to all that is, just as it is. Zen offers particular meditative disciplines and the *koan* as ways of arriving at this realization.

The goal for Pure Land is, or may be, the same. But what the Japanese call *"satori"* comes as a gift to be received in faith rather than as a condition to be obtained by disciplined effort. Christianity sees the primordial order or eternal Word or Wisdom of God as calling us to actualize ourselves in some ways rather than others, prizing the development of character and personality as well as a just social order. But for a process theologian, the Buddhist rejection of substance holds.

I also learned from Pure Land that "faith" must be sharply distinguished from "clinging." For Christians the call is often to give up clinging to things of the world and to cling only to God. But as long as the relationship remains one of clinging, it blocks real trust or faith. This is expressed in full openness both to God and to the world as they are.

My learning went beyond the realization that what Whitehead called "creativity" or "concrescence" has been of enormous religious importance, especially in the East. It gave me a clearer sense of its ontological status. Whitehead called it "ultimate," but when I wrote *A Christian Natural Theology* I could conceive of no ontological status other than the concrete and the abstract. I thought creativity could only be an abstraction from all concrete processes, the ultimate character of all things. My recollection is not reliable here, but I believe my awareness that Whitehead had distinguished a third metaphysical status had dawned before these conversations with Buddhists, and that Del Langbauer's work had alerted me to the relation between creativity and the Buddhist ultimate, *pratītya samutpāda*. But I have no doubt as to the importance of these conversations with Abe and Takeda for the development of my metaphysical understanding and especially its religious relevance.

Whitehead carefully distinguished creativity from both the abstract (eternal objects) and the concrete (actual entities) and accorded to it the status of ultimacy. He thought that every philosophy required some such ultimate that is actual only in its instantiations. In the Aristotelian tradition it was "prime matter." In Whitehead's day, it was sometimes called "neutral stuff." But Whitehead did not pursue this question in the history of either Western or Eastern thought. Limiting his examples to matter and stuff, he was not led to consider the potential religious significance.

As I further considered the question, it became clear that in the medieval tradition, especially in Thomism, the ultimate was Being Itself, an idea that took on new life in the twentieth century in both philosophy and theology. In the East it is Brahman, or Nothingness, or dependent origination, or the Tao without characteristics. Unlike matter and neutral stuff, these understandings of the ultimate have had great religious importance.

At times in the West there have been efforts to identify God with this ultimate. But this has been a source of great confusion and has done the credibility of Christianity considerable harm. Whitehead is not the first to affirm both God and the ultimate and to distinguish them, but I believe he makes this broader picture clearer than any previous writer. There is the ultimate: creativity. There is also God. Creativity is not God, and God is not creativity. But there could be no God who is not an instantiation of creativity, and there could be no creativity without the primordial order inherent in God's act of ordering. And, of course, there can be neither creativity nor God without the world. Arranging these hierarchically makes no sense.

This realization had a major effect on my work as a Christian theologian. Previously, I had been somewhat apologetic about Whitehead's description of God as "a creature of creativity" and even "an accident of creativity." I still consider this language an unnecessary affront to Christian sensibility, because it sounds subordinationist in a way that his account as a whole does not support. It is true that God like everything that is actual is an instance of creativity. But there can be no creativity without God. If one understands that to be actual is to be a being, then to call God an instantiation of Being is not offensive, since the Bible takes God's actuality for granted. If we replace "Being" with the more dynamic term, we move closer to the biblical vision. The overall result is to save theology from much of the intellectual and moral morass in which it has regrettably enmeshed itself. I am no longer apologetic about this feature of Whitehead's thought.

Many of the Buddhist objections to what they have encountered in typical Christian formulations of belief about God do not apply to the Whiteheadian formulations. Some Pure Land thinkers are open to affirming this kind of God. For Zen Buddhists, who find Pure Land teaching of grace objectionable, obviously the stronger affirmation of a divine "other" in process theology is unacceptable.

In 1976 I was a Woodrow Wilson Scholar for six months at the Smithsonian Institute in Washington, and I took the relation of Christianity and Buddhism as my topic for study. In Claremont I taught several times a seminar on "The Christian Interpretation of Buddhism." In 1978 I spent a sabbatical semester in Japan with the same topic in focus. Before going to Japan I visited several places in Southeast Asia where I understood that Buddhist-Christian dialogue was taking place. Actually, little was happening at the time, so that my Buddhist conversation partners continued for some time to be almost exclusively Japanese.

While in Japan I taught on this topic at Rikkyo University and the Episcopal Theological Seminary in Tokyo and lectured quite widely on it. In the United States I had several opportunities to give lectures on Christianity and Buddhism, and these resulted in 1982 in publication of *Beyond Dialogue: Toward the Mutual Transformation of Buddhism and Christianity.* The Buddhism I discussed there was still limited to Japanese Zen and Pure Land.

There was considerable interest in Buddhism in the culture of the seventies and among theologians. But when the Department of Religion of the University of Hawaii organized an international conference (in 1978, I think) to bring Christians and Buddhists together for discussion, Christian theologians, myself included, were notable by our absence. The Christians who went were mostly those who had studied Buddhism. They had a great conference, but Abe and I thought it was time to have another kind of conference, or better, a series of conferences, in which a small group of Christian theologians and Buddhist thinkers would engage in serious sustained conversation.

I wrote to some leading progressive theologians asking them to commit to a series of five discussions over a period of five or more years. I thought that would have an effect on their sense of the context and background in which Christian theology should be formulated in a religiously plural world. Abe invited leading Buddhist thinkers. The response was gratifying. Sadly, we were not successful in raising the money to make these conversations possible.

David Chappell came to the rescue. While teaching at the University of Hawaii, he had organized there the first international conference I mentioned above. I had talked with him about the desirability of having discussions specifically for theologians who might know little about Buddhism. He supported the idea, and he invited us to hold our first meeting as part of a second larger conference he was organizing. We did so. John Berthrong, who worked for the United Church of Canada, took an interest in our efforts and helped us get funding for a second conference at Vancouver School of Theology. One way or another, under his leadership, funding was found for later conferences as well.

They grew in size and, especially on the Buddhist side, in representativeness. Because of Abe's contacts, initially the Buddhists were almost all Japanese. But we acquired a strong contingent of Euro-Americans who were committed to Tibetan forms of Buddhism. We never did as well with Theravada. The Christian side remained primarily, although not exclusively, Protestant.

At the end of the five meetings, participants were unwilling to quit. I was myself in an awkward position. Several years earlier I had been invited to join a Jewish-Christian-Muslim international discussion group. I had declined because I simply did not have the energy to participate in two such ongoing discussions at the same time along with my other commitments. However, the invitation was renewed not long before the fifth and, I thought, final meeting of the Buddhist/Christian theological group. I thought I was then free to accept, and I did so. Accordingly, when the Buddhist-Christian group decided to continue to meet, I had to explain that although I was delighted that the conversations would continue, I would not be able to participate.

The group did continue and flourish. Indeed, there was a major breakthrough after I left. In the early years, finding a shared topic for the next meeting was often quite difficult. Topics that seemed natural to Buddhists were often strange to Christians and vice versa. I recall one occasion when Rosemary Ruether suggested that we talk about "justice." The Buddhists explained that that was not a topic for Buddhism, and that the connotations of that word for them were largely negative. We stuck to more narrowly theological topics.

But in later years, objection to such discussion ceased. One factor, I think, was the success of Sulak Sivaraksa, the Thai Buddhist activist, in organizing "socially engaged Buddhists" on a global scale. He took part in some sessions of the group, and I had other opportunities to make his acquaintance and establish a friendship for which I am very grateful.

Despite my resignation from the group, I kept getting invitations to attend sessions, and occasionally took part. I was delighted to find that, whereas earlier I had thought I had to keep my liberationist and my Buddhist concerns quite separate, they could now be integrated. Any idea that detachment from the concrete realities of history is inherent in Buddhism was ended. In general, I found that my understanding of the global situation and of how we should respond agreed as much with engaged Buddhists as with any Christian group.

This theological discussion group provided part of the context out of which the Society for Buddhist Christian Studies emerged under Chappell's continuing leadership. I was honored by being elected its first president. I accepted that role only on the basis of Chappell's agreement to be the real moving spirit and to tell me what to do. Credit for the success of the Buddhist/Christian dialog overall belongs to him.

Chappell had organized the larger conferences bringing Buddhist and Christian scholars together, nurtured the smaller theological ones led by Abe and me, and founded and edited a journal. One reason for having the society was to stabilize and increase support for his work. I was pleased to give him what help I could. It was actually very little. I was glad also that Abe and I were able to fit into his larger program and make our contribution there. Chappell's death a few years ago was a serious blow, but he had been sufficiently successful in institutionalizing his programs that the work he initiated could continue without him. In any case, precisely because of his success, the institutionalizing is now far less important. Mutual understanding between Buddhists and Christians no longer depends upon special institutions.

My experience in Jewish, Christian, Muslim dialogue was very different. Tensions in Israel-Palestine profoundly affected relations between Jews and Muslims. This was true even though we systematically avoided current events in our discussions. I sometimes thought that the main reason for the presence of Christians was to make discussion between Jews and Muslims possible.

On the other hand, it became clear that in fact Islam and Judaism were very much alike and that Christianity was the "odd man out." Despite the differences between the Torah and the Qur' an, the centrality of textual interpretation and its methods and history are remarkably similar. For both Judaism and Islam, the focus is on law understood as the essential guide especially in the corporate life of the faithful community.

I came to a new appreciation of Paul. I had never liked "legalism" and had been grateful to him for his polemic against it, but I had also been warned against projecting on Judaism the legalism I opposed. This warning was completely justified. The legalisms generated within Christianity are different from (and less justified than) anything to be found in Judaism. What my Jewish and Muslim colleagues were doing had little relationship with the oppressive sexual rules so often identified with Christianity. Nevertheless, for these colleagues it was through the study of the law and the long history of its interpretation that they found the way forward. In no way did they feel oppressed by the law, but I would have felt severely constricted if I had to follow a comparable pattern. With all of our Christian problems with bad doctrines and bad theology, I am deeply grateful that this is my tradition. And I believe that Paul is responsible for what I cherish.

There is also an important difference in our founding figures. In this case, as well, Jews and Muslims have similarities. Both Moses and Mohammed were political and military leaders as well as religious ones. They resemble each other far more than either resembles Jesus or Paul. Precisely because the latter belonged to the politically powerless majority, their teachings are very difficult to apply to those responsible for society as a whole. Within Judaism there were those who spoke against the powerful, and these prophets produced the tradition in which Jesus and Paul stood. Judaism has honored its prophets and preserved, and been influenced by, their teaching. The law is affected by their ideas. But it is the law that subsumes the prophets. I think the situation is similar in Islam. In Christianity the prophetic tradition is central, although in most of its actual history it has been co-opted by the powerful. Again, I find that I prefer this situation with all its terrible problems.

Both Judaism and Islam, of course, reject the deity of Jesus and the doctrine of the Trinity. I explained earlier that in terms of what is often considered the orthodox understanding of these ideas, I share their rejection. But my rejection of the doctrine of the deity of Jesus is partly because it has in fact weakened the call to be his disciples. Feeling justified by believing incredible things has nothing to do with faithfulness to Jesus, and Jesus himself makes clear that calling him "Lord" is not the point. Sometimes I think that one might be a better follower of Jesus if one were a Jew like him. But I fear that following him might be as offensive to Jewish leaders today as it was in his time. I will remain in the community that, at least in principle, respects such discipleship.

There were some fine Jewish scholars in the group, but to be with impressive Jewish scholars was for me nothing new. Accordingly, what I most prize from the experience with this group is the association with Muslims whose thinking I could take with full seriousness. Previously, in my limited encounters, I found Muslims solving all questions with quotes from their scripture. I do not enjoy conversations with fellow Christians who employ arbitrarily selected proof-texts to settle difficult questions, and I was no happier with Muslims who do so. The Muslim scholars in this discussion group were very different. With them real discussion was possible.

For many Christians, of whom I am one, the idea that the biblical text is verbally inspired, even dictated, by God is a highly objectionable one. This objection is not simply a matter of taste. It is that the idea flies in the face of history and common sense even, or especially, for believers. The text nowhere lays claim to this status. Neither Jesus nor Paul treats the received texts in this way. The texts are full of contradictions. They are written in many different styles. The question of which texts should be included in the cannon is itself a complex historical one on which Christians disagree. That in spite of all this there are so many Christian

Fundamentalists is an indication of some deep craving of the human soul for absoluteness. Authentic Christian faith works to counter this craving. Nothing creaturely can be absolute.

In all these respects Muslims are in a very different situation. Their text is a largely coherent body of writings all in one, quite beautiful, style. It repeatedly claims divine authorship. If one enters the community that accepts this text, one can hardly view it as anything but verbally inspired. Such a view introduces only a small fraction of the problems faced by Christian Fundamentalists. But, of course, I still find any such claim offensive, whether Christian or Muslim.

I also learned that in Islam the appeal to the original text is often liberating. Most of the moral problems Westerners observe in contemporary Islam come from the incorporation into Islamic law of patriarchal practices and forms of punishment that express the culture of later times. Our group included two strong Muslim feminists who were able to interpret even the most troubling Qu'ranic texts in inoffensive ways.

I also learned that Muslim scholars can make major distinctions within the Qu'ran. The divine revelation through Mohammed while he was in Mecca provided the general principles applicable in all times and places. When, in Medina, Mohammed was in a position of political power, the divine revelations dealt with the specific situations he faced there in that capacity. Muslims can learn much from these specific instructions as well, but they should not apply them directly to other, very different, situations. Instead their task is to apply the Meccan teachings, with careful regard to each specific situation.

The closest Christians can come to this is in the distinction between Jesus' teachings as in the Sermon on the Mount, on the one side, and Paul's responses to questions addressed to him by congregations he established. We can certainly learn from the latter, but it is clear that they respond to specific needs in particular contexts. We may certainly respect Paul's wisdom, but we must learn to be similarly wise in our very different circumstances.

I was, obviously, not convinced that the Qu'ran is word for word from God. But my prejudices toward Islam were dissolved. I rejoice that we Christians have a scripture that is so obviously imperfect that its human authorship is evident on every page. I rejoice that it gives expression to so many points of view that it cannot be summarized in any set of doctrines. But I can see the attraction of a scripture that is free from most of this messiness, and I can deeply respect those scholars who are claimed by that scripture and work to make it relevant and effective in our time. If one is impelled to treat one's scripture as quite literally God's words, then I recommend Islam.

The group met in the United States and Europe. Some of the Muslim scholars would have been arrested in some Muslim countries, and at first they would not go to Israel. But after Camp David, that changed, and we did meet in Jerusalem. Regrettably, that meeting was our last. The political context was too intense to allow the apolitical character of the dialogue to be sustained. I never had a chance to even present the paper I had prepared, and I was a bit relieved. In the context of the agonizing problems of Jerusalem, its theses seemed abstract and remote.

On the political front, I found the situation deeply discouraging. We met with the most open-spirited and irenic Jews, Christians, and Muslims in Jerusalem. Yet even they were far apart in their perception of the situation. They located what was then happening in very different historical trajectories. What would seem to Jews who sought to establish a relationship of peace and justice with Palestinians to be an act of great courage and generosity would appear to Palestinians as but a small step in the direction of justice. Against this background I was amazed and moved at a later date by the ability of some Israelis and some Palestinians to agree on the Geneva Accords. Would that the United States had thrown its full support behind these! Sadly, I have realized that my country is not really interested in justice in Israel/Palestine.

Engagement with diverse religious traditions in different ways solidified my opposition to approaches to religious pluralism that generalized too easily. My view has been that the relation between Christianity and each other tradition needs to be considered separately. The Christian relation to Judaism is profoundly different from any other. Re-thinking Christian theology in light of the great harm that supersessionism has done may be the most important response to the recognition of pluralism. It is my hope and belief that as Christians change in this respect, Jews will increasingly be able to reclaim Jesus and Paul as part of their history and that Judaism will be strengthened by this.

The relation to Islam is very different, but it is increasingly important. The Qu'ran already has a high Christology. If Christianity could clearly repudiate the idea that Jesus is God and the tri-theistic tendencies of trinitarian formulations that Muslims rightly find offensive, relations

could certainly be improved. Christians could also adopt a high view of
Mohammed as a great prophet without giving up our Christocentrism.
Some object that prophets cannot be men of war. But if the meaning of
"prophet" extends to Moses and David, who were certainly men of war,
highly esteemed by Jews and Christians, why not to Mohammed? And
if we judge by the historical importance of what a prophet has done,
Mohammed was indeed the greatest!

My hope is not for a merger of the Abrahamic faiths but for a time
when they will view themselves more in the way that the several great
historic branches of Christianity now view themselves. There is much to
celebrate in the differences between Orthodoxy, Catholicism, and Protestantism. Our emphases are quite different, and on some points we deeply
disagree. But we can all agree that Christianity would be impoverished by
the loss of any of these. Although we do not object to individuals moving
from one of these forms of Christianity to another, we do not favor
efforts to proselytize.

Perhaps we are not too far from a time when the children of Abraham will all hold in deepest respect Moses, Jesus, and Mohammed. Our
emphases will be different. But we will respect one another as fellow
believers in the God of Abraham, who have come to worship that God
through different traditions. We will thank God for all these traditions.
It would help if Jews and Christians recognized that Islam has already
led the way. Their scripture teaches them high respect for Moses and
Jesus and readiness to respect their followers. The problem has been
the rejection of Mohammed and the Qu'ran by Jews and Christians. I
learned from Hans Küng that there is no reason that we cannot recognize
that Mohammed was a great prophet. Indeed, judging by his historical
impact, he is indeed the greatest.

Our relation to the major religious traditions of South and East Asia
is quite different. I have found Whitehead's distinction between creativity
and God especially helpful here. Whereas many, I think most, advocates
of religious pluralism still affirm that all religious traditions are directed
toward the same ultimate, however great the differences in their concep-
tualization, Whitehead enables us to recognize that this is not the case.
Probably in all of the major religious communities there are some who
orient themselves to the ultimate that Whitehead calls "creativity." The
role of Being Itself in the West, sometimes identified as the Godhead,
and especially important in the apophatic mystical tradition, attests to

this orientation. But this is not the God of Abraham. And it is that God who plays the largest role in the Abrahamic family of religions. The God of Abraham calls forth trust and worship. Creativity or Being Itself calls forth the realization that, at the deepest level, each self is one with the ultimate. Judaism, Christianity, and Islam have room for both, but their focus is on God. The attempt to identify the God of Abraham with the metaphysical ultimate has led to great confusion.

In India and China there are strong theistic tendencies, but the primary focus of the most articulate religious leaders has been on the metaphysical ultimate: Brahman, the nameless Tao, Dharmākaya. These are not worshipped. The religious goal is to realize the already existing identity with the ultimate. That is held to be beyond all concepts, yet at an important level the ultimate is quite diversely conceived. The differences among religious communities oriented to what Whitehead calls creativity are as great as the differences among the Abrahamic traditions. Nevertheless, on the whole, there is greater tolerance of diversity among them. The move toward full mutual respect is not as difficult for them as it has proved to be for monotheists.

Recognizing the metaphysical difference between creativity and God allows for a mutual appreciation between these two families of religious thinking and experience that otherwise is found only by regarding at least one family as profoundly mistaken. Each family is basically correct in what it says about that toward which it orients itself. Obviously this leaves a great deal of room for further argument! But if each makes its affirmations carefully, there is no need for denial of the truth of the other set of affirmations. It is possible both to trust and worship God and also to realize that at bottom we are all instantiations of creativity. This dual possibility is more easily accepted in South and East Asia than in the West, but it is increasingly accepted there as well.

In more recent years I have added to these two families of religious orientation a third: the orientation to the world. This plays a larger role in primal religions than in those that arose in the axial age, the ones with which I was earlier preoccupied. But it has never disappeared from the axial traditions altogether. It has played a considerable role in China throughout its history. The need for this orientation has become apparent in the West in recent times. Sometimes it appears in the form of nature mysticism. It has reappeared among some who are led by the ecological crisis to meditate on their natural environment. It sometimes plays an exclusive role, but it can also supplement both the other families of traditions.

I never wrote a book on religious pluralism although I wrote a number of articles. I am grateful to Paul Knitter who helped me make a book out of these essays. The title did not make clear the subject matter: *Transforming Christianity and the World: A Way beyond Absolutism and Relativism.* The subtitle was intended to stress the point that each tradition grasps and communicates real truth that does not need to be treated as merely relative. On the other hand, its truth, properly understood, does not exclude the truth of other, quite different, traditions.

I also owe a great deal to David Griffin for systematically formulating my thought and publishing his account in 2005 as a chapter in *Deep Religious Pluralism.* This book takes the pluralism a step further. Griffin recognized that the basis for pluralism also differs from tradition to tradition. Hence he organized a Center for Process Studies conference, in honor of Marjorie Suchocki, of people from various traditions, all of whom appreciated the contribution of Whitehead. The book contains essays on pluralism from the Jewish, Christian, Islamic, Buddhist, Hindu, and traditional Chinese perspectives. There is a plurality of pluralisms.

More recently, after both John Hick and I had retired, this kind of pluralist thinking has taken a further step in Claremont. Karen Torjesen, as dean of the School of Religion at Claremont Graduate University, undertook to develop a multi-faith program. Her success was limited, but Jerry Campbell, then president of the School of Theology, picked up this vision for the preparation of leaders of the multiple traditions. He raised money for a university within which the professional schools of the several traditions could be nested. He was enthusiastically supported by the faculty of the School of Theology and most of its constituency.

Meanwhile it was clear that the idea was one for which the time had come. Jewish and Muslim institutions developed in Claremont and other groups were seriously interested. As I write, the total result of the fallout is not clear. But it is certain that preparation of leaders for several traditions will be taking place side by side and with some overlap of curriculum. Claremont Lincoln, instead of being the inclusive whole will occupy a niche in offering programs for the common good that are not otherwise available, chiefly through distance learning. This is quite different from the original dream, but it remains a great advance in institutional expression of religious pluralism.

CHAPTER SIXTEEN

Process Thought in China

My China connections go back to infancy; one might say, beyond. My parents were preparing to be missionaries with China as the intended destination, but problems in China led them to accept the mission board's need for someone in Japan.

For many years my contacts with China were sporadic and occasional. I spent a summer travelling in China in 1936, and changed ships at Shanghai in June of 1939. I visited Hong Kong briefly several times. When visitors to the mainland were again welcome, Tom Trotter invited me to be part of a Methodist group reconnecting with Christian leaders in China and visiting the sites of former Methodist colleges. The man who guided the mainline Protestant churches through the revolutionary period, Bishop Deng, identified himself as a process theologian, and I had occasional direct and indirect contacts with him. But this chapter is about more recent developments.

At our 1998 conference in Claremont, Griffin told us that our goal should be to make the twenty-first century the Whiteheadian one. He evoked laughter from the marginalized folk who constituted his audience. But today the idea does not seem quite so ridiculous. There is widespread recognition that the Cartesian paradigm does not work. More of those who reject the old dualism and materialism recognize the need for a new paradigm. Many of those who study Whitehead's proposal find that it meets the need. Perhaps it is not pointless to hope that this recognition will become widespread and that the intellectual adventure of the new century will be profoundly shaped by it. And most important, the leadership of one country, China, seems to be taking process thought seriously. Working on our relation to China has become an important part of my life.

Indeed, I consider myself astonishingly fortunate. Until this development actually occurred, I would never have dreamed of anything of the sort. For the first time in my life I feel that I have the opportunity of possibly having some effect on the actual course of history. Of course, I know that what happens in China will be the result of many influences and that the influence of process thought, to which I can contribute, is only one of these. But there is in China an openness to new ideas and a readiness to put them into effect that is dramatically different from the United States or other major countries. And the decisions that China makes in this transition period are immensely important, not only for its own future but for the future of the planet.

Some twenty years ago a Chinese man was admitted to the program in religion at Claremont Graduate School. We were glad to have him and tried to support him, but we really had no idea who he was. He wanted help in getting some process-oriented books translated into Chinese and published in China. Actually, he talked more about "constructive postmodernism." He was especially interested in books in the SUNY Series in Constructive Postmodernism that Griffin edited.

It turned out that *The Reenchantment of Nature*, the first book in that series, had made quite a stir in China. Zhihe Wang had been a leading postmodern scholar in China for some time. He became convinced that the constructive version was what China needed. We gradually learned that he was a significant figure in China, having published an encyclopedia of postmodernism. He was a member of the National Academy of Social Sciences, which, in China, includes philosophy. Indeed, he was responsible for their publications. His interest in constructive postmodernism, which he rightly associated with process thought, was in itself a significant breakthrough.

Soon activities in China escalated. At the end of the Third International Whitehead Conference, the Chinese delegation suggested that the fourth be held in Beijing. I thought the idea impractical, but in 2000 the Fourth International Whitehead conference did take place there. It was held at the university where Meijun Fan, Zhihe's wife, had taught before she joined him in Claremont, and she played a large role in organizing the conference.

The conference proved quite successful. Sixty people from countries outside China came, and this impressed our Chinese hosts. They found themselves favorably disposed to the proceedings. The ground was broken for rapid growth.

Under the guidance of Zhihe and Meijun, activities in China developed rapidly. Meijun singlehandedly publishes and distributes a monthly newspaper that reaches fifteen thousand Chinese, some in North America and others in China. It does much to promote interest in process thought.

Seeing that something of a long-term nature was developing, the center gave this work the status of a second "project" alongside Process and Faith: the China Project. It, too, has its own budget, although it has no membership. It has lived from hand to mouth through the generosity of a few enthusiastic supporters. Of special importance in the early stages were Ron and Pam Phipps, who had been doing business in China beginning fairly early in the Mao period. Ron was a student of one of Whitehead's students with a special focus in physics. Participation in the project enabled him to build on his joint interest in Whitehead and China.

Zhihe and Meijun followed up on the international conference with a conference in Claremont on higher education. This was geared to presidents and deans of Chinese universities, and the response was astonishing. Subsequently there have been numerous conferences in China as well as many lectures. A two-week summer academy, taught first by Jay McDaniel and sometimes by Robert Mesle is now an important part of the picture. Although we hope that in due course there will be Chinese scholars fully qualified to teach Whitehead and process thought, for some years yet there will be a need for foreigners.

One of the most amazing things about the rapid development of interest in process thought in China is that its connection with Christian theology does not function as more of an obstacle. It turns out that Chinese Marxists are far less prejudiced against Christian theologians than are most university professors in the United States. They are also less troubled about the marginal status of process thought in the United States. Presidents of major Chinese universities and high government officials visit us in Claremont; see our very modest quarters in the basement of one of the buildings at the school of theology, and are not deterred from cultivating further connections.

I am convinced that many of the Chinese scholars and political leaders are deeply concerned about the future of China and are urgently seeking new responses to their problems. They do not care who provides them. Fortunately, we have been working on some of the questions they face for some time. These include questions such as how to include values in university education; how to improve the lot of the poor without further worsening the environment, how to build sustainable cities, how to relate concern for individuals and their rights to the common good, how to include elements of traditional Chinese culture in a contemporary vision and practice. Given the importance of the decisions China is now making not only for the future of China but for the people of the world, I am awed by the opportunity to make proposals to Chinese who may have some possibility of implementing them.

Although Zhihe and Meijun, as project directors, do the vast majority of the work, the China Project has been an important part of my life as well. We have had many Chinese visitors in Claremont, and I am grateful for the opportunity to visit with them. I chaired an advisory group for the project. It has seemed important to have a separately organized institute, not connected with the Claremont School of Theology, since we hope at some point for support from foundations that do not give money to seminaries. Since our activities in China are not "theological" in any narrow sense, we want to be in position to receive support for fully "secular" programs. We created the Institute for Postmodern Development of China as in independent organization. I am chair of the board. Philip Clayton is the chair elect.

The process thinker initially most appreciated in China was Griffin. It was the first book in his Constructive Postmodern Series for SUNY Press that attracted Chinese attention. *The Reenchantment of Science* argued for the recognition of the presence of subjectivity in the world that science has so drastically objectified. Griffin attended the Beijing conference and lectured at that time.

But Griffin's intense involvement in exposing the truth about what happened on 9/11 forced him to withdraw from active involvement in China. I will return to this topic in the next chapter. Meanwhile, I am one of those who has stepped into the breach. In October 2005 I spent a month in China, visiting many universities there. Wang organized programs for a group of perhaps ten of us foreigners, involving five conferences and numerous lectures.

One result of this flurry of activity is that twenty-five Chinese universities have now officially established centers for process studies. Sometimes the China Project tries to help a little financially in the initial stages. Just how much these centers actually do is certainly very varied and uncertain. But that university leaders want centers in this field indicates that, at present, Western process thought has prestige in China.

Another remarkable indication of the rapid acceptance of Whitehead's thinking in China is in the field of education. At the university level, the interest in establishing process centers is connected with this concern. China has rapidly developed huge universities that are largely modeled on state universities in the United States. Since in most instances they have been created almost from nothing, the remnants of the liberal arts tradition that still influences much higher education in the United States is not present. Instead the model is the research university that aims to be "value-free." The result is brilliant success in educating specialists and technical experts. But many Chinese are concerned that, when education is value free, the only value that is communicated is personal success, chiefly understood in economic terms. This prepares the students more for a capitalist society than a Communist one. These critics are attracted to Whitehead's thought because for him science is not separated from values in this way.

The Chinese government is eager to improve its educational system at other levels. Two of the leaders in this field are women who are interested in Whitehead's educational theories and have visited us in Claremont. One of them was given responsibility for developing a new curriculum for younger students. She tells us that the curriculum she has prepared is Whiteheadian. It was used experimentally. When I inquired at one time how many students were involved in the experiment, I was told that there were thirty-five million! I still find it hard to think in such numbers.

Unfortunately, this project was not continued. It failed because parents were afraid their children would not be able to compete with those who were schooled to do well on the national examinations. It seems to be impossible to change education in the lower grades without first changing the examination system.

A very important part of our work is reflection about environmental matters. The Chinese are fully open on this topic. One of the major reasons for their interest in postmodernism is the obvious weakness of modernism on this point. The government was wholly committed to modernize its industry and its cities, and it has done so brilliantly. But the environmental cost has been very high. This is not something that people have to read about in the paper. It is a matter of daily experience. Chinese intellectuals were disappointed, however, to find that the French postmodernists were hardly any improvement over the modernists in their reflection about the right relation between human beings and the natural environment. Their work was brilliant in its deconstruction of the modern, but did not give much positive advice about an alternative.

In contrast we process folk have all sorts of proposals on many topics, and we have been talking a great deal about ecological matters. This has led to a close connection with Sheri Liao, the organizer of "Global Village, Beijing." This is recognized as the leading nongovernmental organization in China, and she has received several international honors. She has visited us and spoken for us on several occasions, and we work with her also in China. Indeed, our Chinese headquarters are at her place.

Early in the new millennium, leading Chinese, including high government officials, began talking about "ecological civilization." Wang contributed to the interest in this idea. A Chinese government think tank shared this interest with Wang and they decided that we should hold conferences in Claremont under this heading. Soon after the idea was espoused by the Communist Party, we held the first conference dealing with it. We have held such conferences annually since them, with as many as a hundred Chinese in attendance. The eighth was held in April 2014. These conferences receive considerable attention in China and many of the papers presented are published there. I continue to be amazed by the attention given to our ideas in China. The contrast with the United States is dramatic.

One difference is that in China philosophy belongs to the social sciences. This is because the overwhelmingly dominant philosophy has been Marxism, and the Chinese look for a philosophy to provide guidance in the political, economic, and social spheres. Few contemporary Western philosophies do this, and if Whitehead had simply been taught in philosophy departments, his thought would probably have had little application beyond that which he himself gave it. However, as a theologian I have always been even more interested in its application than in "pure" philosophy. First and foremost the application with which I have personally been concerned is in Christian theology and interfaith concerns. But in the Center for Process Studies we have cast our net widely. This has meant that when Chinese wanted to see what proposals come from Whiteheadian philosophy in various fields, we have thus far been able to give answers. We have provided speakers for conferences not only on education and ecology, but also on economics, business ethics, political theory, legal theory, psychology, and eco-cities.

Currently we are facing our greatest opportunity and our greatest challenge. The Chinese government has announced its intention to give priority to agriculture and rural development. This is unquestionably an important and urgent direction. During the past decades, rural China has been largely neglected except as a source of cheap labor.

Nevertheless, the news also arouses anxiety. Thus far when China has "developed" industry or cities or universities it has followed the modern form. Modernization in most of the world has meant replacement of human and animal labor by machinery and fossil fuels. It has involved the replacement of more or less integrated family farms with industrial monoculture. Most of the former farmers have to move to cities.

These changes in China would involve an enormous increase in its use of fossil fuels at a time when we are already near or at "peak" oil. It would replace a form of agriculture that, with all its limitations, has been relatively sustainable with one that will quickly deplete the soil. And it will require building additional cities for hundreds of millions of people and additional industries to employ them. Estimates of the numbers involved run as high as eight hundred million. I believe that modernization of agriculture has done great harm in the United States. It will be a global disaster if China adopts this policy.

Is there another way besides continued neglect and modernization? I have long been convinced there is. My major teacher in this regard is Dean Freudenberger, who has degrees in agriculture and Christian ethics and years of experience in Africa and elsewhere. His two sons have continued to apply his vision of integrated, organic agriculture in Africa and Australia. The Heifer Project works in communities all over the world, including China, to implement this kind of vision.

Part of Freudenberger's vision is that farmers should imitate nature. This principle is central to the work of Wes Jackson of the Land Institute in Salina, Kansas. He notes that in its natural state, the soil is covered by a perennial polyculture. Human beings have replaced this with an annual monoculture. From the earliest period there has been no fully sustainable agriculture. Modern agriculture carries the destructive character of this replacement all the way. Jackson is developing perennial grains that will be as productive as the annual ones now grown. It is this kind of vision that should guide China in its new focus on agriculture.

Can we contribute to making that happen? This is a truly exciting challenge. We have begun trying, and our first venture was remarkably successful. We held a conference on ecological agriculture in an agricultural university in north China. David Freudenberger from Australia gave the keynote address. It was well received and the Chinese translation has been published in three different journals. It was then picked up by a digest read by governmental leaders and was reproduced there in full. We think that the idea must be attractive to some people of influence in China.

In the fall of 2009 we followed up with another conference. This one was co-sponsored with the Chinese Academy of Social Sciences and the governor of the province where it was held. Sadly, for health reasons, neither Dean Freudenberger nor Wes Jackson could go, but they sent papers. The conference attracted high level attention. Maybe, just maybe, the Chinese government will see the wisdom of avoiding the "modern" path. We have also focused on agriculture in several conferences in Claremont, including some in the "ecological civilization" series.

The idea of following nature is traditionally Chinese. Our effort to synthesize facts and values is also traditionally Chinese. Much of what we are promoting in ecological terms as well is traditionally Chinese. We emphasize whenever we can the value of traditional Chinese thought. Whitehead himself noted the similarity of his thought to that of China. If Western process thought succeeds in making a difference in China, it will no doubt in large part be by helping to bring elements of traditional Chinese philosophy effectively into the current scene.

For this reason we are particularly pleased that some Chinese commentators on the public discussions there note that there are just two major movements. One is constructive postmodern thought. The other is the renewal of classic Chinese thought. Since we think of them as allies, we find this picture very promising. But our optimism is tempered by the realization that the most powerful pressure on the Chinese government is from hundreds of millions of ambitious and capable Chinese wanting to better their economic situation.

There is certainly progress in China in renewing its own heritage. The government is now open to China's own traditions. This is a reversal of the position of the intellectual leadership of China since the time that thoughtful Chinese saw that China could hold its own in relation to the European colonial powers only by Westernizing or modernizing. This required uprooting Daoism and Confucianism which were perceived to stand in the way of modernization. The attack on Confucianism reached its greatest intensity in the Red Guard movement.

This has changed in the past decade. As China has realized that Western intellectuals hold ancient Chinese thought in high regard, they have begun establishing Confucian centers in the West. Lectures and books on traditional Chinese thought are gaining a new audience in China. The government has begun using traditional language. We think that Whitehead can help to reassure Chinese that they can re-appropriate many aspects of their tradition without impeding their advance in science and technology. This re-appropriation will be particularly valuable in rural and agricultural "development."

My own travel to China ended with a trip in 2009 that followed the seventh IWC in Bangalore. Jean could no longer travel with me. She needed close attention continuously, and I gave up travel in order to be with her. My arrangements for her in my absence themselves met with problems. My travel and therefore my participation in events in China ended. Since then my interaction with Chinese has been only with those who have visited Claremont.

There has been one exception. Kil Sang Yoon, the director of our Korea Project, has been a frequent visitor in North Korea. No South Korean is better informed about developments there or more trusted by the North Korean government. In the late spring of 2013, he became alarmed that tensions between North Korea and the United States would erupt into massive violence even involving nuclear weapons. He thought that nongovernmental groups, especially the churches, should send delegations to lessen the North Korean isolation. He persuaded me that efforts of this kind might reduce the danger of nuclear war. Despite my earlier decision not to travel, I agreed to go.

Ironically, the tensions eased, and the church groups on which he was working did not materialize. He urged me to go anyway, and by then I had made arrangements for the care of Jean in my absence. So I ended up going at the time that North Korea was celebrating the "victory" that led to an armistice with the United States. Incidentally, this armistice was also claimed by Obama as an American victory. I was seen by the North Koreans as part of an American delegation participating in their celebrations. The delegation was led by Ramsey Clark, whose truth-telling about what the United States did and continues to do to North Korea is much appreciated there. We were treated royally. I enjoyed a memorable and illuminating experience, but it had little in common with what I originally agreed to do.

The visit to North Korea, together with all that I learned from Yoon and my reading, reinforced my understanding of the endless distortions brought about by American imperial ambition. We are led to view the world, not in terms of what is there, but in whatever categories are thought to support the American geopolitics of the time. The "villainy" of North Koreans has nothing to do with any actual crimes (of course, there are some) but with their refusal to be dominated by us. They beg for a peace treaty, which we refuse, and their occasional saber rattling is in response to continuous threats and provocations on our part. We want to maintain our military control of South Korea and our military bases there as part of our containment of China. The image of North Korea as a threat is our justification.

In this chapter on China, the relevance is that travel to North Korea is through Beijing, and despite my expectation not to go any more I had four rich days there. It was in those days that I first became aware of discussions about promoting a new form of Marxism re-formed by process thought. The question was whether to call it "process Marxism" or "organic Marxism." I did not even understand the significance of the question and contributed nothing to the discussion. Only after returning home did I discover that this might prove an important next step in process thought in China. If it can present itself as an updated form of Marxism it can gain a still stronger place in the Chinese scene. Philip Clayton is taking the lead in this project, which may prove our most important. With Justin Heinzekehr, he has written a book, *Organic Marxism,* which has now been published by Process Century Press.

The single greatest contributor to advancing process thought in China from the Western side has been Jay McDaniel. As a graduate student in Claremont he was keenly interested in the Christian/Buddhist dialogue, especially with Japanese. As our connections with China developed he has been a strong supporter, our most frequent and appreciated leader in the annual Process Summer Academy and elsewhere, but also an independent entrepreneur in developing ongoing relations. His amazingly successful website, "Jesus, Jazz, and Buddhism," has not been limited to Americans and Chinese, but it has advanced that relationship. He has also organized Ecological Civilization International to involve institutions on both sides of the Pacific in working together for the advance of ecological civilization.

It is obvious that our work in China is not directly in the promotion of Christian belief or practice. However, our connections in China do not exclude an explicitly religious dimension. Bishop Deng, the Christian leader who maintained some positive relation between the Chinese church and the Communist government through all the years of turmoil, identified himself as a process theologian. The government's department of religion has been very receptive of our ideas, especially our ideas about religious pluralism. The man who ranks second in that department spent four months with us on one occasion. Of the process centers at twenty-five universities, one is on religious pluralism and one actually on process theology.

I am fully identified in China as a Christian theologian, and when Chinese visitors come to Claremont they find the Center of Process Studies to be part of a Christian seminary. They often eat with us at Pilgrim Place, a retirement community of Christian workers. It is my belief that the more positive the experiences that Chinese leaders have with Christianity the better the chances for healthy relations in China.

Many may regard these reflections about our work in China as well as the work itself as not theological at all. Yet this part of my professional life feels to me a part of the whole, and the whole feels theological. One of my deep concerns is that in the West secularism has cut us off from what is most valuable in our heritage from Israel. It is leading us to self-destruction. Its victory in so much of public life makes the affirmation of the most important values of the past awkward and difficult.

Central to our heritage from Israel is faith in God. But belief that there is any reality corresponding to the meaning of the word "God" is undercut by secularism. This means that those who continue to believe do so in spite of the dominant intellectual climate. The more believers adopt an open-minded spirit, the more their belief in God is likely to be disconnected from most of the rest of their thought. Only those who are insensitive to the knowledge developed by the modern world are likely to have a way of thinking in which God plays the central role. Yet a reality that plays only a marginal role cannot be God. None of these options is healthy.

Whitehead belongs to a very small group of thinkers who offer us an alternative. God is integral to his richly articulated cosmology. Since the cosmology is new, the God who is integral to it cannot be understood as just like the one who was integral to medieval or early modern cosmology, just as none of these can be understood just as ancient Israel understood Yahweh or Jesus understood his "Abba." Nevertheless, what Whitehead calls God is the same reality that Christians have worshipped and trusted throughout our history, now freshly conceived in relation to the rest of our knowledge. Whitehead thus offers us the possibility of healthy faith.

The realization of this possibility depends on a major change in the intellectual situation. It does not require that economists, political theorists, physicists, and biologists all believe in God. But it does require that those who shape the fundamental beliefs of the society hold to views that do not automatically exclude the reality of God. If they rethink their fields based on a Whiteheadian event ontology, one that rejects dualism and determinism, this condition is satisfied. Even if most shapers of the cultural mind continue to hold to a fully secularist vision that rules God out, the wide recognition that their secularism is one position among others, rather than the default position for all, would go far to renewing the possibility of a healthy theism. It does not seem impossible that one of these days, the many weaknesses of the seventeenth-century metaphysics that shapes so much of secularism will weaken its hold on the university and intellectual culture. To work to hasten that day seems to me an appropriate theological task.

This is true even if "theology" is understood quite conventionally. However, I have found it important to define it differently. Prior to the modern epoch theologians such as Augustine and Thomas and even Luther and Calvin thought that treatment of all humanly important topics belonged to theology. The only question was whether one was writing from a Christian point of view. They thought that their reflection about what was going on in their day and the best response to new developments was part of their theological responsibility. This is my understanding of my task as a theologian.

It is this understanding that enables me to think of my efforts in relation to China as also theological. Whereas in the West the tradition that needs to be selectively re-appropriated is the God-centered one of Israel, in China the ancient wisdom that secularism has rejected is not clearly theistic. It is my personal bias that in the long run Chinese thought will benefit from interacting with a healthy biblical theism. Through Marxism China appropriated something of the prophetic tradition, but this functioned to oppose Chinese culture rather than to enrich it. The Marxist passion for justice does not have deep roots in China. And cut off from its biblical basis its prospects are not good. I hope, in due course, for a China that has selectively re-appropriated both Marxism and its own traditional wisdom. I think it will then be able to benefit from interaction with a healthy biblical theism. I can see an important role for Whiteheadian thought in that process. But for now, most of the available forms of Christianity do not have the health needed to contribute well to the future China. The priority is the recovery of its own wisdom. Many Christians already recognize that there is much there from which we need to learn.

CHAPTER SEVENTEEN

The Church

In the years after World War II what were then the mainline denominations flourished. Veterans wanted to establish homes and families, and being part of a church was part of that picture. There was close connection between the anti-Nazi cause and Christian faith, and the new Cold War against the Soviet Union was felt to be another struggle for Christian faith, this time against "godless Communism." In short, it was politically correct to be a participating member of a church—or a synagogue. And the denominations that were most favored were ones such as my own, the Methodist.

I gave little thought to this. I took the church as an important social institution for granted. I thought that many individuals within it had trouble reconciling their Christian beliefs with the dominant teaching of the modern world, and I thought I could help them out of my own struggle and thinking. I hoped that would be a significant way to serve the church.

But with respect to the church as institution, my only question was how I should relate to it. My earlier intention of going to a Methodist seminary and becoming a Methodist pastor had given way to the hope of college teaching. But as I explained earlier, with no job of that kind on the horizon, and the need to return to Georgia to take responsibility for my brother, I decided to ask for an appointment from the church.

My parish experience was interesting but not really satisfying. The second year I was happy to be a full-time teacher. I participated as a layman in the life of the campus church, teaching a Sunday school class much of the time. The situation was similar when I moved to Emory

University. The church there also was strong and well-established. My only question was what role to play. I was once asked whether I would consider the role of associate pastor, and I was struck that the position would have involved an increased salary. But I enjoyed my teaching and was not tempted.

The situation changed somewhat when I moved to Claremont. Many Californians related to no organized religion, and Protestantism in California was a small part of the religious scene. The Methodist conference in southern California was about the same size as the one in north Georgia, but the population from which it drew may have been ten times as large. Nevertheless, it was growing and had considerable confidence.

A new church had been started in Claremont. We came early enough to be considered charter members. I and my family became involved in this congregation as we had never been before. The pastor, Pierce Johnson, was really interested in my ideas and I in his. His departure was a blow, but his successors have all been fine ministers with diverse gifts. For the first time, a local congregation came to mean a great deal to me. In recent years my activity has been limited to church attendance, but it is still a pleasure to be part of an active and truly inclusive and faithful community. I think I am now the only charter member still attending

Originally we met in a school. As we talked about building the church, we envisioned that eventually it would be a large one. We would build a small building first that could be the chapel for the larger one we eventually expected. We still had no sense that the church as an institution was in trouble. Of course the local congregation needed time and money from all its members, but the annual conference and the national church were, for me, simply givens. I attended the yearly meeting of the Annual Conference, as all ordained ministers were expected to do, and I did what I was asked to do, but I did not feel any responsibility for it.

However, in the mid-1960s the Methodist Church united with the Evangelical United Brethren to become the United Methodist Church. Both were part of the movement shaped by John Wesley and inspired by the hymns of his brother, Charles Wesley; so their teachings were very similar. Nevertheless, the theological statements of the two bodies were different. The new united church appointed a commission to study "Doctrine and Doctrinal Standards" and to come back to the next General Conference with a recommendation.

The plan was chiefly the brainchild of Albert Outler, who was often called "Mr. Methodist." He was a theologically sophisticated and politically astute church historian, and his scholarship included and emphasized John Wesley, whom he rightly considered to be underappreciated in the wider church and even among Methodists. He was also a church activist. He was admired by persons with a wide spectrum of perspectives. He chaired our group, and for the most part we followed his leadership.

One expression of that leadership I found somewhat amusing but also respected. He had been an observer at Vatican II. As a student of church history he knew that Wesley had adapted the twenty-three articles of religion for his followers in the United States from the 39 articles of the Church of England. Some of those 39 articles had a definitely anti-Catholic character and others were quite problematic. Wesley's elimination of many of them was a real improvement. But Outler knew that the anti-Catholic emphasis of the original 39 had not been eliminated even though Wesley did not personally have anti-Catholic feelings. Especially after Vatican II, Outler considered it highly inappropriate for us to have official anti-Catholic statements.

Unfortunately, there is no practical procedure for altering the Methodist Articles of Religion. Accordingly, he had us recommend to General Conference that it adopt a statement to the effect that henceforth we do not understand these articles in an anti-Catholic sense. General Conference approved unanimously, and he took this action to the Vatican, where he was graciously received. I believe that a cardinal came to the next General Conference to express appreciation. I think that Catholics understand better than most Protestants that one can change the meaning of past statements while leaving the statement as such intact. This was a new world to me.

Since we could not change our Articles of Religion, but since in a number of ways they did not reflect the actual beliefs of many Methodists, we formulated a statement that emphasized our respect for them as part of our historical heritage and then went on to talk about the importance of encouraging serious theological reflection at all levels of the church's life. That reflection should be guided, we said, by what Outler had taught us to call the Wesleyan quadrilateral: scripture, tradition, reason, and experience. One of our tasks was to clarify our understanding of these.

My proposal was that we reverse the order. I proposed that there was nowhere to begin except in our experience; that this provided the material for reflective thought; that we needed to check our understanding in relation to that of others in our community of faith, present and past; and that the heart and norm of the tradition was scripture. I remember vividly that one member of the commission made an impassioned speech against me. He had been a teacher of theology at Emory, indeed, a colleague, before he became a bishop. He said that, of course, that was the way he taught theology, but that if we brought a statement of that sort to General Conference, he would lead a fight against it. I wondered how we could encourage serious theological reflection if we opposed formulating the guidelines in the way that we actually did theology. But, of course, no one picked up on my proposal. We would stick to the traditional order.

In general the discussion went well. But at our last meeting the formulation of scripture was one that attributed to it a kind of authority that I could not recognize. I said I could not vote for it, although if the majority did so, I would accept the decision. Outler was very upset by my position. I have never understood why it bothered him that much. He could easily have won a vote, I'm sure. I would not even have been present at General Conference and would certainly not have agitated against the statement. But instead of outvoting me, Outler modified the wording so that I could sign.

Outler took our report to General Conference and it was approved without much debate. No doubt, confidence in Outler played the primary role in this easy acceptance. But it also reflected the mood of tolerance and confidence that still characterized the church in the sixties.

That situation declined not long thereafter, and one focus of controversy became our formulation. Conservatives saw it as far too permissive. They wanted a statement in which scripture was not one of four criteria but *the* criterion, with the other three as aids to interpretation. I have often wondered whether, if Outler's original, slightly more biblicist formulation had become the official doctrine, the controversy would have been less heated. Perhaps for political reasons, I should have supported him and swallowed my discomfort. I may bear some blame for the theological wars in Methodism.

Eventually the agitation against our statement led to the appointment of another commission. Obviously, this time I was not invited. The commission came up with a statement that was far more restrictive than Outler's formulation to which I had objected. I read it as stating that, henceforth, the only legitimate United Methodist theology would be hermeneutical theology.

I had two strong objections. First, my theology was not hermeneutical in the required sense, and I had no intention of abandoning my convictions. Second, this kind of theology has been very rare among Methodists. The arguments of those who supported it did not conform to what they required. They provided no scriptural basis for their proposals. To me this all seemed profoundly inauthentic. Partly for the second reason, but primarily for the first, I decided that I would have to leave the denomination. I could not function as a United Methodist theologian if the denomination formally and officially declared that my way of doing theology was invalid. I had no intention of making a stir, but I thought I needed to inform my bishop.

This created more of a stir than I anticipated. One of my former students and a truly remarkable theologian and administrator, Rebecca Parker, went to General Conference and attended the committee meetings in which committee reports were received and discussed. She managed to get considerable rewording into the statement. I am deeply grateful for her work both for the sake of the denomination and because I could live with the final formulation. I considered myself to be very much a Wesleyan, whereas I did not think the statement in its original form was faithful to Wesley or to the American Wesleyan tradition. I had no desire to abandon that tradition. Later I wrote a book about Wesley to express my own appreciation for his thought and to claim it for the progressive church.

By the late 1970s it finally sank in for me that what had been the mainline Protestant churches were in *serious* trouble. My own denomination, now the United Methodist, was a full-fledged example. One problem was that there was very little real theology in it, and that meant that very few people had convictions about their Christian faith that were both strong and clear. For a century prior to that time the theological school we call Boston Personalism had given the denomination a progressive center. This had fitted well with the Social Gospel that flourished from the end of the nineteenth century through the first decades of the twentieth. In Methodist circles this combination dominated most of the seminaries and the church school literature until World War II, although some internal critique began in the thirties. This liberal synthesis then came under strong attack from the theological renaissance associated with neo-orthodoxy. This weakened confidence and conviction. The last time the church was able to rally around the earlier synthesis was in its support of the work of Martin Luther King, himself a product of the Boston school, and whose major theological advisor was L. Harold deWolf, the last of the major Personalist theologians.

The Boston school did not seem able to reconstruct itself in light of the valid critiques of liberalism by neo-orthodox thinkers. On the other hand, process theology, as represented, for example, by Daniel Day Williams, was largely reformulated in the context of the neo-orthodox renaissance and hence informed by its critique of earlier forms of liberalism. I believed then, and I continue to believe now, that process theology as expressed in Williams' classic work, *The Spirit and Forms of Love*, could have helped to revise and carry forward the progressive tradition of Methodism. It continued the philosophical theology tradition, but overcame the dualism that made Personalism clearly inadequate as a response to the ecological crisis.

But that was not to be. The new situation evoked considerable interest in theology, and each of the major figures of the period attracted a following within Methodism, although none of them fit the Wesleyan tradition as well as Williams. But instead of engaging in serious discussion of the future of theology for the church, the topic was largely dropped. Theology in general almost disappeared from both preaching and church school literature as well as church publications for lay people. By the seventies, the category of theology for lay people disappeared from the publishing arm of the church.

The only forms of theology that continued to attract attention were the liberation theologies and sharp critiques of the theological sins of the church: its anti-Judaism, its racism, its exclusivism, its ties with colonialism, its sexual repression, its homophobia, and so forth.

In many ways this was a very rich theological period, and any future progressive theology must incorporate the critical insights that were attained. Further, the church was able, to a remarkable extent, to hear these criticisms and to take some account of them. I celebrate this work. But the overall effect of this kind of theology was to call for repentance. It was what we now call deconstructive. It did not help most pastors or lay people to think clearly and with conviction about the positive meaning of their Christian faith.

When liberal-minded church people are offered little help in formulating and reformulating their beliefs in changing times, they are likely to stop trying. Many of them now know what they do not believe. They do not believe that their Jewish and Buddhist neighbors are going to Hell. They do not believe that women should be second class citizens in the church. They do not believe that sexuality is inherently unclean. But they often suppose that the church's theology teaches those things they do not believe. Hence they do not think of their new rejections of such beliefs as part of a positive Christian theology.

Some decide that ideas do not matter, only actions. Others fall back on what they learned as children or assume to be the tradition. This abandonment of progressive theology opened the door to a militant kind of theological conservatism that had played only a small role in the denomination in the past. Some of those who adopt this style do so out of the sincere belief that it is the only way the denomination can find effective moorings in the theological chaos of the time. They have not tried to turn back the clock on the major changes effected with respect to race and gender and anti-Judaism. But on issues of abortion they do try to reverse positions earlier adopted, and they have led the church to refuse recognition of same-sex unions and ordination of homosexuals. Since the progressive impulse toward inclusion and acceptance of difference is still alive in the denomination, this conservative reaction has led to painful division of a sort not experienced in Methodism since the controversy over slavery.

At an earlier point, before the situation had become quite so polarized, I made one effort to help the national church. To me it seemed important that the church have some kind of effective unity. It was clear that this was not to be theological. The alternative seemed to me missional. This had certainly been important to Wesley, and extending "scriptural holiness" across the land, and then to other lands as well, had given American Methodists a sense of mission for two centuries.

Today "scriptural holiness" sounds very conservative, but it did not always have that connotation. The church had dotted the continent, and other continents as well, with its liberal arts colleges and its hospitals. It had often worked against slavery and the worst forms of racism under this rubric. The participation in the Social Gospel movement was part of this mission. The church's work against "demon rum," that now looks so conservative, had a progressive character in many contexts where the money urgently needed for food and clothing for wives and children was spent instead on alcohol by husbands who then sometimes inflicted physical abuse as well.

Of course, there were still many opportunities for United Methodists to give to national and international missions and to engage in local projects. But whereas missional activity had once given a deep sense of purpose to local congregations, now it had become peripheral to the life of most of them. The General Conference every four years lifted up some one cause to be emphasized for that quadrennium, but most lay United Methodists hardly knew what it was. Yet the missional impulse was far from dead.

It seemed to me that the denomination might recover some unifying zeal if it reflected carefully about the needs of the world and the nation and decided thoughtfully what role it could play in response. It had numerous colleges that might contribute. It had excellent resources in its theological faculties. To me it seemed that the problems of the world and of the nation had never been more critical, and that the United Methodist church could make a contribution. I also believed that for its members to understand themselves as playing this role would give them a sense of working together on an important project that would override some of our divisions and recover something of the vitality the denomination was losing.

Accordingly, I teamed up with a professor in another seminary, who was much more of a Methodist politician than I. We drafted a "memorial" to General Conference asking that a commission be appointed to consider the question of the church's mission, and we secured the signatures of more than a hundred professors in Methodist seminaries in support. The General Conference did appoint the commission, and I was made a member. For a short period I thought that I might actually be able to make a contribution to the health of the denomination.

My idea was that we should discuss the general idea of a long-term focus on particular issues around which there would be a large consensus in the church. We could then brainstorm about possible choices. I came up with a list of ten that I thought could spark discussion. I emphasized social problems that I thought would be both eminently worth dealing with and that would, at least initially, not be divisive.

For example, there would be wide consensus that addiction to drugs and alcohol was a serious social and personal problem. The problem is complex and the apparent increase of addiction reflected changes in the culture that needed to be understood and addressed. We would need serious reflection as to how to approach it. It involves both social and

intimately personal considerations including spiritual ones. In addition
to reflection about its many-faceted nature, there is no question but that
proposals for action on the part of local congregations would emerge.
Other proposals would be for relevant courses in colleges and seminaries.
Still others would be for legislation at state and national level. Both theo-
retically and practically the denomination might give local and national
leadership in programs that would both reduce addiction and deal better
with those who are not healed. The denomination would in no way claim
that the problem it chose to deal with was the *only* or *most important*
problem in the nation. It would be most pleased if other denominations
chose other problems so that ecumenically the church would become an
effective agency of change in society.

After identifying a number of such possibilities, the commission
could discuss how to involve as many congregations and judicatories
as possible in selecting the problem judged to be most suitable for the
United Methodist Church's response. This would involve reflection about
the church's history and present capacities locally and at other levels as
well as the importance of the problems themselves. I thought discussion
of this kind would be healthy in many congregations and that it would
also lead to more sense of ownership of the eventual choice. And finally
we could either recommend particular directions to General Conference
or, if that were premature, next steps toward making a decision.

However, I was quickly disillusioned. Apparently among the denomination's leaders there was no interest in having this kind of reflection. I
became aware that the powers that be had decided that this was not a
good idea and that the task of the bishop who chaired the commission
was to suppress all discussion of this kind. I suppose our denominational
leaders saw any proposal of this kind as disruptive of the existing functioning of the church. No one ever talked straight with me about the
reasons for suppressing any serious discussion, but it was clear that none
would take place. The professor with whom I had planned the project
would hardly speak to me at all. We wasted the church's money with two
meetings a year for four years and came up with an innocuous statement
that was accepted and wisely filed in the wastebasket.

I learned that, as an outsider to the church's leadership, any initiative
I took would do more harm than good. I still wonder sometimes whether
a serious effort by a denomination to discern a way it could contribute to
improving the national or global situation significantly might also save

the denomination from continuing decline. But I learned that I was in no position to test this possibility. I narrowed my horizons as a church-man to my more immediate context.

The local situation also changed. Our sanctuary was burned by an arsonist in the late sixties, and when it came time to rebuild, we realized that our original plans did not make sense. We had something like six hundred members, and further growth was unlikely. As we rebuilt, we would enlarge what had once been thought of as the chapel of a larger church and recognize that what we had was the permanent church build-ing. In the old-line denominations, membership had begun to decline. Ministerial morale was also declining.

One year at Annual Conference I spoke on the mission of the church. I was addressing the problem of a church that had not adjusted from the situation of cultural support by the society to one in which, lacking that, it needed to become clear about what it was and what it was called to be. I was invited to tour the conference speaking in the various districts. I fear that I did not know how to take effective advantage of the opportunity.

I decided that such contributions as I could make would be theo-logical and consist in what I wrote. My theological writings had been directed chiefly to students of theology. The new awareness, along with practical experience teaching in theological seminaries, prepared me to involve myself to some extent in the national conversations about theological education. One of its leaders was my friend and dean, Joseph C. Hough, Jr. We wrote a book together on the topic. It received some discussion at the theoretical level, but, so far as I know, our proposals for curriculum reform were not seriously considered anywhere, certainly not in our own seminary.

I began writing for laypeople and writing about lay theology. I am not sure that this has been any more effective than the other efforts, but perhaps it has helped a few individuals. I wrote two books in story form: one on intercessory prayer and one on Christology. I also wrote two books on lay theology. I mentioned above a book on John Wesley that is, I think, readable by laypeople. I have shared in the efforts of the Process and Faith program, mentioned in the previous chapter, to help local congregations. These efforts include contributing to a book on what has come to be called "spirituality."

None of this amounts to much, but it does express a certain change in my sense of vocation. I finally realized that the problems of

Christianity are not just those of individual Christians. The form of
Christianity with which I most identified, including the denomination
to which I belonged, was rapidly declining. The only response I could
see was interest in techniques of church growth. I was deeply troubled
that the leaders of my denomination showed no signs of having any
sense of how it could recover vitality. In that situation, I felt that, as a
United Methodist theologian, I was called to respond in some way. I have
accomplished nothing of importance, but I am still glad that I tried.

More recently the situation has become even worse. The public image
of Protestantism is no longer provided by denominations like my own.
It is given by the religious right. It is now assumed that Protestants are
largely defined by their opposition to evolution, feminism, homosexuality, and abortion and by their support of rightwing economic policies,
American imperialism, and Zionism's most militant actions. Much of this
image of Protestantism has been formed by the prominence of renewed
apocalyptic expectations of a sort that had played no role in my experience
in the church. The spirit of this "Christian right" is far removed from the
broadly conservative Protestantism that was so widespread in Georgia in
my youth. Its methods, as in its takeover of the Southern Baptist Convention, are as shocking to many conservative Christians as to progressives.

Closely allied to this Protestant "religious right" is Catholic neo-
conservatism. Its militancy also expresses itself in its efforts to subvert the
regular leadership of denominations like mine with money coming from
outside the church. I refer here especially to the Institute for Religion
and Democracy. Its board is heavily Catholic, but its money comes from
persons committed to right-wing politics. These people still perceive the
old-line churches, such as the United Methodist, as obstacles to their
complete takeover of the United States. Accordingly, they provide funds
to undercut progressive leadership in these denominations. I have contributed marginally to publicizing the extent to which outside funds were
being used to intensify the problems of the United Methodist Church.

What can progressive Christians do under this onslaught? Not much,
perhaps. But still we cannot be completely quiescent. Since our denominations are not able to give strong progressive leadership, it seems necessary to develop parachurch organizations. These have been important
throughout much of the history of the church.

By parachurch organizations I do not mean ones that work against
the major institutions or are subversive of their leadership. I mean

ones that undertake to give a leadership to the expression of the faith that those with administrative responsibilities cannot give and that the regular budget of the institution cannot support or cannot be used to support. In Roman Catholicism the orders have played this role. In Protestantism much of the work of foreign and domestic missions was initiated by parachurch organizations. In Methodism for more than a century there has been a Methodist Federation for Social Action that has taken leadership in formulating positions many of which have subsequently been adopted by the denomination. Ecumenical and interfaith organizations are often "parachurch."

As noted briefly in the chapter on the Center for Process Studies, in 1995 conversations in our Process and Faith steering committee led us both to feel the urgency of a voice for progressive Protestantism and to recognize that trying to develop this only on the basis on our own rather marginal theology would not work. We needed to support the development of a fully independent organization. I felt responsibility to implement this idea.

For the Euro-American community, the flagship progressive congregation in southern California has long been All Saints Episcopal Church in Pasadena. Its rector, George Regas, had announced his plans to retire. I went to see him to discuss the possibility of bringing together a group of progressive Protestants to consider how to counteract the dominance of the right wing. We invited a group that met in Claremont and initially called itself simply "the Claremont Consultation." Regas and I were joined by Fred Register, the conference minister of the United Church of Christ, and for some time the three of us constituted the leadership of the organization.

For the first few months, Process and Faith and the Center for Process Studies provided logistical support, and for a considerably longer period its office remained that of Process and Faith. We spent a lot of time deciding what we wanted to be and do. Should we be just Protestant, or should we organize in union with Catholics and Jews? Should we be regional, or should we work on building a national organization? Should we focus on theology, on social action, on media, or something else?

It is often striking that about the time one group decides something must be done, similar decisions are being made elsewhere. James Adams came to our first meeting and told us of his plans to organize Progressive Christianity as a network of progressive Protestant churches across the country. We felt encouraged to move toward regional organization of members of churches. Both institutions now exist as do others around the country, notably, at least until quite recently, Protestants for the Common Good in Chicago, which was also established by participants in the process community.

Also, although we did not know it then, at the national level Christians and Jews were organizing the Interfaith Alliance. Learning this confirmed the decision to be a regional organization. Because the range of progressive concerns to which we were committed included some on which we differed with the Catholic hierarchy, we decided to remain predominantly Protestant. Nevertheless, for some purposes we functioned as the arm of the IFA in our region, and we enthusiastically welcomed Catholics, usually lay, who agreed with our goals.

In our region about the time we were taking shape, Clergy and Laity United for Economic Justice came into being as an effective action organization. And after 9/11 a number of leading Jews, Muslims, and Christians came together in Interfaith Communities United for Justice and Peace. We rejoice in this growth of progressive religious movements nationally and locally. Their presence guides our own self-definition.

The Claremont Consultation decided to make itself known through a conference, held at All Saints, and entitled it "Mobilization for the Human Family" to contrast our purposes with those of "Mobilization for the Family," which emphasized conservative "family values." We subsequently changed our name to that of the conference. Later we changed it again to "Progressive Christians Uniting."

In the beginning the whole group worked together on papers to be made available at our first conference. They were perforce prepared in haste, but we did publish a book entitled *Speaking of Religion and Politics: The Progressive Church Tackles Hot Topics* in time to be sold at the conference and to give a sense of who we were and how we thought. Westminster John Knox later published an improved version.

Subsequently the production of such papers has fallen on the Reflection Committee, which develops them at leisure and with greater care before sending them to the board for critique, revision, and, in most cases, eventual approval. I was chair of that committee throughout its life. In 2008 we published a second set of papers, better unified into a coherent volume. It argued that the progressive churches should shift from the model of social "reform" to the more radical model of "resistance."

We concluded our work with a volume on the relation of Christianity to other traditions, entitled "The Dialog Comes of Age."

George Regas was able to solicit a gift of $25,000, but our financial situation has always been precarious. The initial pattern of having the whole board work together on every project could not continue long. We needed more leadership. We employed Richard Bunce on a very limited basis. Although Bunce himself lived in Claremont, he led the organization to cut its nurse-strings to Process and Faith, to move to Los Angeles, and to establish itself in its full independence. That the organization survived was due to his sacrificial willingness to work full time for part-time pay.

When he retired, PCU faced a difficult situation. We needed a full-time leader with some staff, but at best our budget could only pay for part-time help. The rest must come from foundations. Such support was available only for programs. Hence the new leader would have to re-organize around programs. Instead of being a group of active Christians with minimal staff aid, PCU had to become a staff-operated institution only partly supported by members.

Providentially, Peter Laarman was looking for a new challenge, and despite warnings about the risks involved, he took the helm of PCU and reorganized it in the required direction. He has established himself as a leader among progressive NGOs in Los Angeles, developed a multi-faceted program, and attracted support from foundations.

Despite the deep change in its nature, the new PCU has maintained continuity with the old. This is especially true with respect to our work on the prison system. In the early days, we held a conference on the prison system attended by many people with relatives in those prisons and hence vividly aware of its problems and limitations. We raised a little money to produce study materials for churches.

A major reason for the severe overcrowding of California prisons is the criminalization of the use of drugs. There was a successful effort to move California's response to drug abuse away from punishment toward treatment. But those charged with administering the new program were not really supportive of it. We gave some leadership to efforts to monitor and improve implementation in Los Angeles, which has half the state's cases. Any claim we can make for these or other efforts must be quite modest. Perhaps the main result of our struggles to act out of progressive impulses has been to make PCU visible in Los Angeles as a "player."

Laarman built on this work and raised foundation funding to continue and expand our efforts. The new program is called "Justice not Jails," and it has been active at the state level" as well as in Los Angeles county. Progressive Christians strongly support the work of its staff.

Fortunately, this shift to staff-operated programming has been complemented by the emergence of local chapters that function on a purely volunteer basis. The most enduring is the Pomona Valley chapter that meets in Claremont. Its existence and effectiveness is due to the remarkable leadership of John Forney. I try to give support.

Its most important contribution thus far has been to bring significant speakers to Claremont under the rubric of "Agenda for a Prophetic Faith." Vernon Visick had such a program at Madison, Wisconsin, before he retired to Pilgrim Place, and he has worked closely with Forney to continue it in Claremont. The chapter also sponsors a weekly film dealing with social and ecological issues.

When Peter Laarman retired, once again the future became uncertain. A young man, Timothy Murphy, bringing insightful ideas and deep dedication to the church, has succeeded him. Whether PCU can pay his salary depends on the ever more difficult task of raising funds for programming from foundations. To survive without foundation funding will require re-envisioning and re-creating itself.

Perhaps, if there can be several local chapters, PCU can be reconstituted as a network of local groups. Perhaps these can work with progressive groups within the denominations, such as the Methodist Federation for Social Action. We believe the need for a strong progressive Protestant voice is as great as ever, perhaps greater. Perhaps Murphy can give the leadership we need for PCU to survive and flourish. We do not know. It is a formidable task!

With all its limitations and its financially ever-problematic future, I consider this initiative as success. Along with the other progressive parachurch organizations, we have made it a little more difficult for the public, and indeed for many people in the religious communities themselves, to view the religious right as the only, or even the chief, voice of Protestant Christianity in the United States. Rabbi Lerner has carried this shift further with his books, conferences, organizations, and his talk of "spiritual progressives" and of the left hand of God. And Jim Wallis has made it clear that to be an authentic "evangelical" does not mean that one abandons concern for the poor and oppressed.

While my efforts have been primarily to bring together the progressive leaders of the regional old-line Protestant churches, another, very different development is worthy of note. In the more biblicist churches there are encouraging theological stirrings. I have often claimed, in full sincerity, that process theology is more biblical than the philosophical theology that is widely regarded as orthodox. Among conservative Protestant scholars, a kind of scholastic hyper-orthodoxy has reigned. It emphasizes divine omnipotence and is willing to draw the logical consequences of that idea. It claims to justify all this on the basis of its close following of the Bible as the inerrant Word of God. However, it often builds more on Anselm than on Jesus and Paul.

Not all conservative biblicists have been comfortable with these emphases, since some of them belonged to the Wesleyan camp, but they acquiesced in the leadership of the high Calvinists. However, over the last few decades another voice has been heard. The most important figure is Clark Pinnock. He began his career as a part of this high Calvinist leadership, but step by step he moved away. No doubt his own experience was an important basis for this move, but his re-reading of scripture was crucial. He found an emphasis in the Bible on personal decision and responsibility that did not square well with the idea that God controlled everything. He began emphasizing human freedom. He was led by this to speak also of the openness of the future, such that God's omniscience includes knowledge of what will happen if creatures act in one way or another but not of human decisions not yet made. He paid more attention to Jesus and to Paul.

The similarities with process theology are obvious, and Pinnock did not let these stop him from pursuing his biblical study and reflection. Pinnock engaged in dialogue with the process theologian, Delwin Brown, some years ago. More recently we have met with him and other "open theologians" in conferences. Thanks to the initiative of Thomas Oord, process theologians do so regularly now at the American Academy of Religion annual meetings. It seems that issues of how we think realistically of God have virtually disappeared in the academic study of religion except among conservative theologians; so the future of that part of process theology may lie chiefly with them. If the more liberal churches abandon this topic, I think they abandon the future of the church to those who know that how we think of God is important. It is good that among the conservatives there are vigorous thinkers who will not be bound by a particular orthodoxy but are truly open to the biblical message.

Pinnock has paid a price for his openness and theological honesty. He barely survived a vote of exclusion from the Conservative Evangelical Theological Society. One objection to his work has been its proximity to process theology. Hence it is important to him politically, but probably personally as well, to emphasize differences. In doing so he picks up on the idea of God's self-limitation. This makes it possible to retain the idea of God's omnipotence while attributing to God's choice the fact of our freedom and responsibility. Many liberals have made the same move, although process theologians do not. Pinnock acknowledges that the idea of divine omnipotence is not strictly biblical, but he thinks it is too central to the tradition to abandon. Of course, the greater difference between Pinnock and process theology is his commitment to views of scripture that are alien to the "mainstream" theological community of which process theology has been a part.

It may be that a corner has been turned. The Christian right, with the support of President Bush, may have overplayed its hand. The Tea Party has grown out of the Religious Right. Initially it expressed some legitimate resentment at the alliance of the government and Wall Street against Main Street and the middle class. It included many who opposed American preoccupation with military and economic domination of the planet. Sadly, the movement was taken over by the power elite who dominate the popular media. They redirected white middle class anger against Wall Street's domination of Washington toward Washington's remaining New Deal policies of support for labor and minorities and concern to meet the basic needs of those not able to provide for themselves. Opposition toward global domination became opposition to the remnants of humanitarian aid and international cooperation.

Many conservative Protestants oppose this takeover of their faith by politicians exploiting the racism and social conservatism of many of their members so as to serve corporate interests. Some of these authentic conservatives are speaking up. Some recognize that the Bible speaks far more often about justice for the poor and oppressed than against abortion or homosexuality. As a minimum, these moderates want to regain some balance. If our old-line, more progressive denominations continue to fade away, an authentic biblical faith may well reassert itself among open-minded evangelicals. Some of them even adopt views, stemming from the Bible, that are remarkably congenial to process theology. I mourn the continuing decline of the denominations in which I feel most at home, but I feel some confidence that authentic forms of biblical faith will survive and flourish.

As a teacher in a school of theology my most significant contribution to the church has been through students. I believe that, despite its small size and the fact that many of our students have not gone into parish ministry, the Claremont School of Theology can be proud of the service its graduates have given to the church. Limiting myself to those whose committees I chaired, I can say emphatically that I am proud of my students. Of course, claiming that the school or I personally made much contribution to the effectiveness of a pastor is always questionable.

This is particularly questionable in regard to the pastor in whom I take the greatest pride. Cecil Murray (we call him "Chip") displayed his gifts before he came to Claremont. Our teacher of preaching made sure he was invited to be his successor. He would have been a great preacher without a seminary education and certainly regardless of his choice of seminary. He was, in fact, much more than that. He was appointed to a modest size AME church in Los Angeles and led it to become a congregation of 18,000. First AME (often called FAME) was also the center of low-cost housing and social services in the black community in Los Angeles. At least from the perspective of the larger community, Chip became the spokesperson for black Los Angeles. When he retired, with many distinguished persons present and speaking, we saw two videos made in his honor by presidents of the United States. His was a truly distinguished ministerial career.

But my pride in Chip Murray goes beyond that. Through all his success and with all his actual political power, he never wavered in his Christian humility. Indeed, one secret to his success was that no one ever thought he was seeking wealth or status. Everyone trusted him. He is one of my special "saints," and I am indeed proud to have been his teacher. I rejoice even more that he is my friend.

Many others have been effective pastors. For a while one of them was my bishop. Others have taught in seminaries with distinction. Several have been deans and presidents of seminaries. My pride in them is such that I wrote a chapter on them for this book. But I found it really did not fit well into my "reminiscences." This vague and general statement will have to do.

CHAPTER EIGHTEEN

Economism, Imperialism, and Money

I had one course in economics at Emory at Oxford. I have a faint memory of the corn/hog ratio, but nothing else. Accordingly, years later, when I began to recognize the immense importance of economic theory as the real "theology" of our world, I had little basis for entering the discussion. I continue to realize my severe limitations.

Nevertheless, I operate under the slogan "theology is too important to be left to the theologians, philosophy is too important to be left to the philosophers, biology is too important to be left to the biologists, and certainly economics is too important to be left to the economists." I am also one who joins the fools who march in where angels fear to tread.

In Chapter 11, I recounted how my first response to awareness of the ecological crisis was to examine and contribute to the rectification of church teaching. I noted that at official levels, that teaching has greatly improved. Sadly, what the church says on such matters is no longer of much importance in the public scene, where the real decisions about the fate of the earth are being made. That which shapes the most important policies relative to human relationships to the earth is economic theory geared to economic growth. This is measured for each nation by gross domestic product and for the world by gross world product.

From an early point in my awakened state, I saw that aiming at continual increase of economic activity was not compatible with preserving the Earth from further degradation. It remains astonishing to me that only now, in the wake of the global financial crisis, is there a faint beginning of discussion of better ways of evaluating real growth. Nearly half a century after the first Earth Day the simple point that endless growth in production is incompatible with the health of the Earth has not registered widely in the human consciousness. So far as I know, with the exception of Bhutan, regardless of what commitment they may have to the health of the environment, all the nations of the world are aiming at continued economic growth. This has been the shared goal of Communism and capitalism. It is not a topic of debate at the United Nations or within individual governments. It is not a topic of debate in universities either. Even environmental organizations rarely challenge it. Our world may be polytheistic, but economic growth is its highest god. The punishment for failure to worship this god can be severe.

It is especially sad to me that the church challenges this god so little. Jesus was very clear on this point. "You cannot serve God and wealth." But neither the biblical literalists, who claim to take every statement in the Bible as the direct word of God, nor the liberals, who want to follow Jesus, pay serious attention. Of course, there are wonderful exceptions! But the churches as a whole do not really oppose the reign of wealth as god. Still, in the church, unlike the university or the political world, the topic can be discussed.

I told in Chapter 12 about the conference, "Alternatives to Catastrophe," that some of us organized in 1972. I mentioned also that we had found one economist who was trying to revive the old idea of a stationary-state economy as an alternative to the growth economy taught in all our universities. It was certainly not an accident that he was a Christian who actually introduced theological language into his economic writings! He was also very concerned about ecological issues. Establishing a relationship with Herman Daly was for me the most important outcome of this conference. I was clear that there was an alternative to the economic theory that shaped the public world. I hoped that Daly would succeed in drawing attention to it.

Daly has pursued this matter in numerous writings. He did get considerable attention from environmentalists and evoked interest in some sectors of the church, especially the World Council of Churches. But his ideas were not discussed in the guild of economists. Indeed, he was excommunicated in a quite literal sense. That is, the guild would not communicate with him or even about him.

I had not previously realized quite how rigid are the requirements imposed by the various academic guilds for membership. They are much more rigid than the limits imposed by what were at that time still the mainline Protestant churches. These allowed discussion of atheism among their theologians. But the academic guild of economists would not allow any critical questioning of growth as the supreme goal.

The silencing of Daly was quite remarkable. His name did not appear in articles in economic journals even when there was a dismissive mention of his ideas. His colleagues at Louisiana State University systematically failed PhD students who came to work with him. He seriously considered an invitation to join the department of geography, since he would have been welcomed there. It seems that geography and anthropology departments resisted the fragmented approaches to their subject matter favored in the university. As a result such departments have been squeezed out of many universities.

He received an invitation to the World Bank. This would never have happened if the bank had been left to itself. But there was pressure on the bank to institute environmental impact studies of its projects. They needed to make a visible appointment to respond to this pressure, and Daly was their choice. From his point of view, the World Bank had the advantage over economics departments in universities in that the Bank had to pay *some* attention, however limited, to the actual effects of its policies.

Since Daly had lived in Brazil, had a Brazilian wife, and spoke Portuguese, he was assigned to the Brazilian desk. However, Brazil did not want him evaluating the environmental impact of its projects for developing the Amazon, and since it was a chief borrower from the World Bank, it had considerable clout. Daly was "kicked upstairs" to a research position where he was largely allowed to do what he wanted.

Years later a friend and admirer, Robert Costanza, was organizing an institute for public policy at the University of Maryland. He was strongly committed to the importance of the natural environment. The economist he wanted was Daly. However, the university administration could not appoint him to a position in economics without the approval of the economics department, which, of course, was not forthcoming. Only when Costanza raised money for a special chair, titled in such a way that its occupant need not be approved by the university's economists, could Daly be appointed.

Fortunately, while excluded from the guild of economists, Daly has had a significant and growing following. While at the World Bank he received numerous invitations to speak around the world. He has been awarded the Heinecken prize and recognized by the Nobel committee with a "Right-livelihood" award. The declaration of the Buddhist Kingdom of Bhutan that it aims at Gross National Happiness rather than Gross National Product has attracted wide notice. An international organization of "Ecological Economics" has emerged. Some "greening" of the GNP is widely discussed and sometimes implemented. But the world is paying a huge price for the slow pace of change.

There is restiveness even in university departments of economics. It is generally limited to recognizing that policies supported because they claimed to support growth have failed to do so. Some economists are seriously concerned that the supposed rising tide is lifting so few boats. They point to the impurity of programs they have previously supported as the reason they have misfired. This weakens the close alliance between corporations and economic experts. There may be openness to criticize even sacred theories. Indeed, there is now at least one university that has an economics department that takes Daly's work seriously.

I think it was in the late seventies that I began offering an occasional course dealing with economic issues. We read chiefly books by theological ethicists. Michael Novak was giving expression to his great enthusiasm for *laissez-faire* capitalism. It seemed important to examine his arguments theologically. Viewing them from the perspective of process theology, they seemed unacceptable. I gave occasional lectures on theology and economics.

When Charles Birch and I wrote our book on *The Liberation of Life,* (published 1982) we included a chapter on economic development. I have not changed my mind on what I wrote then. Nevertheless, we recognized that what a biologist and a theologian can say about economics is inevitably quite limited. Not long after that I asked Daly if he would work with me on a book on economics. He agreed, and in 1989 we published *For the Common Good.*

In the meantime, together with some students I took on a much more focused project in the field of economics. Not only did I think that economic growth was a poor goal of governmental policy, but also I was convinced that the Gross National Product and the Gross Domestic Product were poor measures of such growth. I mention both terms here, but since the difference is not significant for what we were doing, I will speak only of GNP hereafter. We thought that if the misleading character of these ways of evaluating progress was demonstrated, the critique of present practice might be taken seriously. There might then be support for proposing alternatives, especially if we provided a plausible one. Because of our interest in being taken seriously by economists, we limited ourselves to measures that in principle they approved.

It is universally acknowledged that the GNP, or even per capita GNP, does not measure the economic well-being of the people of a country. For example, it rises dramatically during a war, even while people are suffering all kinds of shortages and destruction. Earthquakes and tidal waves lead to increases in the GNP because of the expenditures on emergency relief, medical care, and especially rebuilding. The reason that catastrophes increase GNP statistics is partly that nothing is subtracted because of the destruction. Similarly, if a Third World country cuts down its forests and sells the wood, its GNP rises; nothing is subtracted for the loss of its natural resource or the erosion and other destruction that follow.

Another well-recognized limitation of GNP is that it does not count housework. Obviously cooking, cleaning, and repairing the home as well as taking care of the yard are economic activities that contribute as much to economic welfare as anything done in the market place. The same is true of childcare. Given this omission, when a second parent goes to work, far more is added to GNP than to economic well-being. The added income, obviously, is counted. But the extra costs involved in earning this income are also added: more meals in restaurants, additional clothing, a second car, and childcare. Whether the reduced parental care is a loss for the child is, of course, not considered at all.

I will not go into further details. I mean only to say, we were not being radical or breaking with the economic literature in saying that a more accurate measure of improvement of real economic well-being would be possible. Hence we hoped that our proposal might be taken seriously even within the establishment.

We should have been forewarned of its actual indifference. In the 1960s there were many criticisms of the overuse of the GNP and calls for a better measure. Nordhaus and Tobin responded with what they called a Measure of Sustainable Economic Welfare. They did a lot of fine work. They showed that by their improved measure, between 1929 and 1965 sustainable economic welfare grew about two-thirds as much as per capita GNP. They acknowledged the difference but concluded that the two correlated sufficiently that there was no need to pursue alternatives to GNP measures.

When one looks at smaller time periods in their study one finds great variety. There are even times when the two measures move in opposite directions. Most important, during the last eighteen years of the period they studied, while per capita GNP grew by 48%, sustainable welfare grew by only 7.5%. That is, during the period most likely to indicate what was ahead, instead of growing at two-thirds the rate of GNP it grew less than one-sixth as fast. Surely it is not rational for economists to conclude that this correlation is so close that there is no need to consider further whether economic policy should be guided only by growth of GNP!

We thought that it might be worthwhile to extend their study another twenty years. This did not prove possible or desirable. It was not possible because some of the statistics they used were no longer available. It was not desirable because they did not include any environmental factors, and these were important to us. Hence we decided to start afresh to study the post-World War II period.

Unfortunately, only one member of the group had the expertise needed to carry out this project, and she did not have the time. We struggled along. Fortunately, my son Cliff returned from international travels, and I cajoled him into taking over the project. He was reluctant because he is highly suspicious of statistical arguments of this sort as was Daly. My argument was not that we would ever have a realistic statistical measure of human well-being or even of economic welfare, but that it was important to dethrone the GNP from its dominant role. Cliff had a masters degree from Berkeley in public policy, which was sufficient background to find his way around in the literature. The index in its completed form is his work.

By our figures, the correlation of our per capita Index of Sustainable Economic Welfare and per capita GNP was quite high in the 1950s. However from 1959 to 1989, while per capital GNP nearly doubled, per capital ISEW grew by only 10 per cent. Furthermore, in the 1980s, while per capita GNP rose by around one-fifth, per capita ISEW declined slightly. (For details, please consult the appendix to *For the Common Good*, 1994 edition.)

Actually, our figures were more favorable to GNP than were those of Nordhaus and Tobin during the period of overlap. The reason was that they included measures of leisure, whereas we did not. Since leisure has declined over the years, and leisure is considered a positive value in standard economic theory, the inclusion of leisure depressed their welfare figures. In their index, leisure overwhelmed everything else in its importance and yet there was great uncertainty as to how to evaluate it. We decided that a measure that omitted it had a better chance of being considered. If we had included figures for leisure, based on any of the ways Nordhaus and Tobin proposed to evaluate it, our index would have shown a considerable loss of economic welfare throughout the period while per capita GDP more than doubled.

We included only one item that economists in general prefer to leave out, that is, a measure of inequality. We judge that people are economically better off when the gap between the rich and the poor declines. Many economists do not agree.

I paid a number of leading economists to critically evaluate our work. We published the results and learned a little from them that led to minor revisions. One insisted that our omission of leisure was a serious weakness. I am glad to say that the organization, Redefining Progress, which took over our work and makes annual reports on their Genuine Progress Indicator (GPI), found a way of introducing changes in leisure that do not overwhelm the index. The results are, of course, more strongly indicative than ours that GNP (or, now, GDP) is no indication at all of sustainable economic welfare, much less human well-being in general. Its continued use as a measure of something desirable is wrong. Basing economic decisions on it is outrageous.

I have written about this project in more detail than it deserves because at that time I was quite absorbed by it. I thought I had hold of something practical with a realistic chance of influencing the direction of public policy. Surely it was evident that governments should not take as their goal changes in economic activity that did not benefit people, even when people's well-being is considered only in economic terms. I thought there was a real chance of getting the support even of some economists.

Step by step I have been forced to recognize that expecting rationality from members of academic guilds is naïve. Faithfulness to the norms of those guilds plays a far larger role. The idea that the university is dedicated to the advancement of knowledge while the church is stuck on arbitrary beliefs is far from the truth. And, of course, the powers that be profit from our dedication to increased economic activity regardless of its effects on human beings.

In spite of the indifference of both governments and economists to our proposal, it has not gone altogether unnoticed. A good many reviewers of *For the Common Good* paid attention to the index. Similar indices have been compiled in perhaps a dozen other countries. Mark Anielski appreciates our work and has carried it much further with some real effects. Indeed, some recognition of the need for better measures is now widespread, and the GPI is recognized as a prime example. There are occasional indications that one government or another may develop some alternative to the GDP, possibly influenced, directly or indirectly by our work. China seems to have gone farthest in this direction. One never knows what seeds may sprout—or where. I judge in retrospect that while our hopes were unrealistic, we did not waste our time.

Daly and I had in our minds as we wrote our book a title like "Economics for Community." What we saw most lacking in economic theory was any interest in relations among human beings other than those of contract and exchange, or in the relation of human beings to the other creatures, animate or inanimate. The result was that economic policies growing out of economic theory consistently destroyed human communities and the natural context of human life. We are grateful that the editor persuaded us to use the much less descriptive title 'For the Common Good," since the use of that phrase as the book title may have contributed to a revival of the phrase and even of the idea. The phrase has taken on a life of its own, one of which we fully approve.

Probably my most important contribution to the book was in the chapter on trade. Economists often write as if the principle of comparative advantage demonstrates that free trade is beneficial to all trading partners. In reading Ricardo I noticed quite naively that he said that the principle works only because capitalists prefer to invest in their own country. It does not work between different parts of the same country because within the country capital moves freely to the place where it can be invested most profitably. When capital is in fact not mobile, the argument from comparative advantage to free trade works reasonably well. I make a special claim to leadership on this point since Daly admits that when I sent him a draft of the chapter making it, his first reaction was that I needed to be educated.

Whereas the relative immobility of capital may have been a relevant consideration in Ricardo's day, it is wholly inapplicable to the world of our time. This means that if there is any argument for free trade in our world, it is not this one. "Comparative advantage" should disappear from the discussion but, alas, it has not done so. Realizing the irrelevance of

this argument to our world has at least freed some of us from any lingering commitment to "free" trade, which in our world means the freedom
of capital to exploit labor and resources wherever they are cheapest. It
certainly does not leave much freedom for nations to protect their people
or their environment. Further, the nations that have successfully developed by standard GDP measures, such as Japan, South Korea, Taiwan,
Hong Kong, Singapore, and China, have done so, not by free trade, but
by skillful management of the national economy. It is true that they take
advantage of the openness of other economies, especially our own.

In structuring our book we made use of Whitehead's "fallacy of
misplaced concreteness." We argued that economists have been particularly prone to this fallacy at particularly important places in their theories. The most obvious of these is with respect to "money." Yet we did
not include a chapter on money or finance. Daly thought the topic too
difficult. When our publisher encouraged us to produce a revised edition, I persuaded Daly to try. Unlike most of the book, in which we both
contributed to almost all the chapters, my only role in this chapter was
to read what he wrote and ask for clarification. Until I could understand
what money is and how it comes into being, I thought, most of our readers would also have problems. To avoid restructuring the whole book,
we made Daly's essay an appendix to the revised edition. I consider it a
valuable addition.

What I learned from Daly is that money is credit, and that credit is
always debt. I learned that what banks lend is not the money of deposi-
tors but money they create simply by bookkeeping. Although the money
is destroyed by repayment, the bank profits by receiving interest on what
it has created out of thin air. And in order that borrowers pay back what
they owe with interest, more and more debt must be created. The system
is inherently unsustainable.

Later I learned how this has played out in history. I learned, for
example, that the tax on tea was a minor factor in causing the American
Revolution. Far more important was the depression that resulted when
the Bank of England got parliament to stop the creation of money by
the colonies. I now understand that the interference of England with the
desire of wealthy colonialists to profit from lands in the west may have
played a decisive role. In any case, my most helpful teacher with regard
to the historical importance of the control of money creation is Ellen
Brown, whose *Web of Debt* was for me a revelation. David Graeber's

Debt: the First 5,000 Years shows us how debt has destroyed healthy societies, turning them into slave societies, for millennia. The necessity for the biblical "jubilee," that is, the occasional cleaning of the slate, is made clear. We return to Brown to learn how to overcome the destructive role of debt. She has laid out the needed policies in *The Public Bank Solution*. Once one's eyes are truly open to the nature of money and how it is created, the problems of all societies and their solutions appear in new light.

When we had finished writing *For the Common Good*, I felt a new confidence in addressing the issues of the real world. For example, I could see immediately that NAFTA would benefit only the capitalists, leaving the people impoverished and breaking the power of unions. Economic issues played a large role in my speaking and writing. To make clear that I was addressing the issue as a theologian, I called what I was opposing "economism." I think it is a good term, but my notion that I was original in coining it was mistaken. I collected some of my essays in *Sustainability* and *Sustaining the Common Good*.

I became keenly interested in the Bretton Woods Institutions and especially the World Bank. With respect to the International Monetary Fund and the successive rounds of agreements on tariffs and trade that led to the World Trade Organization, I felt comfortable and secure to be simply in opposition. But with the World Bank, it was different. It had many fine projects, and many of the people who worked there were deeply dedicated to helping developing countries. Yet it seemed to me that overall the World Bank did more harm than good. I judged that this was because it accepted the dominant neo-liberal economic theories that Daly and I had criticized. Still I thought it worthwhile to study the Bank in some detail. I wrote a book that set a study of the World Bank in the context of a broader discussion of economism. Unfortunately, it ended up being priced out of the market.

I developed the habit of interpreting most of what happened in the world in terms of economic motivations. I often spoke about the succession of "religions" or organizing commitments in European history. I moved from Christianism, whose dominance ended with the Treaty of Westphalia, to nationalism, whose dominance ended with the restructuring of Europe after World War II, and to economism as the now dominant religion. I pointed out that the end of an "ism" seems to occur only through events that display its horrific consequences: the Thirty Years War, which devastated continental Europe in the first half of the seventeenth century, and World War II, three centuries later, which devastated much of the planet and was accompanied by genocide of European Jews.

The only hopeful message I could derive from this periodization of history was the shortening of these epochs. Christianism lasted a thousand years, nationalism only three hundred years. But I fear that the destructive consequences of even a century of economism will be irreversible ruin for the planet. I sometimes feel that the remnants of nationalism provide a healthy check on economism. Islam, which never gave way to nationalism as a genuine "religion" in the sense of binding together, also offers some resistance, but I was not as aware of that at the time I wrote. I looked for signs of the rise and possible ascendancy of Earthism as a vision and commitment that could supersede economism and save the world. In this context I interpret U.S. policies, domestic and foreign, as expressing the economic interests of the elite. I included this theological periodization of history in my book on the World Bank, but because that book was unpurchasable, it has made no contribution to the ongoing discussion.

I find this a fruitful approach. However, it did not prepare me for the type of idealism of the neo-conservatives. I tried to understand them in economistic terms but became convinced this was inaccurate. Theirs was a nationalism that had become fully imperialist. They wanted to impose American hegemony on the whole planet. Some of them, at least, genuinely believed that doing so would be beneficial to the subjugated people.

I remain convinced that the neo-conservatives would not have been able to shape policy as they have without the support of the economic elite. In the long run it may appear that they were used by that elite and then discarded when their actions were no longer in the economic interest of the elite. But at least in the interim, we must deal with neo-conservative imperialist ideology on its own terms.

Their astonishing influence after 9/11 stems, in part, from the fact that they provided a clear vision of where we should go, and no competing visions have been offered. There are many who assume that foreign affairs should be conducted pragmatically with the immediately apparent interests of the United States decisively in view. But they do not put these short-term apparent interests into any large context, as the neo-conservatives do. They may raise objections and cautions with regard to actions proposed by the neo-conservatives, but they do not propose a different direction.

Accordingly I have joined others in decrying American imperialism. As Christians we must oppose it. Catherine Keller held a conference on the subject at Drew in September 2003. Subsequently in Claremont several of us gave lectures to continue the discussion. Westminster John Knox has published (2006) *The American Empire and the Commonwealth of God.* We hope events will make the book out-of-date before long, but it still seems all too relevant.

For one who awakened to the global environmental crisis in 1969, watching the national and international behavior of the United States during the past forty years has been depressing. The eight years of George W. Bush's presidency intensified that depression. Almost everything our nation did was the opposite of what we needed to be doing for the sake of the world. The ultimate crisis became more and more imminent, while corporate control of our government tightened and consolidated in its opposition to any program that threatened its power or profits. AIPAC also tightened its control over American policy in the Near East supporting American imperialism there. The Bush administration reduced the independence of the CIA and the military, reshaping them into centers of nationalist and imperialist thinking. The Supreme Court became more supportive of all these regressive moves. Serious investigative reporting became rarer and rarer, so that the press in general avoided many of the real issues and became largely an organ of the right wing. Punishment of whistleblowers became more severe.

I shared in relief when Bush was replaced by Obama. However, I did not expect much change from the election of a Democratic president. Before he became president Bill Clinton had organized the New Democratic Leadership, which was designed to assure the corporate world that the Democrats were no longer a threat. His election reduced the Democratic opposition, rooted in labor and environmental concerns, to NAFTA, so that it was the Democrats who brought this fateful "agreement" upon us. The Democrats were marginally more supportive of "environmental" policies, but did nothing to postpone the catastrophes toward which the world was headed. By Clinton's time, the actual program of the Democrats was to the right of Richard Nixon.

I became less and less happy about calling myself a Democrat. John Quiring, a key person at the Center for Process Studies, had become an active Green, and when he approached me to join, I quickly agreed. At least the Green Party platform was one I could affirm, and the party was serious in its affirmations. Ralph Nader was never a member of the Green Party, but he was its candidate when Gore ran against Bush. My Democratic friends were quite angry with the Green Party because it took votes that would otherwise go to the Democrats. The Green Party only sought votes in states that were solidly Democratic or Republican so as not to damage Gore's chances in swing states, but Nader himself did not conform to this rule entirely. When Gore lost by so narrow a margin, many Democrats blamed Nader's candidacy. Although Nader's support in Florida was small, it was claimed that it took enough votes from Gore to give the state to Bush.

The problem of a third party is certainly a difficult one in our political system. If there is any significant difference between the two major parties, it does matter which one wins the presidency. Nader virtually denied that there was any difference, since both were controlled by corporate interests. But the great majority of Greens disagreed. If in fact running a third party candidate throws the election to the worse of the major parties, any effort to organize for what one believes becomes problematic. One has to take seriously the argument that persons who follow the Green platform should work in the Democratic Party to move it in the green direction.

However, I remain unpersuaded. In the first place, blaming the loss of Florida on the Greens is quite arbitrary. In fact Gore won Florida. One must consider other causes for his official loss than the Green vote. Further, the Republicans used unethical and almost certainly illegal tactics to intimidate black voters. In subsequent elections such tactics have been developed and greatly enhanced. But the Democratic Party has yet to take strong action against voter intimidation, which is likely in the future to distort elections by the hundreds of thousands if not millions. One could point out that if Gore had won his home state, the election would have been his. Apparently he unwisely took it for granted. At most, if one listed all the ways things might have been done differently that would have made Gore president, the absence of Nader's candidacy would be only one of many.

There is a more important reason for not giving up on the Democratic Party than any responsibility the Greens may have for putting Bush in office. There have been Democrats who would have the strong support of Greens. Kucinich was an outstanding example. He ran for nomination for the presidency in the Democratic primary. My guess is that a

third of Democratic voters or more agreed with his ideas. If most of them
had voted for him in the primary, there would have been a great boost
to his standing in the party and the proposals he makes in Congress. But
most of those who agreed with him did not support him. They thought
they should vote for a "serious" candidate. Many of them had difficulty
deciding between Hilary Clinton and Barack Obama, but they voted
for one of these in order not to "throw their vote away." This attitude of
progressive Democrats insures that they will vote in the primary only for
those Democrats who raise a lot of money. This requires adopting views
accepted by a large segment of the corporate leadership. This means also
that only centrists can be nominated, and the Republicans have been
quite successful in moving the center farther and farther to the right. I
feel the need to support the resistance movement.

The idea of a politics of "resistance" became a serious topic of discussion among progressives during the late years of Bush's presidency, at least
in Christian circles. We despaired of stopping aggressive wars and the
concentration of wealth and power in fewer and fewer hands. It seemed
impossible to deflect policies that hastened disaster for the whole planet.
Yet we felt that as Christians we could not simply allow ourselves to be
swept along without protest. We had to find some way to resist.

Although the idea of "resisting" had not played much role among
progressive Christians, George Pixley persuaded the Reflection Committee
of Progressive Christians Uniting that our next publication should center
on this idea. Under that heading, we put together a group of essays that
worked together as a book, and Westminster John Knox agreed to publish
it. The full title is *Resistance: The New Role of Progressive Christians*.

Ironically, the campaign and victory of Obama, which we all cheered,
changed the mood, so that the title has probably reduced interest in the
book. Obama's election renewed the sense that positive change might
take place through democratic processes after all. In that case, progressive
Christians' role would not be resistance but rather vigorous support.

Actually, the lesson of Obama's presidency is that the structure of
power in this country is now such that even a president is narrowly circumscribed with respect to what he can do. Government is controlled far
more by money than by people. Commitments made around the world
and supported by powerful interests at home cannot easily be undone.
Such critical needs as medical care for all can be enacted only if they do
not threaten corporate interests. A one-payer system that would provide

better results much less expensively is simply not on the table. Still there was a better chance for more people to get coverage under a Democratic government than a Republican one. There was still a difference between the two parties, even if both were subservient to economic interests. If the only way a bill can get through Congress is by forcing more people to buy insurance from the for-profit health care industry, then that is the lesser of two evils.

Similarly, the kinds of changes that might save the world from ecological catastrophe cannot be considered, but marginal improvements are possible, and we should support them. It seems that we need to work the system for whatever gains are possible. But working for incremental gains can easily draw us back into the system that remains fundamentally destructive.

The difficult task is to oppose the system as a whole while continually working within it for improvement wherever that is possible. Far from being outdated, it is clearer than ever that we are called to resist. Perhaps, the prophetic importance of Pixley's message and the book that embodies it will be recognized.

The financial crisis and the government's response re-enforces my conviction. Wall Street dictated policies that led to its collapse. It then demanded huge sums of money, beyond any previously conceived, to save it and restore its wealth. What it demanded it received. It seemed completely indifferent to public opinion. Any difference in the treatment of Wall Street between Republican and Democratic administrations is superficial. Wall Street may allow a few token gestures toward preventing the recurrence of collapse, but apparently nothing more. Neither Congress nor the administration is free to consider real changes that would depose Wall Street's hegemony. We should strongly support those who work for regulations that marginally restrict Wall Street's behavior. But we should recognize that this is not the answer. And we should recognize that by putting Obama in the presidency Wall Street co-opted the energies of liberals and quieted what could otherwise have been strong opposition from Democrats to bailing it out. Our masters are skillful manipulators, and most of us allow ourselves to be used with little protest.

The commitment to global capitalism and to American imperialism has not lessened under Obama. The erosion of democratic practices has accelerated. Human rights have eroded further. Punishment of whistleblowers has intensified. Yes, there are differences between the two major parties, but Wall Street gets its way through playing them off against each other on issues about which it is indifferent in exchange for slavish obedience on matters important to it.

But what form can resistance take with any meaningful chance of making a difference? If we resist simply in order to feel better about ourselves, it is hardly worth it. The best answer I can come up with is that we can resist by identifying fundamental alternatives to the system to which we have become accustomed and spreading interest in these alternatives as far as possible. Thus far, when there is a crisis, few suggestions are made of alternatives that are well thought out and have significant segments of public opinion behind them. We can work to develop such proposals and to gain as much support for them as possible. When another collapse occurs, public anger might be mobilized in support of radical needed change.

For example, an increasing number of people now understand that the Federal Reserve belongs to the banks and is their instrument rather than the servant of a government beholden to the people. It could be nationalized. If it were, money could be issued by the U.S. treasury rather than a bank-owned bank. Even more important it would then be possible to monetize the national debt. That is, we could pay it off gradually by issuing new money. This would end our need to pay interest on the national debt. Banks now create new money as they issue credit many times the amount of deposits. This very profitable role of private banks could be abolished. If the government alone created money it would be able to meet the needs of the people including the needs of businesses to borrow money. Wall Street's domination of the nation would cease.

Short of such changes at the national level, the creation of state banks could alleviate many of our problems. North Dakota has had one for years, and it is currently almost alone among states in having a budget surplus. Whereas the changes proposed at the national level will long be dismissed as impossible or dangerous, the existence of a successful case makes such dismissal more difficult at the state level. Most people, including most legislators, have simply never considered this possibility. Once considered, it might rapidly prove attractive.

Meanwhile resistance can also consist in shouting from the housetops that our present system is rotten and shares in leading us to global disaster. We should not be so fearful of leading people to despair or being dismissed as alarmists that we fail to speak the truth. To speak the truth is to resist the lies that now so widely shape our national life.

When I become completely cynical about the possibility of trying to get needed change at the national level, I note that public opinion and organized popular pressure seem to have recently affected Obama on several points. It has at least delayed his planned military intervention in Syria; it has led him to postpone approval of the tar sands pipeline, arousing the anger of the corporate world; and it has slowed down the granting of fast-track to the Transpacific Partnership. If the people's action succeeds in permanently de-railing any of these, it will show that democracy has not died completely.

My hope that Obama is not simply a creature of the established powers has also been strengthened by his recent speech at West Point. The attack upon it by the establishment suggests that it did not have their prior approval. Although the policies it proposes are very far from those we really need, it proposes more restraint on the U.S. use of military power than the dominant elite desires. They no longer trust him. Perhaps we are discovering the real Obama, in distinction from the instrument of the powers that be. Eisenhower, in his farewell address spoke the truth. Perhaps we can hope for some truth from Obama. But speaking it would take enormous courage on his part. Most Americans would be persuaded by the media to consider him a fool, and many would say they would never again vote for a man of his race. Whatever his courage, he is unlikely to take such a step.

CHAPTER NINETEEN

Censorship and Conspiracy Theory

To speak the truth requires knowing the truth or at least being clear that much of what we assume to be true about public events is false. In a general sense I have long had a skeptical attitude toward official events. I explained in Chapter 1 that attending a Canadian school in Japan as a Southerner from the United States, I could not help but become aware that in authoritative sources, public events are described in very diverse ways. Decades later, President Eisenhower told us on one day that the U.S. had no spy planes and then a few days later had to admit that the Soviet Union had shot one down. I regard Eisenhower as one of our more honorable presidents. Hence the incident made clear that official accounts and presidential statements are instruments of policy rather than sources of information. Some may be true and accurate, but the fact that we are told something by our government is in itself no evidence of its truth.

Sadly, we cannot turn for the "facts" to the media. Of course, much that is reported is relatively accurate. I have general confidence in the sports section of the paper. But with respect to political and international events, the media today do not help in distinguishing reality from "spin." They even add to the spin themselves. The distinction between news and editorial position has blurred badly. As I write there is astonishing spin on support by the United States of a revolt in Syria against an otherwise stable regime by multiple dissidents including Al Qaeda. We continue to promote civil war despite clear evidence that the great majority of citizens want the rebellion to end.

When there were many papers reflecting diverse political views, there was some chance of learning to distinguish facts from spin. But today

235

virtually all the media represent the corporate and official government perspective. Even so, one can learn to trust some papers more than others and some journalists more than others. At times in the past a good many journalists sought the truth behind what was publicly available. But investigative journalism has declined greatly. For the most part when we read our papers or listen to radio or television, we can suppose that part of what we read or hear is true, but which part is another question.

I have lived in the academic world, and the work of academicians is somewhat more reliable than that of the media. Of course, this helps only indirectly to understand what is currently happening, since scholarly articles and books appear only much later. One also learns that truth as such is not the only determinant of the behavior of scholars and scientists. Some are in the service of those with political agendas. Some subordinate their science or their scholarship to the desires of their employers or those who pay for their research. However, I dare to believe that these problems of personal corruption are not really extensive.

The problem is much deeper. Academic disciplines set boundaries to acceptable discourse just as firmly as do corporate interests. There are topics that are taboo, and on acceptable topics there are interpretations of the data that are not acceptable. The taboos are enforced by the guilds through supervision of doctoral research, selection of faculty from among the applicants, financial support of research, acceptance of articles in journals, and acceptance of books for publication. If none of this suffices, and something improper slips through, there remains the possibility of ignoring it or blasting it in reviews. Students learn not to refer to these writings in their term papers or theses.

In an earlier chapter I illustrated this problem briefly with respect to physics and more fully with respect to the economic guild and Herman Daly. The economic guild is committed to the increase of economic activity and organizes itself to study how that is achieved. Daly emphasized that economic activity is already at a level that threatens the planetary future and that economists should be studying how to meet human needs with a steady-state economy. This was not an acceptable topic for the guild; so Daly has been excommunicated. His writings have been excluded from the corpus of acceptable economics.

More briefly, I have described how similar practices obtain in physiological psychology, biology, and cosmology. Indeed, there is a doctrinaire definition of science as such that strongly discourages any suggestion that there can be action at a distance or an influence of subjective experience on what happens in the world. Whole ranges of topics are not discussed and vast bodies of evidence are ignored. I recommend a study of Rupert Sheldrake's career and his description of the present state of science. So far as I can see, he is accurate. The response of the orthodox community is not serious argument or analysis but simply an effort to silence him. This all became publicly apparent through his recent You Tube presentation and the controversy that followed.

More broadly, parapsychology as a whole is excluded from consideration in the American university. This is not based on absence of evidence for particular parapsychological claims. Actually the military and the security establishment are quite interested and try to make use of phenomena of this sort. For a while a few laboratories existed in universities, but no matter how carefully they observed scientific protocol, the scientists involved were marginalized and their opportunity to work in a university context has been virtually ended. For academics in any field to take parapsychology seriously is likely to be damaging to their careers. This is true also in theology, but the whole field of theology is rejected by academia; so the rules are less strict. Nevertheless, academic writings by theologians rarely make positive affirmations about parapsychology or make use of parapsychological ideas.

David Griffin, nevertheless, recognized the important role in religious literature of reports of faith healings and other occurrences that belong to the sphere of parapsychology. He considered the topic worthy of systematic attention and devoted a year to reading the literature in the field. His book, *Parapsychology, Philosophy, and Spirituality: a Postmodern Exploration,* was greatly appreciated by the extra-academic parapsychological community but ignored in theological circles and the academy generally. Especially since it is written from the perspective of process thought, I regard it as the most reliable guide into this important and neglected field.

More recently I have marginally extended my suspicion. I am sure that the great majority of academics and even leaders of major guilds do not intend to simply be servants of the rich and powerful. Nevertheless, I now have little doubt that they often function in this way. A key case is economics. I once, naively, supposed that economists seriously studied money and finance. Since finance is now unquestionably the dominant element in the business community in this country,

understanding it would seem to be a central goal of economic research.
It is not. Money is naively defined and then ignored in mainstream
economics departments.

There is now an excellent body of writing on this topic, but its
chief authors, such as Stephen Zarlenga, Thomas Greco, Ellen Brown,
and David Graeber do not teach in departments of economics. Further,
it appears that their writings are not studied there. This may be only
because there are no courses in which they fit. But if the reason is only
that economics is defined so narrowly that it excludes major discussions
of money and finance, one would expect openness to a new department
focused on money and finance. My suspicious mind has come to the conclusion that the financial institutions do not want finance to be studied,
and that the universities cooperate in insuring that the "experts" they
produce remain ignorant of the more important matters.

My disillusionment with the academic establishment has led me to
examine some of the books and periodicals my peers had taught me to
dismiss as irresponsible. In this literature I have been introduced to ideas
and attitudes that I continue to find repugnant, but also to facts and to
features of past events of which I had not heard. I remain surprised that
the relevant guilds seem to suppress so much evidence.

I now take it as at least highly probable, for example, that some
undersea ruins of large stone buildings were flooded at the end of the
last ice age. This seems to be the physical evidence. But if so, the story of
human civilization that I have taken for granted is drastically misleading.
I have been taught that the first cities were built around 5000 years ago.
I now learn that some were destroyed 12,000 years ago. Perhaps this is
being vigorously discussed in academia and in "respectable" journals. But
I am shocked that I had to learn it from "unrespectable" sources. I cannot
see that economic interests are here at stake; so I assume that we are dealing with the conservatism of the relevant guilds. My view of the modern
university is not improved.

Process thought has not suffered complete exclusion from academia,
but participants in this movement know that our work is marginalized
in almost all fields. Hence our antennae are up for the possible value of
what is marginalized or even wholly excluded by the various guilds. This
attitude of skepticism toward the current "authorities" is deep seated. We
are fully open to the evidence on any topic that the authorities are correct, but we need the evidence. Their systematic exclusion of "heretics"

and their frequent efforts to silence them, increase my suspicion that they often have no evidence to offer.

What does this have to do with conspiracy theory? The relation is indirect, but important. The label "conspiracy theory" is used to cause people to ignore or reject whatever those who control the media choose to describe in this way. It is implied that it is foolish to suppose that groups of powerful people plan any of the events that change the course of history. Or more accurately, it is foolish to do so if any of those powerful people are thought to be members of any branch of the American government or leaders in the American plutocracy. There is no objection to attributing conspiracies to the rich and powerful in countries that are not allied with us especially if they are Arabs or Muslims.

I am not aware of any evidence that the rich and powerful in the United States and its allies are incapable to the sort of actions that similar people have engaged in throughout history and continue to act out. The appeal to "American exceptionalism" has never been convincing to me. I am certainly not aware of any evidence that such powerful people never consult with one another about how to achieve their shared ends or that their morals are such that they would never consider killing their enemies. I have been explaining that in other fields I have long opposed this method of blocking thoughtful consideration of alternate theories.

Since I do not regard the government, the media, or the university as reliable sources of real understanding of the world and what transpires in it, I am left to sift what evidence I can. With respect to the assassinations (and attempted assassinations) of key progressive leaders, such as, but not limited to the Kennedy brothers and Martin Luther King, the fact that the official story is always that a lone gunman conceived and executed the killing does not convince me that in fact the reality is always a lone gunman. Indeed, my inclination is to think that this explanation should be accepted only after other, more plausible, theories have been disproved.

It is *possible* that the shooter has had no encouragement or assistance from anyone else and has acted without consultation with anyone, but the weight of evidence in favor of that account would need to be considerable in order to convince me. One would expect an inquiry into his connections and into those with whom he has been in contact. But no such inquiry is conducted. How our government always knows so quickly that no one else is implicated I cannot imagine. And in fact the individuals who are credited with outwitting the entire security establishment of the United States, without assistance from anyone, do not appear to be of the caliber of the comic book superheroes who might pull something of this sort off.

When a leader who is feared and hated by very powerful people is assassinated, my initial guess is that some of those people are behind it. I have seen no reason to give up this more intrinsically probable expectation. Yes, it is a "conspiracy theory." No, that is no reason to doubt it

The clearest case is the assassination of Martin Luther King. The official story was totally unconvincing to the King family. Their efforts to get the government to investigate based on evidence they provided got no result. They hired an investigator who found a great deal of evidence about what actually happened. Since the government provided no place for presenting this evidence, they brought charges in court against a minor participant in the plot. They persuaded a Memphis jury that the government at several levels participated in the assassination. The transcript of the trial is available on the King family website.

About the time of this trial there was another one, of O.J. Simpson, which was very well covered although it had little actual importance. However, no newspaper sent a reporter to cover the King trial. To its credit, at the very end the *New York Times* reported the verdict, but of course did so in such a way as to attract minimum attention. I am told there was an obscure report in the *Washington Post* as well. But due to the unanimous judgment of the media that the question of who actually killed King was of trivial interest, very few Americans know about this trial and its outcome. So much for a free press!

Years later a friend launched a truly magnificent magazine, which he called *Empirical.* He explained that he referred to the radical empiricism of William James and Alfred North Whitehead. He advertised his commitment to truth. I asked him if he was serious, and he said he was. I then asked whether he would publish the first article ever about the King trial. He had no previous background in the conspiracy world, but he investigated and agreed to publish. The article would just report the facts about the trial and the lack of publicity. It would take no position on whether the verdict was correct or why there was no publicity. Another friend, Matthew Witt, very well versed in these matters, wrote the article and it was published. Sadly, soon after that, the man whose financial support had made *Empirical* possible died abruptly. I hope his death was not the result of the courage of the editor. I do not want to feel responsible for the death of an individual and the demise of a wonderful magazine. But it is hard not to worry.

On September 11, 2001, no one supposed that a single individual was responsible. All theories about this event are conspiracy theories. The question is only who conspired. We were quickly told that it was the work of Osama bin Laden and his followers and that they had no assistance from any American. Apparently we could know this latter point before any investigation was conducted, even though we were told that we were totally ignorant about the attacks in advance. Since the media picked up this story and told it to us over and over again, the great majority of Americans, and indeed people elsewhere in the world as well, believed it.

Part of what led to credence on the part of thoughtful people was the situation in the Middle East. That the policies and actions of the United States in the Middle East, along with its unqualified support for Israel, would generate the hatred that would lead to this attack was believable. David Griffin, like so many of us, accepted this "blowback" account and continued pursuing the research in which he was engaged.

However, Griffin did read the writings of some skeptics who pointed out the inconsistencies and obvious impossibilities in the official story. Since 9/11 was used as the justification of an increasingly aggressive foreign policy and radical attacks on traditional American liberties, the truth of the story seemed important. Griffin began to study the evidence with care. His first book argued that the official story cannot be true, and that some involvement of some government officials at least contributed to allowing the attacks to occur. He called for a new investigation. The book reflected his usual careful investigation and formulation of alternative possibilities. I was fully convinced that he was right.

Griffin stayed at the cutting edge of the 9/11 Truth Movement for many years, establishing himself as the leading scholar in the field. He systematically exposed the failure of the government to explain any of the major elements in its story. There is, indeed, no evidence that Osama bin Laden was involved in any way, and there is some doubt even that the supposed hijackers were aboard the planes. The FBI acknowledges the former point. On the other hand, there is a great deal of evidence that our government has taken extraordinary steps to conceal the truth and to prevent any serious investigation. Later discovery that nanothermite was used to bring the three World Trade Center buildings down is virtual proof of the involvement of leaders in the U.S. establishment.

People saw the Twin Towers hit by planes, and whatever skeptics said, most of them thought that this explained what happened. Peculiarly embarrassing to the government account was that a third building, not hit by a plane, fell in just the same way a few hours later. This was televised at the time. Indeed, on television the collapse was announced before it happened!

Since no explanation was available, the solution was to cease any mention of this building. Of course, the media cooperated. The majority of Americans forgot about the third building. Everyone spoke of the terrorist destruction of the Twin Towers. Imperial policies abroad and the destruction of civil rights at home proceeded on the basis of this story.

Even so, memory of an event that was witnessed by tens of millions of people on television could not simply be erased, and eventually the National Institute of Science and Technology was given the unenviable task of showing that fire alone brought the building down. There are good scientists in NIST, but it is a branch of the Commerce Department, and the scientists were not invited to consider what theory is most plausible. In 2004 they provided an interim report that their fellow scientists roundly criticized. They came out with their final report four years later. No informed independent person supports it, but it stands as the position of the United States. As Griffin points out, this means that our government affirms the occurrence of "miracles" in the sense of supernatural violations of physical laws.

Eventually, for health reasons, Griffin gave up leadership of the 9/11 Truth Movement. However, by then Architects and Engineers for 9/11 Truth was well established. It seems that anyone knowledgeable about the way buildings are destroyed can tell immediately that none of these buildings were brought down by fire as the official account states. They all fell as buildings fall by controlled demolition. But it was the total failure of NIST with respect to the third building that removed any lingering doubts. Two thousand registered architects and engineers are now calling for a new investigation despite the risk incurred by each one in doing so.

Since it is harder to dismiss more than 2000 recognized professionals in the relevant field than one lone theologian, the public strategy has been to say as little as possible about them. But they are finding ways to force public attention on the matter. Currently they are trying a new tactic. If in fact three buildings of the World Trade Center collapsed from fire, one would think the city would be concerned for the safety of other buildings of similar or inferior construction. No such concern has been shown. The truth-seekers are asking the people of New York to demand an investigation as to why buildings of this sort are uniquely vulnerable to fire. Since the city leadership was in fact complicit in 9/11 and knows that other buildings are in danger only if targeted by powerful people, it seeks to suppress any such inquiry.

Griffin has taught me the term "false-flag" operation. We know that the CIA uses false flag operations. For example, in Italy it blew up a bomb in a public square and blamed this on the Italian Communists in order to prevent them from winning an election. It is now almost certain that when the United States wanted to go to war with Spain, it sank the Maine in Cuban waters and blamed Spain. When Japan wanted to attack China, it blew up a bridge in Beijing and blamed the Chinese. When Germany wanted to invade Poland it dressed prisoners in Polish uniforms and had them attack German troops. It is now almost certain that when the United States wanted to conquer Afghanistan and Iraq, it enacted the attacks on the Pentagon and the World Trade Center and blamed al Qaeda. Years later, Pres. Obama cited "9/11" as the reason for intensifying the war in Afghanistan.

I have done no independent work in this field and have spent most of my time on other topics. But I accepted Griffin's leadership and continue to celebrate his accomplishments. I have certainly not wanted to conceal my participation in "conspiracy theory." A few times I have brought up the topic in public lectures and essays, and I have occasionally had the opportunity to speak about it in churches. My only significant role has been as one of three editors of a book entitled *9/11 and American Empire: Christians, Jews, and Muslims Speak Out.* Many of the writers declined to commit themselves to any particular theory, but at least they were willing to contribute to a book in which this was a major topic.

Sandra Lubarsky, as Jewish editor, is a former student in whom I take great pride. She had the most difficult role. The ties between the neo-conservatives and militaristic forces in Israel are well known. The covert operations of the United States and Israel are often interconnected. It is unlikely that a full account of 9/11 would fail to bring some of these connections to light. Most of the Muslim contributors to the book are hostile to many of Israel's policies, and the sympathies of several of the Christian contributors are strongly with the Palestinians. One effect of

9/11 and the War on Terrorism was to give Israel full support of its brutal treatment of the Palestinian opposition. In a time of rising anti-Judaism, finding Jews willing to support a serious inquiry into the events of 9/11 was not easy.

While accepting the difficult role of Jewish co-editor, Lubarsky was wisely determined to make sure that the book did not fan the flames of anti-Judaism. Her negotiations with the Muslim editor, Kevin Barrett, who actually coordinated the editing as a whole, increased my admiration for both. It also made me realize my lack of sensitivity to some of the issues and terminology that others rightly see as of great importance.

This book, like most of Griffin's work on this topic, was published by Olive Branch Press, a marginal publisher. Other marginal publishers have published other books of the 9/11 truth movement. The mainstream publishers work with the government, the universities, and the rest of the establishment to suppress discussion. Even leftist magazines will not touch this topic. There is more readiness to speak about a conspiracy on the libertarian right than anywhere else.

Accordingly, publication of one of Griffin's books by Westminster John Knox was an act of great courage and a major breakthrough on the part of publishers. For this act not only Griffin but also WJK were attacked vigorously by the editor of the leading ecumenical Protestant magazine, *The Christian Century.* The two WJK editors who showed this courage are no longer with the press. No doubt editors of other mainstream presses will take notice. Informal censorship is very strong.

As I have been increasingly convinced that there are conspiracies behind most assassinations as well as such historic events as "9/11," I have found the behavior of the media ever more depressing. The increasing evidence that the official story is a tissue of lies is convincing to anyone who cares to study it. But even if bits and pieces of this evidence are occasionally mentioned in one place or another, readers are not encouraged to connect the dots. Those who do so are not considered serious participants in the discussion.

There is a vast literature written by those who have investigated what goes on behind the scenes. One important writer for me has been John Perkins. Whereas the writers on 9/11 are all outsiders probing the facts, Perkins writes as a participant in a pattern of operations that he finally decided to expose. I have seen nothing to cause me to doubt his veracity and basic accuracy. Clearly deceit, bribery, threats, and assassinations have been a major part of American foreign policy, at least in relation to "developing" countries, since the Eisenhower years.

Michael Rupert first entered the public discussion by exposing the role of the CIA in introducing drugs into the ghettoes of Los Angeles. Once he saw the great gap between reality and the spin that is the world that most Americans inhabit he devoted himself to discovering and exposing the reality. He made me aware of the close connection of Wall Street and the CIA, a combination to which he traces many of the actions of our nation.

Recently I have read more about the Bush dynasty. Here, too, one learns that much that has transpired has been very different from the standard spin. I have found particularly fascinating a convincing account of the downfall of Nixon quite unlike what I had previously understood. He appears in this picture more as a victim than an actor, with the older George Bush pulling the strings that destroyed him. What we have perceived as brilliant investigative reporting now looks more like participation in a plot against Nixon. Whether this is the deepest truth I do not know, but it reminds me of how extensively we can be deceived.

In this vast literature of investigation beyond the official story, there is much that is itself twisted and biased. The decision about whom to trust and what to believe is as difficult here as anywhere else. It may well be that my cynicism about the truth of what we are told may make me too credulous toward those who expose the lies. To some extent we can make our judgments less arbitrary by factoring into account the expressed convictions of the writers. But on many, many questions I can only remain agnostic.

One personal experience has warned me against myself. Somewhere around thirty years ago there was a Lebanese student in the Department of Political Theory at Claremont Graduate University. Because of his interest in Whitehead, he audited some of my lectures and visited with me from time to time. He wrote his dissertation on the political theory of the late Sartre and did some teaching at one of the Claremont colleges. Then I lost touch.

Around fifteen years ago he showed up in a one-week summer course I was teaching on the problem of evil. He was almost blind and had other physical ailments. He told the class that he had lost his sight when being held for three years as a hostage by Hezbollah in Lebanon. He indicated that he had been serving in cloak-and-dagger work there, at least partly for the United States. I assumed he was telling the truth. He wanted to be a visiting scholar of the Center for Process Studies, and we agreed. He did a quite fine job with a lecture on Whitehead's political views. I invited him to visit from time to time.

We talked about Whitehead and other topics, and I avoided asking him about his cloak-and-dagger activities. But he dropped hints, and gradually some of them became fleshed out. I thought I was hearing from an insider. He depicted the situation in the United States as ultimately under the control of a patriarch on Wall Street. Different factions struggled for his support. One of them, led by the Hunt family, had been favored for some time. But he expected that soon there would be a shift of support to the Kennedy family. He was himself involved in persuading one key actor to move in that direction.

About the time this picture was taking relatively clear shape, he fell while riding a train and, not long after, died. I was asked to perform the service, and I did so, believing that he had been working behind the scenes in important ways for the sake of a major shift of power in the United States and wondering whether his rather strange death was in fact an accident. Afterwards I received an anonymous letter from two members of the family who had decided to tell me that this was mostly a con job. At first I was not sure what to think, but fairly soon I decided that they were right. As time passed what was transpiring did not seem to fit what he had told me. But I am still not sure. The last chapter of this strange experience was a brief visit by a young man who told me he had been working with my deceased friend. He asked if the family had informed me that he was a fraud and assured me that, in fact, he was not. He promised to come again, but he did not. What am I to think?

I am indicating that I do recognize the dangers of becoming a "conspiracy theorist." One may well become too suspicious. There are many unusual events that occur by accident or whim. There are those who invent or imagine much that has not occurred. We need to be as suspicious of this or that conspiracy theory as of government propaganda

Nevertheless, when strange things happen and are quickly blamed on Muslims, I think it is well to wonder. The Boston Marathon bombings are a case in point. I was suspicious at the time, but largely kept my suspicions to myself. I now believe that this was an FBI operation. The evidence has accumulated. But I still worry whether I am allowing my general suspiciousness to influence my judgment too much.

On the other hand, there is also danger that I, like many I criticize, decline to consider evidence that might lead where I don't want to go. I will confess two instances where I acted in this way. One was with a woman who studied at the School of Theology and who on more than one occasion talked with me about the Satanic cult in which she was raised. She believed that Satanism is an important movement in our country and wanted support in understanding it, exposing it, and working against it. I preferred to think it was a minor eccentricity that I could ignore as I dealt with more important things. I had no evidence for my view and clearly I did not want to hear hers. Accordingly, I never gave her a real chance to make her case. Like almost everyone else to whom she turned, I suspect, I turned a deaf ear. I do not know what would have followed from really listening, but I know I should have listened.

The other case is more extreme. At Esalen, I think, I met and listened to David Mack, a psychiatrist who dealt with those who claimed to have been taken up into spaceships and experimented on. Shortly after returning to Claremont, I was chatting at the library desk with one of the staff. I mentioned this experience and how impressed I was by Mack's openness in believing that his patients spoke the truth. A young woman standing beside me said that this had happened to her. I'm sure that if I had expressed interest she would have been glad to talk, thinking that she had finally found someone who would take her seriously. Instead, I hurried away. Clearly I did not want to be pushed to take the reality of such experiences with full seriousness. I am not proud of my refusal to listen to her story. But at least my avoidance of dealing seriously with evidence of visitors from other parts of the universe helps prevent me from being condescending toward those who refuse to consider the evidence about 9/11.

My conviction that the attacks on the World Trade Center and the Pentagon were self-inflicted leads me to remain anxious about the future. There are those with great power who will stop at nothing to get their way. My fears were reinforced by the strange incident of a military plane in North Dakota being loaded with nuclear bombs and sent to a Louisiana army air force base that had been used in the bombing of Iraq. Fortunately, it was stopped there, and the bombs were removed, but it seems that someone with considerable clout had intended a different outcome. My suspicious mind guessed that Cheney, who was pushing hard for an attack on Iran, decided to carry it out on his own. Once an American plane bombed Iran with a nuclear weapon, there could have been no turning back.

In military affairs, these events are not necessarily held to be the work of a single person, but they are blamed on low-ranking personnel. The likelihood that an Air Force colonel would engage in such strange behavior without authorization from higher up is minimal. But the official investigations into this obvious breach of rules and laws, like those into Abu Graib, were designed to limit blame to the low-ranking perpetrators who got caught.

It is a great relief to have Cheney out of high office. Perhaps someday we will learn that he was not really as powerful and independent an actor as it now seems. But I think it more likely that we will be confirmed in our judgment that he was truly dangerous.

The question is whether we are any safer with Obama. The man we elected and the administration that followed are quite different. With respect to the issues dealt with in this chapter there has been no improvement. The geo-politics of American global domination has been continued and extended. There is no worse example of U.S. aggressive destructiveness than in the Ukraine. Our alliance with fascists and our use of thugs is more blatant than ever before. Our efforts to provoke Putin into military action that would justify us in launching a war have been shameless. We are losing what shreds of respect we still have so far as morality is concerned, and we may also be displaying the limits of our imperial reach.

At home, there is continuing advance of the policy of limiting freedom for the sake of "security." There have been fortunate breaches of this security by whistleblowers, but no previous administration has gone so far in treating whistleblowers as terrorists. To be a "terrorist," it is now clear, is to act against the interests of the United States as perceived by the powers that be. It has nothing to do with the form of the action. Any threat to the ability of the government to keep its vicious plans secret is now "terrorist."

The Obama administration has controlled the media as tightly as any. The case of the Transpacific Partnership is illustrative. It is by far the most extreme trade agreement yet, that is, it goes furthest in empowering corporations to run roughshod over people, removing political and legal restraints. It has been three years in negotiation, but it has been reported only in what is considered "irresponsible" press. Even when it was brought to Congress, the mainstream media long ignored it. It is still barely mentioned as a struggle of enormous importance to all of us goes on in Congress over whether it should be fast-tracked. The extent to which the elite can keep people ignorant of the struggle in Congress has surprised even this suspicious and skeptical observer.

When the Republicans were in power, many Americans thought that Democrats believed in democracy and human rights. Now it is clear that on these matters, a Democratic administration is no better than a Republican one. On the other hand, there are Democrats in Congress who do care. Probably no one can be elected president who does not commit to the financial-military-security establishment. All this is the situation at a time when this establishment is leading the world to ecological self-destruction! Is there anything that ordinary citizens can do to make more likely an improvement in international affairs that would also allow the world to change its behavior in the direction of sustainability?

Perhaps not, but we are called to try. I believe that we are called to work with God for the salvation of the world. Today that means first and foremost the avoidance of dramatic climate change, the death of the oceans, the exhaustion of fresh water and productive soils, and other equally important dangers. To act wisely and relevantly requires that we have a reasonably accurate idea of how the really important decisions about the fate of the Earth are made. The quest for truth is a profoundly theological one.

The theologically difficult question is about sharing the truth. The great majority of Americans grow up, as I did, believing that they are citizens of a great and good nation. Their positive feelings about themselves are bound up with their pride in their country. On the whole this positive feeling about one's nation is a contribution to psychological health and, through that, also to national health. There is in fact much that is good and great about the United States as there is about each nation. If I did not believe that I would not be so concerned to learn the truth about its history and current power structure. But what is good and great is also corrupted and exploited for ends that are neither good nor great. And what is truly good and great is seriously threatened.

I know from personal experience how painful it is to move from a naïve celebration of my nation to a more realistic recognition of the role of crime in its history and present life. Without widespread recognition of the truth, the changes that alone can save us from continuing decay will not be made. But what would be the response to the full recognition that our own leaders, just the people who have stirred up our feelings about the villainy of the 9/11 attack, are those who enacted it? Would it move us as a nation to restore the rule of law, our personal freedoms, and the respect for the right of self-determination on the part of other peoples? Or would it simply intensify the divisions within our nation making civil discourse impossible? Or would we turn to a charismatic reformer giving him dictatorial powers so as "to free the government from corruption." I recognize that many who suspect the worst about 9/11 oppose exposing the truth for fear of the consequences. Are they right? Is it better to base our policies on lies than to face the truth?

I think not. In the long run, and usually even in the short run, lies lead to more lies, the web of deception becomes so complex that even the liars no longer know the truth. And actions based on lies enmesh the actors in more and more disastrous ways. Truth is often painful. But salvation depends on passing through that pain. Perhaps the truth will make us free.

CHAPTER TWENTY

My Last Hurrah

In Chapter 19, I expressed my distress that so many good people allow themselves to be socialized into the acceptance of so much falsehood. I wish that I could make some contribution to openness to truth. What people would then see might be very different from what I see. I know that I have also been socialized into limited perceptions. It is always good when I can exchange views with others who have been liberated from contemporary orthodoxies of all sorts, so that I can check my perceptions against theirs.

Among those who are free from the understanding of world affairs that governs our media and our government and corporate propaganda, not all agree as to how current events are best understood. We need to check our views with one another. A new vision needs to come out of discussion of multiple possibilities, and we are unlikely ever to agree fully. Disagreements on many points are healthy. When I can, I participate in these discussions and support efforts to expose the deceptions used to justify vicious policies.

On the other hand, my own judgment is that even this discussion often presupposes a worldview that is inherently destructive. I think that the previous chapters have made clear that my personal focus is on what I consider this more basic level. Breaking through deceptive socialization at any point helps to open one to breakthroughs elsewhere, but today it may be that the worldview level is the one where a major breakthrough is most possible.

In every culture many of the most moral and honorable people defend the existing orthodoxy. In the name of that orthodoxy, some do terrible things to those who threaten it. Usually the defense of orthodoxy is bound up with the power structure of the time. Hence legal, political, military and economic instruments are used to enforce it. Sometimes those whose orthodoxy is more purely ideological are troubled by the violence used to defend their beliefs. Sometimes they are also troubled by the tendency to suppress those who raise questions without answering the questions. Sometimes they are sufficiently troubled that they begin to reformulate their own views. Eventually, one orthodoxy gives way to another.

During the Medieval period it was common to tell stories of the earlier Christian martyrs. The early church was intensively persecuted by the defenders of Roman imperial rule whose beliefs were symbolized by the sacredness of the imperial office. To be emperor was to be "God," at least in the sense of being the object of ultimate loyalty. Without that faith, the justification for the empire and even its actual power were endangered. The refusal on the part of Christians to worship the emperor was a serious threat. Accordingly many were killed. Eventually their numbers became too great to solve the problem by persecution. The emperor gave up the claim to *be* God, claiming instead to serve God. A new kind of order emerged in which political power and religious power were separated, although they usually cooperated. A new Christian orthodoxy became dominant and legitimated the power of both state and church.

Today it is orthodox to view the Christian orthodoxy that preceded the modern world in terms of its errors, its crimes, and its failures. We like to make fun of the epicycles used to defend the classical astronomy and of the refusal of the Aristotelian scientists to look through a telescope at the moon. We like to point to the horrors of the Crusades and the Inquisition. We feature the burning of Giordano Bruno at the stake for his heretical views and the persecution of the Waldensians. We like to talk about the corruption of the papal court. And on and on. There are many evils to report. Eventually scientific evidence, revulsion at the corruption of the church and its use of political power to enforce dubious ideas undercut the hold of its orthodoxy and thus also of its power. A new system arose of nation states determining the religious life of their people. The wider ideology was rationalist and supportive of scientism. The latter eventually came to dominance.

I have no desire to defend the Roman Empire or the orthodoxy of "Christianism." No doubt the picture of Roman cruelty when Roman history is told from the viewpoint of Christian martyrs is one-sided. No doubt the picture of Medieval Christendom as told by moderns, and especially the contemporary scientistic story, is one-sided. But the crimes were real and terrible.

Now I believe we are in a period in which the limitations of contemporary orthodoxy and the crimes that are committed in its name are becoming more widely recognized. Its defense is becoming hollow. More and more of its subscribers are uncomfortable with its defenders and willing to listen to the critics who have been so harshly treated. A change is coming.

This confidence does not lead me to inaction. In one respect, the current orthodoxy is the worst the world has seen. This is because of the instruments whose use it determines. Currently it is leading civilization to suicide. Anything that can be done to break its stranglehold over so much "expert" thought and public policy should be done, and done as soon as possible.

Obviously, the academic defenders of the scientistic ideology deny that they have any responsibility for what is done with the information they generate. That information, they point out, is often badly needed. For example, objective scientists generate information about climate change. They are not responsible for the failure of governments to act on the information they provide. The problem is with those who fail to adopt their reverence for science and the worldview they identify with it.

The situation is similar to that of most monks in Medieval Europe. They were totally devoted to orthodox Christianity. They felt no responsibility for the persecutions instigated by distant church authorities and governments. And indeed their actual responsibility was very indirect. Yet it was the orthodoxy to which they gave moral support that could easily be interpreted as justification for killing those who did not accept it, even if the real reasons may often have had more to do with political power than with religious conviction.

Similarly today, the scientism supported by the innocent scientist includes economic theories that support "free trade" and global capitalism and justify their enforcement by means that lead to millions of deaths. The slaughter thus justified exceeds anything done by the Roman Empire or by the medieval church. And the work of innocent scientists, often directly in the service of the military, contributes quite directly to this slaughter, sometimes called "shock and awe."

Orthodoxies are typically accompanied by excommunication. We moderns associate this with something done by churches. But it means simply the exclusion from a community of someone who has been, or aspires to be, part of it. This is common practice of the guilds that together make up the institutional heart of scientism. They have their own specific versions of scientism applied to their particular subject matters. And if someone has ideas about how to deal with this subject matter that differ from the orthodox ideas, she or he is likely to be excluded. In earlier chapters I have described how this works in some instances. Of course, for the most part those who do not fully agree still accept the permitted parameters and do what they can within them. As with all the orthodoxies I have mentioned, refusal to stay within prescribed limits is costly.

My point in all this is to emphasize that more and more scientists and scholars, including those now working within the orthodoxies of their guilds, are uncomfortable with these limitations. They would like to be free to explore forbidden topics and to follow the evidence rather than be required to support established orthodoxies. They do not like the fact that their work is used to advance economic and political directions with which they disagree. They are ready for a change. Some of them are implementing changes.

Meanwhile there is a wider public that is not waiting for better leadership from the guilds. Thinkers are exploring topics forbidden within the guilds and providing different interpretations of others. Those who seek to make a practical difference in life often look elsewhere for guidance and develop excellent programs. An alternative system of beliefs has already emerged and functions extensively in society.

One might say that given all this, the problem is resolving itself. We should just let matters evolve. The problem is that the guilds have a monopoly on declaring who is authoritative, who is "expert." The governments, the corporations, and the other major institutions, even the churches, seek advice from these experts. The massive recognition of a different truth plays little role in determining the policies of the major institutions.

It is at this point that change seems possible. If most people recognized that the experts produced by the university are specialists in narrowly defined problems that often are not really the problems that need to be solved, then policymakers might look elsewhere for assistance. They might even seek to be guided by common sense and its advanced form—wisdom. Then pulling the world back from the threshold of self-destruction might be recognized as more important than an economic growth that fails to benefit any except the rich. That change would be a great gain.

Indeed if other institutions began looking for advice elsewhere than to the "experts" produced by the guilds, the universities would begin to change. The disciplinary organization of knowledge might give way to one that aimed to respond to the real questions of the real world. The scientistic assumptions that now control the guilds might become subject to critical examination. Truly a new day might dawn. It would be good to have made a contribution

I realize that removing all semblance of rational justification of particular policies might have little immediate effect on those favored by the powerful. But I dare to believe, that when power is exposed in its sheer nakedness, it inspires a revulsion that can undercut it. At least that is my hope.

It is this judgment about the present situation that has led me to undertake a project that I have described as my "last hurrah," a conference designed to show that there is a well-developed alternative to the ideology that now rules the world. To be successful, it will also need to show that this alternative would provide far better guidance for constructive action. It will have to be both comprehensive and focused. It will have to attract public attention. I have failed in several of my projects in the past, and I know that I am likely to fall far short in this one. But it is time to try.

There was, of course, the matter of cost. Small academic conferences can be organized inexpensively. The organizer can use the facilities of a host school without cost, participants pay their way, and a registration fee covers expenses. But for what is needed in this case, there is no host university. Space must be rented. The cost of planning and organizing is high. Technical equipment and staffing alone are expensive. The major effort I envisioned could not be carried out without considerable funding. One could spend years in a fruitless quest to find such funds.

Fortunately, Jean and I had received inheritances from parents on both sides. These came too late to help us when we were putting our sons through college. So we had not spent the money and had no need to do so. It would be inherited by our children, but only long after they were comfortably retired. I checked to make sure that none of them were

anticipating such inheritance with any sense of need, and I was assured
that they were not. They freed me to spend their inheritance. So the
money to cover costs, as long as these were carefully controlled, was available. John Buchanan, as always, also helped and persuaded his mother to
do so as well.

The Pomona Valley Chapter of Progressive Christians Uniting held
a conference around Bill McKibben. It was successful. I asked McKibben if he would return in 2015 for another, larger, conference, and he
agreed. Vern Visick did the nitty-gritty work of organizing. I asked him
if he would work with me, and he agreed. From the beginning Ignacio
Castuera has helped in innumerable ways as he has so often before. And
from an early point Eugene Shirley, a documentary film-maker and long-
time friend and ally, has taken on support of the conference as a major
project. We four have been a kind of inner planning committee. A larger
group of a dozen meets monthly for discussion and action.

More than two years ago I proposed to my colleagues that the
Center for Process Studies ask the International Process Network if we
could host the tenth International Whitehead Conference here. I offered
to take the lead in its organization. Since I will be ninety at the time,
Roland Faber rightly wanted to be sure that, if I could not carry through,
someone else would take over. Because his hands are full, he did not want
responsibility to fall on him. David Griffin agreed to be back up. Faber
accepted this plan, and IPN accepted our invitation. Planning began.

We had three years. I roughly aimed in the first year to develop the
overall structure of the conference, secure the plenary speakers, and get
commitments of people to organize the breakout groups where the serious thinking of the conference would take place. The second year would
be for the organization of the tracks. The third year would be for detailed
preparation of the event. Of course, this sequence in any rigid way is
not realistic, but in a very general sense we have followed it for the first
two years. We are on the verge of registering and working intensively on
detailed planning and local arrangements. Much remains to be done, but
much has been accomplished.

My assumption has long been that the world is in a crisis of unimaginable proportions and that responding wisely to that crisis is of utmost
importance. Having Bill McKibben keynote is an indication that at no
time in the conference should we forget that the context is one of urgent
need for different action. McKibben's call is for action NOW. We will

affirm that call and discuss what can now be done, even without philosophical transformation, with respect to nuclear war, famine, economic collapse and political collapse, as well as climate.

However, I am convinced that responses that operate within the now dominant worldview will at best buy us a little time. To do more than that, we need an ecological worldview, and Whitehead provides this. Unfortunately, Whitehead has not been able to get a hearing, since the only ideas that can be considered in university, governmental, or corporate circles are those that fit the established worldview. Even the need for change cannot be discussed, because part of the controlling worldview is that there is no alternative. From its own point of view, the prevailing worldview is not *a* "worldview" at all. It is just *the* truth that we have learned from science.

Obviously, there have always been those who have disagreed. Here and there real alternatives have been espoused. But they have been marginal to the determinative discussion. Whiteheadians have worked at these margins and undertaken to build connections between the fragments to be found there. This has been the work of the Center for Process Studies from its inception. As we reflected about what should be done, we rejoiced that in China there had been a breakthrough. Perhaps, we thought, it could happen elsewhere.

There were signs that the situation might indeed be changing. More people recognized, at least vaguely, that the world's problems were not resolvable without deep changes. That these changes involved the way we thought was a message that began to gain traction. Occasionally, when I would say we need a new metaphysics, people would not turn away immediately. It became apparent to many that it is not wise to orient all our policies to economic growth when increasing pressure on sinks and resources is just the opposite of our need. Perhaps if an attractive and plausible alternative is spelled out in some detail, people will pay attention. Perhaps we can ride a cresting wave. We can hope.

We have secured some fine plenary speakers. In the evening, Bill McKibben's keynote will be followed by women from India and China. Vandana Shiva is a widely known Indian physicist who cares passionately for the Indian people and especially for the poor. She understands that it is the poor who suffer first and most from the destruction of the environment. Sheri Liao developed the first nongovernment organization in China. She is deeply concerned for China's environment and for

its common people, convinced that modernization has worked against
them. Since the Szechuan earthquake she has been working to rebuild
peasant communities in sustainable and prosperous ways.

Our banquet speaker will be David Griffin. I noted in Chapter 13
that at the third International Whitehead Conference he urged that we
make the twentieth century the process century. Jeanyne Slettom's Process Century Press picks up on that idea. David will comment on where
he thinks we have come and send us out to move forward.

In the mornings we want to show what has already been accomplished by process thinkers. We think that agriculture and economics
may be the two most important fields for fundamental changes. We will
present Wes Jackson and Herman Daly. Wes Jackson calls for a perennial
polyculture to replace the annual monoculture that has been the standard
for ten thousand years. In order to demonstrate the possibility and begin
to actualize the new farming he has developed a new perennial grain
that is just as productive as the current annuals. Herman Daly has long
recognized that the expansion of the human economy cannot continue to
expand in the context of a nonexpanding natural economy. He has called
for a stationary state economy, and he has written extensively about it.
He is the father of the growing field of ecological economics. Both Wes
Jackson and Herman Daly are members of the process community. We
think they show that our call for seizing this alternative is not a vague,
utopian dream but a practical challenge.

The conference is named "Seizing an Alternative" with the subtitle:
"Toward an Ecological Civilization." This is the tenth International
Whitehead Conference, and the alternative we recommend seizing is, of
course, a Whiteheadian one. The idea is that the goal will be to develop a
civilization that is sustainable but much more than that. We are interested in human fulfillment in the context of a thriving ecosystem.

The first section will consist in immediate responses to urgent
threats. In addition to climate change, these include massive hunger,
nuclear war, and economic and political collapse. Then there will be a
section on Whitehead's philosophy and another considering how we
came to be so alienated from nature that we began abusing it as we have.
The rest of the sections will deal with the rethinking of all aspects of
life. Two sections will focus on what are often called "world religions,"
although we prefer to call them wisdom traditions. These sections will
conclude by listening to the wisdom of indigenous communities.

Since the modern worldview had its home ground in physics and mathematics, we want to show that Whitehead's different assumptions work well in those fields. Since he was a mathematician and physicist, this should be easy. However, the situation is, in fact, complicated. Whitehead's work with Bertrand Russell, *Principia Mathematica* is a classic in its field, but, in their own estimation, not quite successful. Of course, there is no fully successful theory, but the general dislike of Whitehead has allowed this "failure" to be an excuse to disparage him or, to ignore any suggestion that he offers the way forward.

The problem in physics is similar. I treated this at length in Chapter 14. Whitehead's greatest contribution to physics was his theory of relativity, and this was declared to be a failure. This has been taken to mean the Whitehead is a "has-been," and that the dominant community had been right to follow Einstein. A more objective view would note that similar "failures" with accepted theories are occasions for further research and proposing adaptations. But a failure in a theory that is not favored is reason enough for total rejection.

Those of us who find the assumptions of Whitehead's theory far more realistic than those of Einstein have much work to do. We believe, however, that we can show that a Whiteheadian theory, one developed on Whiteheadian assumptions, would have significant advantages. In Chapter XIV, I proposed that the course of events may be leading to the end of an era in physics and that Whitehead's thought may guide a new beginning. The discussion at the conference will be at a much more sophisticated level.

Meanwhile, although Whitehead did very little with quantum theory, physicists in that field were attracted to his thought. There is an established interest there within the mainstream. Sadly mainstream physics as a whole, while respecting quantum physicists in their own domain, regards the ideas they have to employ as anomalous rather that suggestive. Showing Whitehead's usefulness there still leaves his thought marginalized.

We believe that if there were a level playing field, there would be great interest in Whitehead in logic and physics as a whole. Interest has, in fact, increased. Category theory, which is now regarded as cutting edge in logic, is remarkably Whiteheadian. Quantum theories of relativity are discussed. If mainstream physicists actually replaced Descartes and Einstein with Whitehead, this would have effects throughout the

academy. These comments about the "hard" sciences may be indicative of
the seriousness with which we view our task.

Whitehead is remarkable for the breadth of his thought. He published most in mathematics, logic, and physics, but his greatest influence
may be in educational philosophy. I and many others have been enlight-
ened and inspired by his comments on theology. Social and political
theorists have built on his insights. Most of the conference will deal
with a wide range of personal and social matters. I will not engage here
in discussion of additional individual topics, but I assure the reader that
we ambitious for all of them. We have been working on these matters
for decades. Perhaps we can get our proposals before a wider and more
receptive public.

The conference has attracted keen interest and taken on a life of
its own. This interest has led to vast expansion of the topics to be dealt
with in what we are calling "tracks." These tracks will be workshops in
the presence of an audience. Or we could call them team efforts to work
through important issues in public. We began with twelve. We now have
seventy-eight. No doubt some will fail to materialize, but most will succeed. We hope that they will show that a change of world view opens up
a world of attractive possibilities.

Not all of the time will be spent in thought and rational discourse.
Artists have long been in the lead in working out of an alternative vision.
We had hoped to include Pete Seeger, who considered himself a part of
the Whitehead family in the program. He feared he could not, but made
a video for us just months before his death. We will include some of it in
the opening plenary. Many other artists recognize connections between
what they see and what Whitehead describes. Perhaps their performances
will enable a breakthrough into a new consciousness.

We envision that more important than the conference itself will be
the potential of what is produced there to influence thought and action
in the future. We hope that most tracks will produce material that will
be useful to others. Process Century Press will be available for publishing
books. Some tracks may work toward courses to be offered on the web.
In any case we expect to make a great deal of material available, hopefully
in accessible form, on a new website.

Plans for this website have developed quite wonderfully. Originally
we thought of it as a website to be created by Shirley to promote the conference and to organize the material it generates. But his plans became

more ambitious. He wants to make process and ecological civilization ideas accessible and attractive to a wide range of people. The website must be popular and inviting. The ambitious goals delayed its inauguration, but it has now been actualized.

Shirley wanted a way a name the conference as a whole that would be more memorable and catchy. He has skilled friends whose help he enlisted. At a weekend workshop they decided that the ideal name would be "Pando Populus." Pando is the proper name of an aspen grove in southern Utah. Aspen groves appear to be composed of many individual trees, but in fact, they have a common root system. The health of each tree is bound up with the well-being of the whole grove and the whole grove provides sustenance even where local resources to not suffice. Thus aspens provide a good symbol of some major teachings of process thought.

Pando may be both the largest and the oldest organism on Earth. Its survival testifies to the strength given by mutual support. However, human activities, directly and indirectly, now pose greater threats than Pando has ever encountered before. Its survival is in question. This too makes it an effective image for our conference.

We did not change the name of the conference itself. However, "Pando Populus" is the name of the new website, and the image will be featured at the conference. Further, Shirley's friends, a group with truly unusual gifts and experience, became enthusiastic about the whole project, and together we have created a new organization to run the website, support the conference, and make its materials available. During the early years I will chair the board.

Over the years Pando will find other ways of promoting process ideas. The goal is to influence a much wider audience than the one process thought has reached so far. Indeed, we hope to nurture a popular movement. This may prove to be the most important consequence of the conference.

CHAPTER TWENTY-ONE

God

Many Christians in our society who grew up in devout homes and chose a professional career in the church have found in their old age that they have moved a long way from where they began. Years of study and reflection have undercut much that they believed as children. Some have come to find almost any idea of God incredible or offensive. For some Jesus has become one good and wise man among others. Some rejoice in their liberation; some are pained by their disillusionment.

My situation is different. I rejoice that in many ways my childhood faith, while transformed, is not denied or watered down. I reaffirm the trajectory on which it sent my life. I believed then that God is Love. I believe that now. I found God then the great companion who understands. That is how I find God now. I looked to God then to direct my life. I look to God now to direct my life. I thought then that the supreme calling is to love God with all that I am. I think now that this is the supreme calling.

Why is my situation so different from many others? I think there are two answers. First, I was very fortunate in the kind of piety that characterized my family. Universal love was at the center, and I experienced my parents' unconditional love. They reflected some aspects of the culture that I have rejected, but they certainly understood that our calling was to love God, not to commit to, or absolutize, cultural teachings.

Second, the contrast of my theocentrism and modern thought hit me early and powerfully. It came close to destroying my faith entirely. But because I recognized fairly quickly that it was the assumptions of modernity and their pervasiveness throughout the cultured world that destroyed faith, I was led to examine those assumptions. Whereas immersion in the vast literature that expresses those assumptions strains and often destroys theistic belief, direct confrontation with them can go either way. For me, it led against accepting modernity and toward beliefs that are "postmodern," but far more continuous with the pre-modern vision of Jesus and Paul than modernity allows.

Before I explain why I find theism well supported, let me say once again, my argument is for the One whom Jesus called "Abba," not for an omnipotent ruler of the cosmos, or a moralistic and narrow-minded lawgiver, or a supernatural being located somewhere else who occasionally intervenes in our planetary affairs. Those who were nurtured in a piety related to any such idols had every need for liberation. For them atheism could certainly be a gospel. However, I believe that a turn to Jesus would have been a truer and deeper liberation than what can be found in Western atheism.

The theoretical question for me is not then whether there is a supernatural being who intervenes in the world. There is not. The question is not whether everything that happens is willed to happen by one supreme will. It is not. The question is not whether one can derive from a book that is called "God's word" a set of moral rules strict obedience to which will get you into heaven. There is nothing of that sort. The question is certainly not whether somehow in the divine realm three persons can be one God, or whether one being can be simultaneously fully God and fully human. I see that as a theologian I must help people think about such things, but I wish that the course of theological development had not created these unnecessary puzzles. To reject all such things did not take me away from the trajectory of my childhood faith.

The question for me was, and is, whether I am loved and called to love. It is whether there is a purpose that transcends individual human purposes and gives them meaning. It is whether there is purpose in the universe as a whole. It is whether it makes sense to worship. It is whether there is a "whole" that I am called to serve.

These are not easy questions to answer. The modern answer is of course negative. But even when one rejects the modern assumptions and asks the questions in a more open context, we cannot presuppose that we will find support for belief in the God of my childhood faith. My point is only that it is an open question, not one foreclosed by arbitrary assumptions. And I want to sketch the reasons that I answer "Yes." There will be few surprises for one who has read the early chapters.

First, however, because we are all socialized into modern thought,
I need to make fully explicit what in modern thought has demanded a
negative answer to all my questions. To say it briefly, it is the enormous
successes of science based on a purely objective or materialist vision. This
vision, when articulated, is really incredible, but the success overwhelms
this objection. For this reason much of the preceding chapters has been
devoted to pointing out the limits of this success. If people recognize that
further advance of science will be facilitated by a changed worldview,
they will be open to considering that worldview. Outside the university,
many already are. But resistance to change is fierce in the university and
the guilds of which it is composed.

The assumptions are clearly articulated by Descartes. Nature has no
subjectivity; that is, apart from human beings there are no feelings or
purposes in the world. There is also no spontaneity or self-determination.
Every event can be explained by antecedent events, and each event is an
instance of matter in motion. Living things are simply more complex
instances of matter in motion.

Great advances were made by natural science following Descartes.
The first great challenge came when Darwin showed that human beings
are part of nature. One response was that if human beings are part
of nature, nature is not a machine, lacking subjectivity and purpose.
This response led to radical empiricism and neo-naturalism. This move
impressed me as a student at Chicago. Within the university, it later
lost out to the extension of the understanding of the Cartesian view
of nature to include human beings. We, also, are part of the world
machine. Our purposes are no more real than the apparent purposes of
other animals.

In my opinion, no one really believes this. Nevertheless, it is this
move that puts an end to belief in God. Descartes certainly did not
intend this result. He thought God was the creator of the world, but he
excluded God from any other causal relation to the nature studied by
science. He enforced that exclusion by denying subjectivity to any natural
thing. For his followers this meant that a dog's yelps of pain were like
the squeaking of an unoiled door hinge. If there is no subjectivity in the
world, the only relation left would be one of acting as one external force
among other external forces. God could only act, therefore, as a miracle,
overruling the laws discovered by physics. There were excellent reasons
for banishing God altogether from a role in natural events.

Descartes' dualism left fully open to theists the discussion of how God works in human experience. They could assume that human experience is not mechanical. Instead it is purposive and unpredictable. God could play an explanatory role there without disturbing science or interfering with its explanations.

But when human beings were viewed as part of nature without a change in the understanding of nature, God was excluded from any explanatory role with respect to human beings as well. Inevitably the thinking that takes place in this context cannot pay any attention to the hypothesis that God plays a role. Anyone immersed in that literature will become, functionally atheist. If one is allowed to believe in God, it must be a God who makes no difference to what happens in the world. That is not the God of Jesus or of the Bible in general.

Now I have said that this view of nature, especially when the reflection about nature is understood to be part of nature, is really incredible. At least as a thought experiment, please set it aside and suppose that the entities that make up the whole, certainly human experiences, but some or all of the others as well, do exist in and for themselves, that is, are subjects as well as objects. We are now in a different world of thought from what is called "modern science." This one corresponds with our experience far better than the modern one. Its *a priori* rejection now seems absurd.

The question, in this new context, is *where* subjectivity is to be found. We will all agree that it occurs in humans, most, that it characterizes all animals, some, that it is present in all living cells, and a few, that even quanta have, or are, subjective experiences. These are important questions, but we need not decide them here. The question about God is whether there is a unified subjectivity throughout all that is in addition to the many distinct subjects.

My view is that there is a great deal of positive evidence. The universe is fine-tuned to support life, and physicists agree that the occurrence of the needed combination of factors is extremely remarkable. The chance of this having happened by chance is infinitesimal. Based on this negative assumption, it has become common to posit an infinite number of universes. If there are an infinite number of universes, then the probability that one of them will be just like this is high.

Thus we are offered two explanations, both compatible with the evidence: there is God, or there are an infinite number of universes. Until recently scientists were emphatic that a theory is not scientific unless we can provide some indication of how it can be tested. In principle, the theory of infinite universes cannot have any evidence in its favor since the universes must have no effect on one another. There is only one reason for its adoption: the *a priori* belief that there is no God. In such a situation I find it far more reasonable to posit God's reality. It violates Ockham's razor far less.

Actually the advantage is far greater than just satisfying Ockham's razor. Let me try to spell out the sort of theory that is required to satisfy the reasons for positing them in the first place. If the same name, "universe," is to apply to each of these posited entities, presumably all must be somewhat like ours. Presumably each would consist in some distribution of mass/energy. If it does, then it must be spatio-temporal. But to be spatio-temporal is to be related spatio-temporally to everything else that is spatio-temporal. It becomes meaningful to ask where these other universes are located. If there is a spatio-temporal continuum that contains them all, then the idea that they are truly distinct universes should be abandoned. There would be one universe containing in various regions various distributions of mass/energy.

We are certainly violating Ockham's razor, but we have an intelligible theory. In itself it does not accomplish its goal. One must add another *ad hoc* hypothesis. Whereas all the universes resemble one another in being spatio-temporal distributions of mass/energy, they differ from one another in terms of the values of the constants.

With an infinite number of such universes in one spatio-temporal continuum one would expect that ours at some point would have collided, or at least interacted, with another. That this has never happened may also be a matter of chance, and we then have still another inexplicable marvel.

If the advocates of an infinite number of universes respond by saying that they are not in a common spatio-temporal continuum, they must posit that they have different numbers of dimensions. How entities with different numbers of dimensions are related is sufficiently mysterious that I will not guess at the physical consequences. But if that is the view, then the marvel that the one universe that has four dimensions, and also has just the fine-tuning required for life, would not be diminished.

There is one other way of formulating this theory that initially seems more plausible. Perhaps the universes are successive. If ours began in a singularity and will end in a collapse, this could be imagined to give rise to a new universe. Perhaps this goes on forever, each universe with different constants. Then one may affirm that it is a matter of chance that one of them has just those constants that make life possible by chance.

But on reflection one sees how implausible this is. For the sake of argument, contrary to my personal judgment, let's suppose that our universe did begin in a Big Bang and will end in a Big Crunch. Let us grant that this will be followed by another Big Bang. In terms of what I have heard, the character of the universe that would lead to an eventual Big Crunch is very specific and limited. There is the possibility, even in the case of this universe, that it will expand forever. But to have an infinite number of successor universes, each one must follow expansion by contraction. They must, in other words be very similar, and it would seem likely that they would have the same constants. However, the whole argument that there is an alternative to theism depends on the *ad hoc* assumption that each Big Bang would express and bring about a different set of constants. The chance that all of these divergent constants would lead to expansion followed by collapse would be infinitesimal. We would then need an explanation of how this infinitesimal chance happens to be the one that is actualized. All of these *ad hoc* hypotheses end where they begin—with extreme improbability.

I am almost ashamed to spend time puncturing the balloon of ridiculous proposals. But silliness of this sort is now rampant, almost orthodox, in contemporary cosmology. One is forced to take it seriously. And since its proponents toss it out as a solution with no explanation, one has to try to offer one. The more one elaborates, the worse the proposal appears.

Arguing for God from the fine-tuning of the universe is based on recent discoveries, but it is in continuity with deep intuitions that have long led to belief in some unified reality that is far greater than ourselves. For the most part people have been interested in how particular things came into being, but occasionally the question has been more inclusive. Who or what is responsible for the whole of things? Once seriously raised, the idea of a "creator" has been widely accepted. In Europe few doubted it as late as the nineteenth century.

It lost its self-evidence through two major developments. The first has already been noted. Tough-minded thinkers rejected any role for purpose or any other subjectivity in the explanation of objective reality.

Subjectivity was to be explained by what is objective. Any "Creator" would have to be an objective occurrence, such as the Big Bang, whereas "God" is identified as a cosmic Subject.

The second was evolutionary thinking applied not only to living things but to the cosmos as a whole. If we suppose we must directly explain the universe as it now is, creation must be an event that cannot be conceived as continuous with any of the developments we observe. Science then seems to be the description of a world that is given for it, not of how that world came to be. However, it turned out that science could show how the present world came into being from a much simpler one. The role of a "creator" receded.

The role of "creator" became the giver of the "laws" of nature that science was discovering. The word "law," so important to early modern science, implied a lawgiver. But many of these "laws" in turn could be scientifically explained. Some proposed that what were called "laws" were in fact generalizations of behavior rather than objective restraints on behavior. The discussion has been confused, but the self-evidence of a lawgiver ended.

However, the fact that what are called "laws" are often better understood as descriptive generalizations does not mean that no "laws" are givens. The "givens" have reasserted themselves as "constants." And it is especially the amazing nature of these "constants" that we call "fine-tuning." When the recognition that this universe is fine-tuned to support the increase of value is combined with the removal of the prohibition of treating subjects as causes, the reasons for affirming a "Creator" are much as they were before the cultural triumph of scientism.

Many scientists have been deeply troubled to find that at the present level of analysis so many fundamental elements of the world are so like what one would expect if a cosmic spirit had selected them. They are just what are required for a world supportive of life to exist. In the early stages of science, the faith that God created the world led to the discovery of mathematical laws reflecting intelligence and beneficence. Now commitment to atheism is so fully established that the discovery at a deeper level of just such laws drives physicists to seek another explanation.

I understand that the theory of supersymmetry has attracted vast amounts of time and money largely because if it is proved true it would reduce the mystery of fine-tuning. There was great hope that CERN would turn up some evidence in favor of this theory. Some still have hope, but so far there is no evidence. The poor scientists will be thrown back on the theory of innumerable universes of which we happen to be in the one that supports us.

One might, of course, argue that the theistic explanation of the fine-tuning of our universe is just as lacking in evidence as are the myriads of other universes that are required for the scientistic explanation by "chance." But the two are not on just the same grounds in this respect. So far as I know, the defenders of multiple universe theory do not suggest that their explanation of fine-tuning explains anything else. Those who posit God claim the usefulness of this hypothesis in other ways.

Consider as a crucial example the universal assumption that we have some responsibility for what we do. The metaphysics of scientism informs us that this is an illusion, but the very act of informing us of this assumes that the informer feels some responsibility to do so. One may assert that we are all zombies, and in principle those committed to scientism do so, but no one can live as if this were so.

Because of undeniable physical evidence, scientists have been forced to a very uncomfortable acknowledgment that at the subatomic level there is indeterminism. But thinkers have long recognized that even if the metaphysics of modern science were adjusted to allow for this, it would be no closer to allowing for the universal experience of responsibility. Responsibility assumes self-determination. Only a metaphysics that allows for self-determination will fit the actual assumptions on which human life is based. That of course requires the inclusion of subjects or subjective experience as causal in the objective world.

Even if we made that move, we could argue that any evaluation of how self-determination operates is arbitrary. One expression of self-determination is as good as any other. More plausibly, we could recognize that some expressions have better results for the organism than others. Still more realistically we could judge that every society benefits from instilling views in its members about which uses are better than others. Much about the universal sense of better and worse, of right and wrong, can be explained in these ways. Just as we now see that much that was once called natural law is better understood as universal patterns of behavior that have evolved over time, so we now know that much that we once considered God's moral law is a product of particular cultures.

Nevertheless, just as the relativization of natural law finds its limits in the constants, so also the relativization of morality or ethics seems to find its limits. The most sensitive and reflective people in all cultures, while critical of the particulars of cultural mores, still find some self-determinations truly better than others. In the view of my mentor, Alfred North Whitehead, human experience attests that "there is a rightness in things" partly realized and partly missed (*Religion in the Making*, 66)

For him, and for me, the best explanation is that God has ordered reality for the production of value and that the right decision in each moment is the one that contributes most to that end. This is, of course, a contemporary formulation of the old assumption that the source of natural law and moral law is the same. Whitehead goes on to overcome the dualism. In his complex and convincing system, the same purposeful ordering of potentiality in relation to actuality that influences the natural world to generate greater values in the form of life and consciousness also influences individual conscious occasions of human experience to aim at whatever value is realizable in the circumstances.

I do not want to be misunderstood. This is not a proof of the existence of God. Proofs depend on assumptions, and alternative assumptions are always possible. My argument is that if we move away from the assumptions of scientism, we can develop an intelligible theory in which God explains both the fine-tuning of the universe and human responsibility. The alternative hypothesis used to save scientistic assumptions throws light on nothing except the possibility that the wonderful fine-tuning of our universe may be a matter of chance. For my part, I do not find it attractive.

To show the multiple gains of theism over chance, I will note one other. We all know, whether we can explain it or not, that holding an opinion does not guarantee its truth. There is a strong sense that things are as they are and that it is good to conform our opinions to this objective reality. This leads us to accept the authority of those who we suppose have more experience and information than do we, beginning with our parents and teachers.

As time passes, we become aware that our seniors do not all agree. We are forced to decide whom to follow. Some of us decide that it is well to consider the evidence and to engage in reasoning ourselves. We do so on the assumption that reality is as it is and that learning more about it brings us closer to the truth. This has led in the past to the idea that truth exists, transcending all human opinions. This truth was called God. Sadly, this has given rise also to the claim of some individuals and institutions to be peculiarly authorized to proclaim this transcendent truth, foreclosing further thought and experiment and even leading to violent action based on these beliefs.

Modern science would not have arisen apart from a strong sense that it was important to learn more of God's truth. The scientists assumed that there was a rationality in things, reflecting God's perfection, that was not obvious on the surface. They dug deeper and opened up new worlds of understanding. But their metaphysics gradually undercut this part of their assumptions. The resulting atheism has raised profound questions about objective truth. It is hard for an atheist to affirm any truth beyond the consensus of experts. Where else can it be?

Nevertheless, the same atheists who make these affirmations know that the current consensus is not final. The truth transcends even the most reliable human opinions. None of the nontheistic theories about truth correspond with assumptions that seem ineradicable.

Perhaps this is most obvious in relation to past events. No one really believes that the consensus of current historians about what happened in the past guarantees that their opinion is accurate. We have, I think, an ineradicable sense that what happened happened. It is not changed by changing opinions about it. Its occurrence is not erased by the lack of memory or current evidence.

I may of course be wrong. You may tell me that you believe that the truth about the past is limited to what is currently known. The past as such has no reality against which opinions may be checked. I will have difficulty believing you, but that may just be my problem. In any case I cannot pretend to think what I cannot think, and I think that the rejection of the understanding of truth as the conformation of thought to reality cannot be correct. This suggests that my ineradicable convictions are better understood in a theistic context.

Again, I am not offering proofs to those who want to explore other options. I am confessing that I do not find such exploration needed. My experience of truth and rightness fit with what we know cosmologically through the hypothesis of God. It is enough.

Let me sum up. We have two alternatives. One is modern atheism. It is based on the assumption that objective events are completely explained by other objective events. Subjective experience can play no explanatory role. Accordingly, we must believe that there we have no freedom and responsibility, that there is no real distinction between truth and falsehood or good and evil, and that the world is to be explained entirely by necessity and chance. Since it cannot be explained as necessary, it must be explained as the result of chance. Since the probability of this one is infinitesimal, we must posit a virtually infinite number of other universes unconnected with this one. Even if the idea made sense there could be no evidence of their existence.

The other is theism. Sadly because of really terrible mistakes that have been made in the history of Western theology, this is sometimes taken to mean the belief that one omnipotent being controls everything or at least can do so. The evidence against this idea is overwhelming, unless one is prepared to attribute all human and natural evil to the direct causality of this being. In that case, the character of that being becomes utterly offensive. In any case, we must give up our hardcore belief in responsibility. Further, by explaining everything, this doctrine explains nothing. If this were the alternative I would stick with modern atheism.

However, this is only one form of theism. In indigenous traditions, in some branches of Hinduism and Buddhism, in philosophers such as Plato and Aristotle, in the Bible generally, and especially in Jesus and Paul, there is a quite different theism. It has attained its most fully developed form in the philosophy of Alfred North Whitehead.

This theism assumes that ultimately causality is rooted in subjective decisions rather than anything that can be observed in sense experience. It explains the most basic structure of our universe in terms of the decision of the Cosmos as a Subject. It explains what happens within the universe as affected by necessity, by chance, and by creaturely decisions made possible, and influenced, by the order of possibility created by the Cosmic Subject. This order also explains the "hardcore common sense notions" of responsibility and objective truth. It even explains rare religious experiences.

For me there is no contest between scientism and this kind of theism. Actually, I am no longer much interested in most of the non-theistic answers to questions of the sort I have listed. They require me to adopt beliefs that conflict with hardcore common sense and to affirm as real what are truly inconceivable and untestable entities. Or they may simply substitute description for explanation and profess satisfaction with the result.

However, there is one alternative to theism that remains very interesting indeed. That is Buddhism. Buddhism does not provide different answers at the level at which I have asked the questions. Instead it challenges the worthwhileness of such questioning. It asserts that we should focus instead on the transformation of experience. The suggestion is that when we immerse ourselves in what is truly most important, we will cease to ask the questions that lead to positing God.

The issue is, then, about importance, and that is a very "important" question. In the trajectory in which I stand, the deepest calling today is to redirect history away from the self-destruction of the human species. In the Buddhist trajectory, the point of beginning must always be the structure of human existence or the spiritual status of the individual. In my trajectory the Buddhist questions are certainly important, but they need to be dealt with in a wider context. Truly loving God and neighbor and immersing oneself in God's work for the salvation of the world will transform the human spirit. In the Buddhist trajectory, moving toward personal enlightenment will lead to attitudes and actions beneficial to the world. Buddhists have every reason to point out that very often the ego distorts efforts to save the world and makes the situation worse. Christians complain that Buddhist analyses of history have rarely given adequate guidance for social action.

Speaking now, purely confessionally, I am a Christian and I struggle with the problems of Christian action. The question of God remains for me central. History is the context of my thinking and acting. I hope that I gain some of the benefits of Buddhist enlightenment, but I do not plan to engage seriously in the disciplines that move one forward in that direction.

Thus far I have spoken only of God's universal role. The Whiteheadian cosmology confirms the biblical view that it is also very particular. It works universally only by working in each event individually. What it contributes in each event is unique, because the possibilities open to that event are unique to that exact location in time and space. There remains the question whether the many claims to still more personal experiences of God can be given credence.

Perhaps the most common form of personal experience is the call. The sense of being called is widespread and in Whitehead's vision arises from the fact that in every moment we are called to realize what is then possible. But the Bible testifies to dramatic experiences of being called. Amos speaks of having been called as if it were a quite definite momentary event in which God's will for him became clear. Paul's experience on the road to Damascus reversed his previous understanding of his calling, leaving him temporarily blind. Isaiah speaks of his vision in the temple. Moses meets God in a burning bush. In this case the blaze is said not to consume the bush.

My belief that this kind of experience occurs is strengthened by my own experience of call. My experience was far less dramatic than the famous ones. But since in one moment I knew what I was to do when I had not known before, it would be easy for me to say that God "spoke" to me. Perhaps in Paul's case he did hear a voice, others report having done so. But if he experienced a blinding light and simultaneously an awareness of what he was called to do, that would suffice. I am at least confident that sometimes God's will, not just for the immediate moment, but for the future as a whole, becomes abruptly and startlingly clear.

There still remains the question: is God acting differently in those occasions than others? It feels that way to the recipient. And the recipient's belief in the reality of God feels confirmed as well. Of course, it may all be explained by the firing of neurons, but so may all the observations through microscopes as well. What explains everything explains nothing.

I told of another experience as well, one of feeling God's totally accepting presence. This experience is certainly not unique to me. I read recently the account of the experience of the Harvard neuroscientist who described his experience while he was scientifically dead. It sounded just like mine, although I was fully alive.

Of course, experiences of this kind are at best episodic. I have lived most of the time with a vague sense of being accepted, just as with a vague sense of being called. But it would be easy to attribute this vague sense to the belief system that I hold. The difference is that I cannot myself attribute the one occasion on which this sense became so vivid simply to my beliefs. The Harvard neuroscientist cannot either. One knows that it is possible to be deceived by experience, and it is possible verbally to deny what one experiences so as not to offend the modern mind. But the feeling remains as it is. It is the feeling of being loved by another. The vague and general belief that God loves everything and the unimaginable joy of vividly experiencing that love seem quite different. Does that mean that God was relating to one differently in that moment?

Rationally, it is very hard to believe that the Cosmic Spirit I call God would relate to one individual on one tiny planet in an insignificant part of the universe in certain moments in markedly different ways. But experiences that encourage that interpretation have been reported too frequently in our history to be easily ignored or dismissed as evidences of what Whitehead called a "particular providence for particular occasions" (*Process and Reality,* 341). He even provides a conceptual explanation of the difference. Whereas in most of our prehension of God, God's consequent nature plays a negligible role, at times it becomes important, even dominant.

I do not know; but for me evidence trumps beliefs of what would seem rationally probable. I do not believe in "miracles" in the modern sense of divine violations of natural law. But I do believe in miracles in the biblical sense of astonishing events in which "God's hand" appears. In a confessional chapter I should not worry about my reputation among moderns. Let them snigger. I should tell the truth. That Whitehead found room in his cosmology even for such miracles is one of his most astounding accomplishments.

WORKS CITED

Whitehead, Alfred North. 1926 *Religion in the Making.* New York: Fordham University Press, 1996.

___. *Process and Reality.* 1929. Corrected Edition, Ed. David Ray Griffin and Donald W. Sherburne. New York: Free Press. 1978.

CHAPTER TWENTY-TWO

Jesus

I have, I think, made clear that the piety of my childhood and youth was theocentric rather than Christocentric. My companion was God, not Jesus, and I did not merge them. Jesus no doubt was with God in "heaven" but not now with me on earth. On the other hand, the God who was my intimate companion was the Abba of Jesus. It was what Jesus said about God that shaped my theocentrism.

Obviously I imbibed my piety from my parents, and no doubt they imbibed theirs from their parents. For many in those days this seemed unproblematic. My mother's mother was a devout, well-read believer, who devoted herself to her family and her leadership in the Sunday school of the then Methodist Episcopal Church, South, in Newnan, Georgia. She was aware of controversies such as those about evolution and the deity of Jesus. No doubt she took them seriously and had her own opinions. But her solution was simple. She taught her children that they should affirm the first four words in the Bible: "In the beginning God." Note that she stopped before "created." Later I recognized this as her way of responding to the question of creation versus evolution. For her, and for my parents as well, struggles over theory were perfectly acceptable, and complete freedom of thought should be allowed, because they did not feel that their theocentrism was threatened. The difficulty was to live and think as a theocentric understanding directed.

Needless to say my parents took for granted the importance of Jesus. They spent their lives as Christian missionaries in Japan. In some other parts of the world the situation would have pushed missionaries to articulate the importance of Jesus. In Japan the only serious threat to Japanese affirmation of the emperor as ultimate had been the Christian teaching of God. This had led to the greatest internal struggle in Japan's history, and the most extensive martyrdom of Christians in all of history. For centuries, being Christian was a capital offense in Japan. The Buddhists and Confucianists did not threaten Japanese tribalism and were fully accepted into the family. When the Christian mission was renewed, the issue was again theism, not the nature or role of Jesus. This time their threat to the tribal society was joined by a small group of converts to Communism. Such limited opposition to Japanese militarism and imperialism as existed in Japan came from these groups.

I do not think my parents or other missionaries, at least the Protestant ones, fully understood the depth of the issue for Japanese. No other people have so successfully maintained a tribal consciousness through the process of developing a high civilization and even the external trapping of its modern form. This consciousness is responsible for much that is truly admirable in Japanese culture. It requires a symbol, and this symbol has always been the emperor. To adopt explicitly and practically the view that the people individually and collectively owe their highest allegiance and devotion to something else shatters their tribal unity.

Christians should ask whether this is a proper goal. In many ways the Japanese have attained a social order that we can only envy. Does it make sense that we bring a message that disrupts it?

Before simply saying that at the spiritual level we should leave them alone, we should note that alongside the wonderful consequences of their unique tribalism, its maintenance has painful human consequences. Foreigners are welcome as guests, and I can testify to the wonderful hospitality they receive. But they are expected to remain guests. If Japanese marry these foreigners, they and their offspring can hardly find a place in Japanese society. Ethnocentrism has problematic consequences.

The Japanese are also capable of terrible evils. The most glaring of these expressed itself in Japanese imperialism. Obviously, Western nationalism also led to imperialism. Many Japanese see Japan as simply following the modern Western model when it set out to create a co-prosperity sphere under its divine ruler. The "Christian nations" are in a poor position to criticize Japan.

Nevertheless, it is an indisputable fact that those who suffered for even a few years under imperial Japanese rule hate the Japanese with a depth that is astonishingly lacking in their critical feelings toward European and American colonial rule. Despite the shameless exploitation and condescension they experienced from "Christians," it seems that they did not feel quite the same contempt and ruthlessness from those rulers as from the Japanese. We Europeans and Americans are forgiven, perhaps too easily. The Japanese are not. I can only conjecture that the centuries of teaching that our devotion is owed to the universal creator who cares also for other peoples had some mitigating effect even on those Westerners whose Christianity was superficial and badly distorted. In a tribal society there is no comparable teaching, and the Japanese behaved accordingly. Despite the lack of really good examples of historical outcome, I remain convinced that ultimate devotion to the finite needs to be overcome. Shinto, Buddhism, and Confucianism do not challenge it. Neither does atheistic modernism.

Most of the Christian missionaries in Japan were enthusiastic about many features of Japanese society. We in the individualistic West have much to learn from Japanese culture. The question remains: is it possible to preserve these wonderful characteristics of the culture while recognizing that supreme loyalty is owed to something inclusive rather than tribal? I think that only Japanese Christians have a chance of working this out.

This excursus may help the reader to understand how the issue of theocentrism is reinforced in one who has grown up in a Christian mission in Japan. Those who have lived only in post-Christian societies often suppose that inclusiveness of concern is a product of reason or universal experience. They do not realize how very special are the circumstances that develop a genuine acceptance of our common humanity. If they did, they would prize their inheritance from Israel through Jesus more highly. They might also see the importance of theism in this process. The relapse of post-Christian societies into idolatries of nation, of ideologies, and especially of wealth should warn those moderns who hope to retain humanist values without theism that the task may not prove possible. Thus far, at least, the project has had no lasting successes.

Moderns, both in and out of the churches, have been highly critical of Christian missions. I have commented that the mission in which I grew up was more ambiguous than the missionaries recognized. Nevertheless, I affirm their work. Those of us who believe that theocentrism is needed to overcome the we/they distinction that is so threatening to the future of humanity must try to encourage it, even when it threatens to undermine much that we admire. We must also, of course, do all we can to reduce the losses that are entailed.

I say this, even though I know that Jesus' only comment on trying to convert people was harshly negative. In his time there were Jewish missionaries seeking to convert Gentiles. Indeed, many Gentiles were attracted to Judaism. But Jesus thought that when Jewish missionaries persuaded Gentiles to accept the Jewish law, they put them into bondage rather than liberating them. No doubt this has often been the result of the Christian mission as well. We free people from one closed system and bind them into another that may well be worse. The proper task of Jesus' followers is to turn them to the God who frees them from all closed systems, overcoming all we/they oppositions.

In *Christ in a Pluralistic Age* I argued that we can and should mean by "Christ," God as present in the world. In traditional terms, "Christ" is the incarnation of the Logos, which is God. Christocentrism then becomes a form of theocentrism. The more Christocentric we are, the more we are open to others and ready to learn from them. I stand by that.

What is newer to my thought, and what I want to emphasize in these reminiscences, is a strongly Jesus-centric view of history. Perhaps I always assumed it, but it has become more important to me to articulate it. Of course, I want to do this in a pluralistic context that appreciatively recognizes that other communities have had other centers and have much to contribute. To emphasize the importance and uniqueness of Jesus in no way reduces the appreciation of the importance and uniqueness of Gotama or Plato. The only issue is whether in our overarching understanding of history and personal life, from what perspective do we locate the value of each of the great figures. I find that I do so from the perspective gained from Jesus. Indeed, speaking of the perspective in terms of an overarching view of history already indicates that this is what I do. Hence I am confessionally, and unapologetically, Jesus-centric.

Again, my understanding of pluralism emphasizes the distinctive contributions of the various traditions. We need them all. But this does not exclude judgments of importance in particular circumstances or even more broadly. My Jesus-centrism is the claim that today the most needed understanding of who we are, where we stand, and what is needed comes from viewing the whole from this center.

I can state the argument briefly. We live in a moment of history that could be its last. Continuation of history depends on how we respond to terrible threats. Assuming some survive, how this remnant reconstitutes itself is of enormous importance. Thus far, the efforts of historically oriented people have been to respond to the crisis with the already accepted cultural values and institutions. These efforts have failed. We need an approach that appeals beyond what is now culturally acceptable to a higher authority than dominant experts. It must be countercultural, and it must look at reality from the bottom up rather than from the top down.

In this context, of course, understanding history from the perspective of the rich and powerful will not help. But taking as one's center, teaching that is focused on what is true at all times and places is also not what is most needed. This can lead to profound illumination of some very important matters, but it can distract from attention to what is unique in our time and place. We need historical thinking, and we need the kind of historical thinking that calls us to involvement and action. We may find bits and pieces of this here and there in many cultures, but its sustained development and recognition as important was in the prophetic tradition of Israel. The prophets were countercultural, viewing reality from the perspective of the poor and oppressed.

There is another need. We need to view the situation globally with a profoundly inclusive concern. On this point the prophets made an important contribution but cannot be said, as a group, fully to meet the need. Understandably, and even desirably, they were ethnocentric. If was Israel and Israel's behavior and destiny on which they focused. But they did not celebrate Israel's superiority over others. If Israel had a special status, some recognized, this was a special responsibility for the larger human community. They went some distance to transcend the we/they opposition of Jew and Gentile. But they did not fully overcome it.

I believe the trajectory leads in the needed direction. I believe that many Jews have followed that trajectory and achieved in this respect the historical understanding that is needed. However, historically, the decisive achievement occurred in Jesus and in his immediate followers. Jesus began his mission focused on Jews and only Jews. He encouraged communities that were inclusive of all Jews. A Syro-Phoenecian woman taught him that this was inadequate. Jesus' ministry and teaching became inclusive. His illustration of the neighbor we should love by a despised foreigner was a clear attack on ethnocentrism. His teaching that we should love our enemies and his call for the forgiveness of those who crucified him went beyond standard prophetic teaching.

Even after Jesus' resurrection his closest followers were ambivalent about this issue. The book of Acts describes Peter's hesitation to accept Gentiles and how it was overcome by a vision. Paul recognized that the gospel was equally for Jew and Gentile. The communities he established were inclusive. In this respect I see Jesus as the fulfillment of the prophetic tradition and the one through whom it entered into the wider stream of human history.

There are two other respects in which I believe that Jesus fulfilled, and to some extent transformed, the prophetic tradition in a way that I find crucial for the needed response to our crisis. Neighbor love was part of the Jewish tradition as a whole and fundamental for the prophets. Jesus' emphasis was no departure. However, Jesus' personal embodiment and expression of love enriched the understanding of what it means. It goes beyond treating the neighbor justly to a deep personal concern. I am not suggesting that this is wholly new with him, but it is strikingly presented in the gospels and plays a special role among his followers, or at least in Christian ideals.

Further, Jesus' is more obviously opposed to violence against human beings than the prophetic tradition generally. In Israel, Moses and David were both considered as prophets, and they were also military leaders. The expectation of the "Messiah" was often of a military leader. Mohammed stands in that prophetic tradition. Modern Communism has continued it. There is much to be said for the use of violence in the quest for justice and freedom. I am not here arguing for absolute pacifism.

But as I size up the current need, the violence taking place in the world is overwhelmingly destructive. The chances seem minute that any form of violence can play a positive role in resolving global problems. I am not interested in arguing whether Jesus would be a pacifist in all circumstances or whether thoroughgoing pacifism is the correct position for Christians at all times and places. But today the only promising form of resistance is the nonviolent form pioneered by Gandhi on the basis of his reading of Jesus' teaching. Martin Luther King developed it both directly from Jesus and through Gandhi. This reinforces my judgment that it is Jesus' transformation of the prophetic tradition that has saving power today.

My reference to Gandhi should allay fears that I am calling for everyone to join Christian churches. Islam already assigns Jesus a very high place. A few Jews want to reclaim Jesus for the Jewish tradition in which he obviously stands. If joining a Christian church means failing to continue a Hindu, or Confucian, or Buddhist, or even a Western atheist tradition that has a distinctive contribution to make, only to bind oneself to exclusivist doctrines, then doing so would be express the proselytism against which Jesus spoke so harshly. So poorly have we who profess to follow Jesus done so, that even with respect to that question, we have much to learn from Hindus such as Gandhi, but also from Jews and Muslims, atheists, and others. Nevertheless, I celebrate the fact that we keep Jesus before the world by reading the New Testament in our weekly services. We have this treasure in earthen vessels. May the treasure be widely shared!

I have described a Jesus-centered understanding of salvation history without reference to God. I think his role can be described in this way, so that nontheists can recognize his importance and possible contributions. Perhaps they can also follow him, and some may do so better than most theists. Nevertheless, Jesus' being was so bound up with his life with his Abba that when we abstract from that we are not dealing with the historical Jesus. Thus far his most faithful followers have shared in that relation. The ability to love your enemies goes beyond rational beliefs. For me to follow Jesus, even very partially, is to center my life and understanding on the One with whom Jesus lived so intimately.

In Chapter 21 I explained that I am a theist, and a rather confident one. Since I believe in God, and since I even believe that God relates to the world in complex ways, it is natural for me also to think and speak of God's way of being in Jesus. I am aided in this by Whitehead's vision of all causality as indwelling. My experience in one moment is causally effective in the next moment by participating in its constitution. The sound I hear in one moment continues to be present in the next moment. Without that there would be no music or even oral communication. This is a much more realistic view of causality than the billiard ball model that collapsed under Hume's still unchallenged analysis.

This means that if God has any causal efficacy in the world, and in my view this is essential to the coming to be of any event whatever, it is by indwelling. God participates in the constitution of every individual thing. We could say in the most literal sense that every fleshly entity enfleshes or "incarnates" God. But we can also make stronger claims about how God is present in Jesus.

Since God is present in human beings as a call to realize what value can be realized in that moment, and human beings respond more or less fully to this call, we can certainly say that God is more fully incarnated in some than in others. Perhaps Jesus more fully actualized the possibilities God provided him than has anyone else. I do not know. Certainly he was a front runner. In any case, I believe that Jesus' modeling of extraordinary responsiveness to God's call, despite the enormous cost, is of vast importance in human history and to us today,

But I do not believe that the most important issue is whether he was more responsive than anyone else. Perhaps there have been others who were more fully obedient. Perhaps not! The question in the earliest church was not that of the fullness of his faithfulness but whether he was the expected one. The issue was the uniqueness of his mission. Was he the one who fulfilled the prophesies? Those who agreed that he was became his disciples.

That was the form that the issue took for many Jews of Jesus' day. This led to somewhat questionable readings of the scripture and interpretations of Jesus' life by his followers. Calling him Messiah or Christ had ambiguous consequences. Nevertheless, at a deeper level, I believe this is the right approach. What makes Jesus decisive for me is not just that he fulfilled his calling but that his calling was of decisive importance for human history. God called him to liberate the prophetic message from its remaining ethnocentrism, to deepen and enrich it, and to make it available to all. What a calling! And to what a remarkable extent Jesus' remarkable responsiveness led to the realization of God's purpose.

Jesus created the possibility of a new kind of community. Paul brought such communities into being. Much of their distinctiveness faded with the passage of time, but some elements survive in many churches and occasionally such community is realized quite wonderfully even today. What Jesus called the Holy Spirit is real there.

At one time I worked extensively on a different question. I believe that through Jesus a new type of individual existence came into being. Many years ago I wrote a book on *The Structure of Christian Existence*. It may be my most original book. I wrote that book at a time when existentialism was the focus of much theology and philosophy. I thought the goal of authentic existence was important, but I thought that existentialists in general, and Heidegger in particular, were wrong in regarding the existence he described as universal human existence. Heidegger himself noted that he was not describing the existence of indigenous people. I thought he was brilliantly examining the existence of post-Christian

Westerners. I wanted to historicize the structure of existence and then to locate what is distinctive about Christian existence in that context.

I described what I considered to be the structure of existence of hunting and gathering societies and then the changes brought about by civilization. I argued that with civilization came variety. I described Buddhist existence, for example as quite different from Western existence. In Greece I talked about Homeric existence and the new form of existence that came into being through the axial philosophers. In Israel I talked about the experience that comes to expression in the ancient prophets and the new form it took in Jesus. I called this spiritual existence.

I understood the distinction to be primarily one of a new kind of transcendence. One's motives become objects of one's attention. Self-criticism of subjective experience becomes a natural activity. One discovers that one cannot do what one wills to do. Self-love takes on new and problematic dimensions and the authentic love of the other also has a new character.

I still think that what I wrote there is important, and that part of what we owe to Jesus is a development in the possible structures of existence. But soon after writing that book my awareness of the ecological crisis shocked me into a realization of how I had allowed existentialism to draw me into a radically individualistic anthropocentrism when what we need is community among human beings and with other creatures as well. I recognized that such community was the focus of Jesus and Paul as well. I bracketed what I had done in that book and started over. But in the wider scheme of things I want to recognize that at this point as well, Jesus' work was transformative. I also see that, as formerly Christian cultures become secular, the distinctive features of Christian existence are disappearing, even in the churches. Perhaps if we prized them more and understood their historical uniqueness, we would also prize the beliefs and practices that made them possible.

Finally, given my understanding of multiple structures of existence, I have reflected also about that of Jesus. I came to the conclusion that for us who follow him, the God who calls us remains, for the most part, an "other" to the deciding center that we call the self. On the other hand, in Jesus, at least during important periods of time, that otherness disappeared. God's presence in him was fully synthesized with Jesus' prehension of his personal past, and this unified element in his experience became the deciding center, the human self. Accordingly, he could speak for God in a way we cannot. This gave me some appreciation of traditional efforts to describe the unity of God and Jesus, although the metaphysics employed by the tradition led, in my view, to poor results.

I am not sure how important these speculations may be. I think there would be some value in displacing traditional doctrines of incarnation that seem in the end to deny the humanity they initially tried to preserve. I think what I offer is close to what the Antiochenes were saying with a different anthropology. I am comfortable in saying that, so far as we know, the way God was incarnate in Jesus was unique. Of course, that does not satisfy those who want to give a supernatural or at least superhuman status to Jesus, but I think Jesus would have preferred my formulation.

Although I believe in real difference and even the possibility of important uniqueness, I also believe in continuity. Uniqueness is uniqueness of synthesis of elements that are shared. It may be the ways of synthesis can be further clarified into structures, and that there can be uniqueness of structure. I have pursued that line of thought with respect to Jesus. But I would like to close this chapter with reflection on more widely shared experiences that help us to imagine that of Jesus.

Our language typically suggests that there is an "I" who reflects and decides. It even suggests that this "I" is a distinct substance that persists through time. Close examination of experience reveals that this is not the case. Buddhists are right that there is no substantial "I." Each experience is a synthesis of aspects of diverse given elements. Whitehead speaks of "prehensions" as the way that elements of the past participate in constituting the present. My judgment is that in what is for us normal experience the prehension of the personal past plays the central role. It determines what is "self" and what is "other."

There are methods of "mind control" that build on the possibility that other relations may take the central role. The results are, for the one controlled, pathological. But tendencies to be excessively influenced by a parent, for example, occur within even a normal range. Sometimes also the supposedly rational "I" is overwhelmed by repressed rage or fear or love. These take over the role of organizing the experience as a whole and "deciding." This too easily becomes pathological, but all of us understand it to some extent.

In Whitehead's view and mine there is another element in experience, what he calls "the initial aim," which can also be described as the presence of God or the Holy Spirit. This "aim" is transformed into the "subjective aim" that actually determines the "decision." This transformation is the effect of the integration of the prehension of God with the many other prehensions, among which the prehension of the personal past is usually dominant.

In this picture there is nothing incredible about the idea that sometimes the "initial aim" is the most determinative element in the subjective aim and, thus, in the final decision. If we approach our own experience and the reports of others with the recognition of this possibility, we find plenty of evidence, mostly vague and pervasive, but sometimes dramatic. I will begin with a personal experience just a night or two ago.

As an old man, I do not enjoy "a good night's sleep." My bladder does not permit it. I hope for a succession of pleasant naps. There is typically a time of mental relaxation when I am not dreaming but when I am not thinking of anything. On the occasion which is my present example, "out of the blue" there came to me the idea that I should take out of my concluding chapter in this manuscript the section on planning the tenth International Whitehead conference, make that a separate chapter, and then add a section on life after death. I was certainly not thinking about these matters at the time the idea "popped into my head." Consciously I was taking pleasure in feeling that my work on the manuscript was almost complete. But suddenly, abruptly, I knew that this is what needed to be done. I have done it.

Of course, in communication with other inhabitants of the modern world, I am accustomed to putting a good face on such experiences. To do so, I would say that "I decided" to make these changes and explain the reasoning that led to the decision. These are the sorts of little deceits by which we demonstrate our acceptance of the modern world view. But the more accurate description is that in a state in which the usual press of other prehensions was lessened, the prehension of God came to dominance in a relatively pure form.

It is also the case that sometimes I become absorbed in my writing in such a way that I seem not to be in control. I start a sentence with no clear sense of how it will end. The writing seems to take on a life of its own. This is a minor part of my experience, but it helps me to understand the way in which some artists explain their experience. They feel "inspired." To say that for a while their experience is organized around the initial aim or the Spirit seems a reasonable interpretation. To say their art is inspired is, for me, a quite straightforward claim. It is a claim also about one of the ways that God works in human life.

Accordingly, I am fully convinced that there are many inspired writings in the Bible. Very likely the inspiration of the Qu'ran is even more extensive. Further, inspiration is divine, and it gives authority. Sadly, those impressed by this inspiration and this authority have seriously misinterpreted it. They sometimes speak of verbal dictation, for example, which would be an entirely different matter. And in order to bolster authority, they speak of "inerrancy." Thereby they discredit the true teaching. The inspiration in no way sets aside the other aspects of normal experience. It expresses itself in language or forms that are not alien to the preceding experience. Very rarely does it provide information that is not otherwise accessible. In short the outcome of inspired art or writing is historically and biographically conditioned as are all other human experience and creations. Nothing creaturely is inerrant or in any other way guaranteed to be right. But much *is* inspired, and its true, and truly important, authority is lost when misleading claims are made about it.

It is my conviction that the role of Jesus in the contemporary world could benefit greatly from an understanding of the reality and the limits of inspiration. Jesus was a man of his time. He thought about the issues of the society of his day and in the lives of the individuals who made it up. He took the domination by Rome for granted. He was a Jew, and he saw the world through Jewish eyes. He was immensely indebted to the prophetic tradition of Israel. In all these respects he was like many others.

What is astounding is the extent to which he transcended and transformed all this. He did this so drastically that his teaching is felt to have direct relevance and authority by people in many cultural and historical circumstances. Equally impressive is the extent to which he lived from his own new vision of reality, paying the full price of doing so. He was inspired in such a way that the claim that the Spirit was enfleshed in his life is not unreasonable. In this quite straightforward sense I believe that he incarnated God. His words and example have decisive authority for me. I seek to be a faithful disciple.

CHAPTER TWENTY-THREE

Winding Up and Winding Down

In 1990, we retired—I, from teaching; Jean, from the library. By then our children were grown and well-established in their diverse careers. All four were married, and we had five grandchildren. Since then we have acquired two great-grandchildren. We moved across town to what is for us an ideal retirement community, Pilgrim Place.

Pilgrim Place was established in 1915 by the president of Pomona College, who wanted his students to have a chance to interact with missionaries who knew other parts of the world, especially China, first hand. A few homes were acquired for missionaries on sabbatical (called "furlough" in those days), and these evolved into a retirement community, primarily for Congregational missionaries. Later others who have spent their lives in professional Christian service have been included, but nearly half of its residents, even now, have spent extended time in other parts of the world. More recently the doors have been opened to persons of other faiths and to those who have worked for peace and justice in institutions that are called secular.

My parents had been residents since 1965. My father died in 1989 at 96, shortly before we entered, but my mother lived on until 1997, when she was 102. The quality of her life in the last two years had not been good. She had the good fortune of being able to end it in a socially and legally acceptable way by declining to have her pacemaker replaced.

I sometimes say that Pilgrim Place is the "social gospel" in retirement. The popular image of "missionaries" is different, but many were progressives inspired by the desire to "build the Kingdom of God" globally. The tone of Pilgrim Place continues that tradition. It has its limitations, but it is for me a comfortable context. Residents play a larger role in their own government than is usual for retirement communities, and we feel responsibility for one another. We raise several hundred thousand dollars each year to support fellow Pilgrims who need help. We now call ourselves an "intentional community" in that we reflect together about how to be more responsible also in our ecological footprint. A community of this kind is a new and exhilarating experience for most of us.

One dimension of reducing our ecological footprint was supported by economic considerations as well. Water is already scarce, and the scarcity will become more severe. The cost is very high. As long as it was cheap, southern Californians poured it freely on the ground to make their landscape like that of the well-watered towns of the East. Now it is clear we must change. Pilgrims decided to make a major effort to reduce and in five years cut their water usage in half. This was done while retaining vast grass areas. Now we are engaged in a second major and far more complicated effort, requiring major changes in landscaping.

A very different kind of change has occurred in the area of food. When we arrived, the meals were typical American "meat and potatoes." When more vegetarians came in, they were told they could just skip the meat. They organized monthly meatless meals and invited the staff in order to show them that good vegetarian cooking is possible. Gradually things changed, and a vegetarian option has been offered at every meal.

For many years, I was not a vegetarian, thinking that moderate consumption of meat was alright. This was in spite of the fact that many Whiteheadians had stopped eating meat largely out of respect for other animals. I comforted myself with the view that the best ecological practice in farming was integrated small-scale production including animals, and that killing them was really part of the natural ecology. However, over time I realized that whatever might be ideal, the reality was that the meat I was eating was produced in meat factories that were not only extremely cruel but also ecologically destructive in other ways. Furthermore, as grains were becoming globally scarce, their use to produce meat priced them out of reach of the poor in less favored parts of the world. I finally changed my habits, grateful to the work of the vegetarians who had insured that meatless meals at Pilgrim Place were available and delicious.

Jean and I both did well for some time in terms of health. We continued active in the church and became active in Pilgrim Place. I continued to be involved in the Center for Process Studies, to teach a little for a few years, and to write. I took several trips to China. However, Jean began to have health problems and by 2004 the decline of short-term memory was apparent. We had the chance to move from independent living into Pitzer Lodge, the intermediate care facility, in 2005, and the excellent assistance we have received there enabled us to continue to live together until recently.

For several years, Jean has lived quite fully in the moment, with hardly any memory or expectation. Most of the time, she seems fairly content. During this period, caring for Jean has been my consuming responsibility. It became clear that someone needed to be near her at all times. I did not need to be that person, and Pitzer provided supervised activities in which she enjoyed participation. Also there were many activities both in Pilgrim Place and elsewhere in Claremont to which we could go together. When necessary I could call on friends to stay with her. Still, the responsibility was mine, and usually I was the caregiver around 22 hours a day.

I continued occasional trips and planned a major one in 2009 to attend the International Whitehead Conference in Bangalore and lecture in China. I made elaborate arrangements for Jean's care. Although no harm was done, the problems during my absence led me to decide not to travel any more. I made an exception for the trip I described in Chapter 16. Mainly, I continued to be able to think and write, and it was possible for groups to meet in my living-room. So my life continued to be quite full.

Recently, Jean's condition became more difficult to deal with. Through the years she often resisted doing needed things such as dressing or undressing or taking a bath, but overall she was cooperative, and we could find ways to overcome the resistance. But increasingly there were times when we could not. Since I could leave her only when others took responsibility, her refusal to cooperate meant that I could make no commitments other than to her as long as I was directly responsible. Since I was not prepared to give up all my activities, I was forced to move her to the Health Services Center, the Pilgrim Place nursing home. I fear that the staff there is also finding it difficult to deal with her. It is very nearby; so I can get to her in a few minutes.

I am enjoying my new freedom. But, of course, there is a downside also. It takes time to adjust to living separately after 67 years of life together. Downsizing in preparation for moving to a smaller apartment is part of the adjustment.

The more difficult change is in my financial situation. I have had resources and income to support causes in which I believe. These include the conference discussed in Chapter 20. An $8000 monthly bill for Jean's care dramatically ends my ability to be generous. My immediate concern is about our work with the Chinese. My contribution has not been so large, but it is essential. I hope that before there is a serious economic problem, an MA program for Chinese can be initiated in Claremont in which Meijun can teach for a stipend that can keep the program going.

In these aging years, I spend all too much time reflecting about my past, who I have been, and what I have accomplished and failed to accomplish. These reflections are, of course, also about my hopes for the future. Writing these "reminiscences" is part of that activity and also an expression of its results.

My evaluation of myself is that I have aspired to be a radical. I do not mean that I have wanted to act like the proverbial "bull-in-a-china-shop," although I know that sometimes I have done that. I do not want to take pleasure in upsetting people, although I have done that too. I do not want to weaken reformist efforts, although I would like to deepen them and sometimes to redirect them. To be a radical is to go to the roots of the matter—on any and all matters. It is then to decide on actions from that perspective. Often one will choose to be quiet or moderate as a matter of tactics, but one bears in mind the need for more fundamental understanding and response.

When one tries to be radical, one realizes how rare radical thinking is, and one appreciates even more highly its historical achievements. It has made me less critical of those who in the past have taken for granted what we see as wrong. On the other hand, it makes me more critical of those today who are condescending toward their ancestors in these ways but are now taking for granted false ideas that are even more destructive.

We today have more resources for thinking radically than ever before. We have used them well in exposing the racism and patriarchalism of all preceding civilizations. But Americans who have largely overcome racism and sexism continue to allow their thinking to be shaped by the modern worldview and the propaganda that passes for news. They may be critical of capitalism, but they take the present world order more or less for granted and continue to participate in the culture of consumerism. They may be critical of atheism and nihilism, but they quietly accept the dominance of an ideology in their system of higher education that promotes just these views.

I think of the Aristotelian scientists who were seriously committed to advancing science but would not look at the moon through the telescope. I think of my Cobb ancestors who worked to support the union against the secessionists (until secession came) but who took the institution of slavery for granted. I think even of the abolitionists, the most radical thinkers of their day, some of whom paid a high price for their radicalism, but most of whom were still racists. I think of highly moral and committed Christians during the Nazi era who worked politically for peace and human rights against Nazism, but whose attitude toward Jews was still sufficiently shaped by centuries of Christian anti-Jewish teaching that they did not vigorously oppose Nazi policies.

How hard it is to be truly radical! Our failures in the present do not justify the failures of others in the past. But they should reduce our condescension toward them. I aspire not to be the scientist who refuses the evidence, the Southerner who could not condemn slavery, the abolitionist who was still racist, or the German Christian who tolerated anti-Jewish policies. Accordingly, I have tried to expose the erroneous assumptions that shape our culture, like every other culture.

My recognition of the power of our socialization to blind us to the truth has intensified my appreciation of Jesus and Paul. With the help of the Syro-Phoenecian woman, Jesus overcame his ethnic bias, and ministered to Jew and Gentile alike. Paul made it even clearer: "There is neither Jew nor Greek; there is neither slave nor free; there is neither male nor female." (Gal. 3:28) What about economic distinctions? They existed, but certainly the rich were not favored! What about the physically handicapped? I could go on. Jesus called for inclusive table fellowship. Paul brought into being communities that believed that God is no respecter of persons. Both took care of those who had needs. They set a standard of which we individually continue to fall far short. The communities in which I have lived also fall short, but I have been wonderfully fortunate all the same. The influence of Jesus and Paul is alive in them.

Given my strong identification as a Christian theologian and a radical critic of my social context, I reacted ambivalently to the recent announcement that I had been honored by the academic establishment by election to the American Academy of Arts and Sciences. They do not admit theologians as such; so I learned that I was admitted as a

philosopher. I genuinely feel gratitude to those who nominated me and
am honored that I was recognized for my contribution to philosophy.
I would like to think that my election is an indication of a softening of
boundaries and a more self-critical spirit, but I doubt it. And if this community is as complacent and as irrelevant to urgent global needs as I take
it to be, I do not want really to identify myself with it. Still I consider
this honor to be part of my good fortune.

Indeed, my life overall has been wonderfully fortunate. I am truly
content. Of course, there is sadness and regret. There are initiatives that
amounted to nothing. There are those I have failed and hurt. There are
mistakes that can never be corrected. But I am confident that God for-
gives, and I have forgiven myself.

There is also much cause for celebration. I will begin with something
trivial, but still meaningful to me. The name "Cobb" was in some danger
of dying out in my branch of the family. My father was an only son as
was his father before him. I had a brother, but he died without heir. My
sister had sons, but they were "Foleys." Now the danger is past. Jean and
I had four sons, and among them they had three. There is even a great
grandson as well. The "Cobbs" have a future.

I wonder why I *feel* that this matters. Genetically I am as much an
Atkinson as a Cobb. Actually, I have always thought that I was more
like the Atkinsons. Certainly this is true of my height. I felt closer to my
mother. When we were in the United States, we lived with my Atkinson
grandparents at 19 Temple Ave., Newnan, Georgia, a great old Victorian
house where my mother was born. For a while I lived there alone with
my grandmother. It is the only address about which I feel sentiment

We were part of Atkinson family reunions. I took pride in my
mother's family. The Atkinsons were at that time a far more prominent
family than the Cobbs. My Atkinson grandfather had a brother who was
a governor of Georgia. We named our first son "Theodore Atkinson" after
my mother, Theodora, and her father. In spite of all this, I have never
thought of myself as an Atkinson. My identity is "Cobb." I suppose it is
just a matter of the name. It is hard for me to admit that a name affects
me so deeply.

My far deeper identity is as a Christian, and within that broad movement, a Methodist. To be a Methodist is not to suppose that a particular
denomination is *the* correct form of Christianity. Our founder regretted
the separation from the Church of England which was forced on him

by the lack of Episcopal priests in the new United States. Our reason for
existence is, therefore, practical rather than doctrinal. Nevertheless, in the
teaching and practice of our founder I believe we have a treasure that can
still benefit the larger church and the world.

Together with Ignacio Castuera, I am working, fitfully, on a plan
that *might* revive an ailing denomination. The decline of the United
Methodist denomination is part of the decline of mainstream Protestantism, brought about largely by its failure to respond intelligently to the
dominance of an inhospitable cultural and intellectual climate. My whole
career has been a counterattack on that climate. However, we judge that
the weakness of our denomination is intensified by the lack of any articulated shared convictions. We think that its health in the second half of
the late nineteenth and early twentieth century was enhanced by a widely
shared acceptance of Boston Personalism. When this theology collapsed,
nothing replaced it. We have had to learn to get along, with no consensus
or even center. In Chapter 17 I acknowledged my own contribution to
this situation. Yet it may still be possible to contribute to healing.

I consider that in many ways the process theology I have advocated is
an updating of his thought and a suitable replacement of Boston Personalism. I noted in Chapter 17 that I thought a wide Methodist consensus
could be gathered around Daniel Day Williams' *The Spirit and Forms of
Love*. However, since that approach is not possible, it occurs to me that
the church might rally around Wesley himself.

To express my appreciation of Wesley, I wrote *Grace and Responsibility: A Wesleyan Theology for Today* (1995). Writing this book strengthened my conviction that serious study and reappropriation of much of
Wesley's theology would greatly deepen and invigorate the spirit of the
church. Proposal of a renewal of Wesleyan theology would not face the
insuperable obstacles to agreeing on a contemporary theology. Perhaps
it is not too late to encourage a movement in this direction. This effort
may prove as much of a failure as my other initiatives with regard to the
denomination, but with Ignacio's leadership it deserves a try.

Still, even for the sake of the Wesleyan movement, my identification with the process movement is still stronger. In this regard, I am
comforted. I have lived long enough to read about this movement of
thought in histories of theology! Somewhat surprising, and therefore
especially gratifying, is the attention our tradition receives in James C.
Livingston's *Modern Christian Thought*. The new edition devotes the

entire second volume to the twentieth century. This deals with the whole range of Christian thought globally. Theologians in the process tradition have often felt ourselves to be marginalized in both church and academy. Accordingly, I was truly pleased to find two chapters of the first ten devoted to a sympathetic account of our contribution. Chapter 2 is on "American Empirical and Naturalistic Theology" and features Henry Nelson Wieman. Chapter 10 is on "Process Theology."

I have just two quibbles. The connection of process theology to the American empirical and naturalistic tradition is not made clear, and a reader could easily suppose that the naturalistic tradition completed its work in the fifties and process theology, in the seventies. In the six subsequent chapters, treating recent theological issues topically, empirical, naturalist, and process-oriented theologians appear occasionally, but without the label. I am glad we are part of history, but I hope we are still alive and kicking.

It is less surprising that a three-volume history of American liberal theology gives considerable attention to the Chicago school. Gary Dorrien devotes to it two chapters of the second volume, which is on the first half of the twentieth century. The second chapter of the third volume, on the second half of the twentieth century, describes the Chicago faculty with which I studied. It begins by referring back to the figures discussed in Volume two, then introduces Whitehead as background and describes the thought of Charles Hartshorne, Bernard Loomer, Bernard Meland, and Daniel Day Williams. Chapter 4 picks up the story under the title: "In the Spirit of Whitehead." The Claremont faculty is featured.

Because of the concluding historical chapter, Chapter 8, there is much less danger in this account that process thought appear to belong to the past. It is entitled "Rethinking the Traditions," and it begins and ends with Claremont graduates (Thandeka and Catherine Keller). More than half of those who come between are, broadly speaking, from the Chicago School or Whiteheadian tradition. Dorrien does not make a point of this, but perhaps the significance is stronger because he does not. I am very proud of my students and of their multifarious contributions. Together with those who have come to process thought through other channels, I am confident that the future of process theology is in good hands.

Of course, my hope is for more. A healthy theology should be continuous with the best thinking of the time. I hope that someday Whitehead will be recognized as the great philosopher of this age. I hope that someday the role of Whitehead will feature prominently in histories of science. I hope, indeed, that when the history of these terrible times is written, process thought will be recognized to have played a positive role. But I am prepared to wait for all this, grateful that recognition has not been so long delayed in theology.

This joyful conclusion has not made me sit idly by. A number of books mentioned earlier were written since retirement. Here I will note a few others.

For many years I hoped to produce a glossary to help students of Whitehead's difficult *magnum opus, Process and Reality*. Finally, in retirement, I found the time to do this. It is freely available on the web, or it can be purchased in book form from P & F Press. Jeanyne Slettom is now planning to republish it with Process Century Press, making it more widely available. It is, in one sense, a very simple book, but I believe it may help a few students of Whitehead to read *Process and Reality* with more understanding.

My good friend and close associate, Will Beardslee, was indirectly responsible for a venture into biblical scholarship that was quite unexpected and rewarding. He published a commentary on II Corinthians with Chalice Press before he died. Other process-oriented biblical scholars persuaded Chalice Press to publish additional commentaries. I was quite startled when David Lull asked me to write one, and I told him that I was totally incapable of doing so. I could barely make out Greek words and knew no Hebrew at all. However, he proposed that we write a commentary on Romans together, and I was happy to accept this quite different invitation.

I learned that my inability to participate in biblical scholarship had been an even greater handicap than I had previously realized. Lull opened up to me the variety of ways in which the text of Romans could be read. I became convinced that even the best translations have hidden Paul's real meaning on key points. My own way of understanding the gospel has been affected by this fresh encounter with Paul. I am deeply indebted to Lull. I think we have shown that Paul was a fine process theologian!

In Chapter 13 I mentioned a book written in retirement years that grew out of a conference on evolution. I owe to that conference, and to my subsequent work on editing materials from it, my current confidence that neo-Darwinian theory is a dogma that conflicts dramatically with the evidence. We called the book *Back to Darwin* to make clear that we were in no way questioning the fact of evolution. For us Darwin represents the demonstration of the fact that humanity evolved gradually from pre-human ancestors, but he also represents considerable openness to diverse explanations. It is this openness that is needed today. We claimed it and shared in a widespread movement of developing alternative explanations.

Neo-Darwinism insists that all evolution can be explained by the random mutation of genes and natural selection by the environment. Thus it excludes the actions of evolving organisms at every level. The evidence is that the activity of organisms participates in the evolutionary process at every level, beginning with bacteria. This was the special field of our most distinguished guest, Lynn Margulis. She has demonstrated that the eukaryotic cell came into being symbiotically—not by genetic mutation. She deeply resented her treatment by the neo-Darwinian establishment. This establishment defunded research that she felt sure over time would show that many evolutionary changes in advanced species have come about by symbiotic relations between bacteria and the larger organism.

Equally important is the role of epigenetic elements of the cell which account for Lamarckian elements in evolution. And especially significant to me are the obviously intelligent actions of animals in changing circumstances. Often behavioral changes precede genetic ones and determine the selection of the latter. These are only examples of the many contributions to evolution obscured by the dominant doctrine. Long after I finished the book, I learned that there is evidence that even genetic mutation is not purely random. Neo-Darwinism is an increasingly desperate effort to exclude purpose from a process in which purpose plays a large role.

Abingdon Press approached me about writing a book on secularity, and I happily agreed. It is called *Spiritual Bankruptcy*. The title suggests that I find no promise for a healthy response to our global crisis in secularism and the institutions it has generated. I criticize as examples of secularism—modern philosophy, modern science, the modern university, and economism. I see them all as cutting themselves off from the broader stream of human experience and the wisdom it has generated. They try to construct the system of beliefs from which we are to live out of what can be derived from immediate experience, especially sense experience. This project has failed us. I see them all as cutting themselves off from the broader stream of human experience and the wisdom it has generated.

On the other hand, traditional religions that undertake to maintain their "religious" or "sacred" character also do more harm than good. They cannot bring the wisdom their traditions embody to bear on the critical problems of our day. What is needed is modeled on the ancient Hebrew prophets who secularized the religion of their day, and the Greek philosophers who secularized theirs. Hence against both religiousness and secularism, I am calling for the continuing secularizing of the wisdom traditions.

My major effort to support others has been in relation to the work in China to which Chapter 16 was devoted. Almost everything described in that chapter has taken place during my years of retirement. Supporting the extraordinarily effective work of Zhihe Wang and Meijun Fan has added intensity and excitement to my retirement years. It seems to bear some hope of actual political and social change.

The question for me during this whole period has been whether I am called to anything further. I put the question this way because this book is a matter of "theological reminiscences." In Chapters 21 and 22, I explained the importance of theocentrism for me. Its practical meaning is to live by calling and grace. These are not sharply distinguishable. I experience the sense of being called as itself a gift. The "call" is also "empowerment." I have felt "called" to make a major effort to influence the cultural and intellectual character of our society. The conference organizing that has been my response is described in Chapter 20. Here I will try to clarify what this talk of "calls" means.

I am not speaking, in this instance, of a dramatic moment as when I realized that I should serve the church professionally, what is traditionally described as "a call to ministry." That happened only once. But over and over again the sense of a need and a new possibility and my role in its actualization emerges. I could explain what happens in terms of sizing up a situation and reflecting on what should be done. That happens to a certain extent, but in part this rational activity, which I judge to be important, follows from prior judgments and decisions responding to what I term a sense of being called.

Hence I will write a few paragraphs in this concluding chapter in terms of how it has "felt." What does it mean, for example, to say I "feel a call" to climax my career by breaking new ground?

Such feeling is not separate from judgment. I judged that it was time that we made a serious effort to put Whiteheadian thinking "on the map." No doubt, the fact that it was "on the map" in China contributed to the sense of possibility. The occasion that presented itself for consideration was the Tenth International Whitehead Conference. The Ninth IWC was to be held in Poland, but there was no offer for holding the tenth. A "tenth" could be taken as an occasion for something special, something different. It "felt right" that the tenth be in Claremont, and that it be a different sort of conference from the first nine. I "felt called" to try. The "feeling," closely related to the judgments, is that one is being involved in something larger than oneself.

My sense that a larger Wisdom is at work has been heightened as the process has continued. What is emerging is far different from anything I, or anyone else, envisioned. It has resulted from a synergy over which I have no control. My part is important, but so is the role of others. The good that occurs results from the generosity, the experience, and the knowledge of many that create novelty out of interaction.

Henry Nelson Wieman described this process of creative interaction and creative transformation brilliantly. He identified it with "God." This was, in my opinion, and in terms of my experience, an unfortunate compromise with modernist assumptions. What really happens is that many are empowered by, and respond to, a call, and their interaction produces what is of value. At this juncture I judge that, important as it is that our plans succeed, the planning itself will have been of value even if it does not succeed. I think of this process as "winding up" my career.

I have described the plans for the conference in Chapter 20. If it does work out as I now expect, one benefit should be increased membership in the Center for Process Studies. I have mentioned the change in my financial situation. I will no longer be able to support the Center in terms of funding. I hope to leave it better able to support itself.

And when the conference is over, what next? At present my sense is that it will be time for me to begin "winding down." I will be ninety. I live in a community in which there is much winding down. It is part of the aging process. It is remarkable that so many people continue to live vigorously and joyfully, serving others faithfully, in this process. But each change is one of diminishment. We leave leadership and even more personal decisions to others. We move to smaller residences, giving up our possessions including our libraries. We stop driving our cars. We become more dependent. We reduce our responsibilities. None of this is to be mourned. It is as it should be. We hope that we can diminish gracefully.

Winding down is not abruptly quitting. There will be much to be done in the aftermath of the conference. The work of Pando will be just beginning. For some time I will continue to be busy. But I will not look toward any new initiative. I will look more to see how to turn over responsibilities to others.

There are times when I think how fun it would be to read novels again. Perhaps it will be a time to escape from this suicidal world to a remembered or imagined one where the problems are not quite so severe. Perhaps my health will be such that there is little choice. So far as my *plans* are concerned, I will wind down. I think the project in which I am now engaged is one for which my career had prepared me, perhaps uniquely. I am proud to have been able to contribute to its realization. Whether my efforts will matter in any larger scheme of things will depend on others and on developments over which none of us have control. That, too, is as it should be.

On the other hand, "my plans" are not decisive. Perhaps there will be something else to which I am called. I rather hope not. But I also hope that, if there is such a call, I will respond. God knows far better than I whether there is more that I should do. When the time comes, I will know, too.

However that may be, before very long I will welcome "sister death." That, too, is as it should be. No one now depends on me. When we die, we leave a hole, a unique one that no one else can fill. But the needs of others are met in different ways. Life goes on. There is sadness in parting, but no reason for grief. I look forward to the new adventure.

I really hope that death will not be too long delayed. I have seen so much of human bodies that have outlived any real life! The huge expenditures and efforts devoted to extending life are worse than a waste. Far better to die while still humanly alive! My one dread is a long drawn-out, useless, and helpless dying. I wish that I could count on the medical profession to help me avoid that. Perhaps I will move to Oregon. Or, far better, perhaps the Oregonian pattern can be adopted in California. Sometimes, eventually, common sense and genuine concern to work with God for the sake of the well-being of real human beings prevail over legalism, habit, and bad dogma.

Actually I fantasize a different death. I am a bit embarrassed to admit it, but I would prefer to die a martyr. The term hardly fits, since a nonagenarian sacrifices so little by being killed. I would be deeply honored, however, if the powers that be took my efforts to expose them with sufficient seriousness as to consider me a real threat. It would be even better if I were considered a sufficient threat that they would arrange an accident or a mysterious poisoning. And all this would be best if my friends, many of whom cling to their faith in American exceptionalism, were a bit shaken and opened to the recognition that the American Empire is much like all the empires that have preceded it. Foolish hopes, I know, but I have long played the fool who rushes in where angels fear to tread.

What ceremony there will be when I have died are for others to decide, but there is one song about which I feel great sentiment. Perhaps I should ask that it be included in any memorial service. It is Jim Manley's "Spirit." I would delight, in it in any case, claiming it as a great hymn of process theology, but that he dedicated it to me touched me more deeply than I can say. My hope is that whatever occurs may be an occasion for feeling that Spirit and joining ever more fully in its work in the world. Unless a ceremony has that effect, I would prefer that it not occur.

And for me, what comes next? If death is the end, I will have no less reason for gratitude for life, no cause to complain, and, in any case, no opportunity. But I doubt that there is nothing more.

In our dominant culture, serious discussion of what comes next is virtually taboo. There are some good reasons for this. It is in part a healthy reaction to the early modern period in which in both church and culture it was supposed that only belief in rewards and punishments after death would support the needed social virtues here and now. In polite circles, the idea of hell has become, to say the least, unfashionable, and if "hell" is understood as a place where God inflicts suffering on people, then belief in hell is, in fact, much worse than unfashionable. What remains in the liberal church is a vague assurance that all will be well. Since no content is even suggested for the imagination, the assurance is, for many, not very reassuring. The result tends to be that Christians cling to even a rather miserable existence here rather than eagerly anticipate a blessedness beyond.

The rejection of otherworldliness is a great gain. Whatever else there may be, our calling here and now is to serve our neighbor here and now in this world. We are called to love the world that God saw to be good. We are not called to use this world as a way of getting to another or treating it as of secondary importance. I respect the decision of some of my

friends to assert without qualification that when we are dead we are dead.
If one belongs to the late modern world, there is no real alternative, and
this clarity has the great advantage of ending any danger of treating this
life as preparation for another.

On the other hand, the avoidance of one set of problems and distortions has led to another. Not, of course, in each individual case, but
overall, culturally speaking, despite rhetoric to the contrary, there has
been a decline of respect for individual people. This is perhaps clearest in
the academy. Nothing in the structure or teaching of the modern value-
free research university grounds belief in the inherent value of individuals. The lingering role of Christianity in the culture checks, but does not
stop, the decline. Increasingly we are valued, and value ourselves, in terms
of our role in the economy. That human beings are more than instruments of the economy can and should be affirmed without reference to
life after death, but its full articulation nevertheless reopens this question.
Historically, the rise of concern for individuals as individuals was very
much connected with belief in life after death.

I make this point only to say that the taboo of discussing this topic
is not the healthiest response to the legalistic projections that deserve
rejection. To affirm the goodness of life here and now and deny that God
imposes suffering on anyone does not require an end to discussion of life
after death. Indeed, it need not end discussions of a "hellish" existence
beyond death! To oppose projections of wish fulfillment on an afterlife
need not end discussion of possible blessedness. What has really ended all
such discussion in respectable society is the materialist worldview. If we
are bodies, if our bodies are part of the physical world and this is understood in Cartesian fashion, then clearly when they are no longer ani-
mated and cease to be organisms there is nothing left but decaying flesh
and bone. If this is our real belief, then at most we can be polite to those
who fantasize about something more.

Those who rejected the reduction of human beings to Cartesian
nature and called instead for re-thinking the nature of nature moved in
a quite different direction. William James sought to explore experiential
connections with those who had died. Whitehead was never personally involved in such matters, but for him, whether there was some kind
of continuation of experience beyond death was a matter of fact, to be
decided by evidence rather than metaphysical assumptions. Thus, in principle, he supported James's approach. As a strong believer that this kind

of neo-naturalism is the responsible direction of thought, I have occasionally speculated about it.

First, what could survive physical death? And perhaps, even prior to that, what would end? A moment of human experience is a creative synthesis of what Whitehead calls "prehensions" or "feelings" of other occasions. These include pure physical feelings, which are the feelings of the physical feelings of their neighbors. These neighbors include the immediate past experience and some neuronal events. I assume that with physical death these feelings would cease. According to the late modern scientistic metaphysics, these are the only real feelings, the ones by which everything else must be explained. However, Whitehead does not agree, and neither do I.

For Whitehead, in addition to pure physical feelings, there are also "conceptual feelings." These are feelings of possibilities or potentials. He believes there is evidence that all experiences, even the most elementary, include such feelings and are constituted by the integration of such feelings with the physical ones. Nevertheless, there cannot be purely conceptual feelings where there are no physical ones. By themselves they give no indication that experience could continue after death.

The break comes when we recognize that much of our physical experience is of the conceptual feelings of other experiences. My memories of my past experiences are of this sort. So is much of my experience of other people. If we affirm that there is experience of God, it is also primarily of this sort. Whitehead calls these feelings "hybrid physical feelings." Our experience is largely a mixture of pure physical feelings, hybrid feelings, and conceptual feelings. Whitehead discusses this mixture and the more complex feelings that arise through it at great length. Conscious experience is dominated by hybrid and conceptual feelings together with more complex feelings that integrate these with pure physical feelings.

In terms of what I value, much would be lost with the ending of the purely physical. On the other hand, much that I prize will be enhanced. The dominance of the physical and sensual aspects of experience obscures, in this life, many dimensions of relationship with other people. Above all, it obscures the relationship to God. For one who truly loves God and neighbor, the positive aspects of the change would outweigh the losses.

This opens the door to understanding that life after death would not be uniformly blessed. For one whose satisfactions are overwhelmingly sensual, the loss would be greater than the gain. And for one who does not care for others, who has related to them only as instruments and competitors, experiencing them only in their subjectivity and realizing how one has affected that subjectivity might indeed be hellish. Also, there may be those whose experience is so limited to the physical that there is no continuation at all.

In any case, without the dominance of the immediate physical environment, the foundational and personal relation to God would dominate experience. For some this would be the beatific vision for which they have longed. For others, the exposure of all self-deception and hiding would be nightmarish. Heaven and Hell may be very real indeed.

But "where" could such continuation occur? I criticized the view of "other universes" on the assumption that they must have a spatio-temporal relation to this one, at least if their existence is to show that the fine-tuning of this one is by chance. Would the existence of experiences continuous with ours after our physical death require some such location?

I confess to great discomfort in speculation about "location." However, I understand that space-time is a function of physical relationships. In my understanding, the temporal dimension would continue, but the three-dimensional space would not. I incline to think there would be something like spatial relationships, but so different as to be to us unimaginable. Perhaps without the purely physical base, there is a single dimension of space. Since physicists can speculate about spaces with more or fewer dimensions than ours, I do not consider the limits of my imagination to be, in this respect, the limits on what may be. We have then the question how a world of different dimensions intersects with a world with our dimensions.

From my perspective, these are all factual questions. We should approach them free of the prejudices so deeply instilled by our culture. We should free ourselves also from inherited ideas of reward and punishment. We should be open to the wisdom of all traditions and also recognize that the actual experiences on which most are based are also highly interpreted. We should try, of course with limited success, to disentangle what has been experientially learned from the ways it has been interpreted.

David Griffin has showed that if we are truly open to the evidence, we have reason to believe that death is not the end of experience—at least in some instances. Many people have had encounters with their deceased loved ones. To dismiss them all as hallucinations expresses *a priori* assumptions rather than careful examination of the evidence. Without the resurrection experiences of the apostles, there would have been no Christian church. For Christians simply to dismiss all of this because of the dominance of a really incredible worldview is a sad commentary on the power of "faith."

The experiences of those who seem to have tasted death and returned give us no reason to dread this future or to suppose there is none. My own experience in this area is extremely limited, but once I was with an uncle when he died. His last words were: "It is so beautiful."

I have spent very little time examining the diverse beliefs in this area and sorting them out, despite my conviction that this is a legitimate and desirable activity. I am ready to be surprised. I look forward to a new adventure.